Reviews for the First Edition

'This extraordinary book charts the development, implementation and evaluation of the UK Government's highly successful Teenage Pregnancy Strategy for England, which reduced the under-18 pregnancy rate by well over 50%. It highlights the principles – of evidence, of partnership, and of the need for a holistic approach – that brought about the change. And it signals the important role that Government can play in promoting young people's sexual and reproductive health. Reflecting on her own experience and the voices of the strategy's participants, Alison Hadley identifies key lessons for the future. A key resource and a compelling read. Strongly recommended to all who seek success in sexual and reproductive health.'

Peter Aggleton, *Scientia Professor in Education and Health, UNSW Sydney, Australia, and Visiting Professor, UCL Institute of Education, London.*

'Inside find an important story of success . . . Teen pregnancy is influenced by social forces that shape adolescent opportunities - particularly education and employment - for a successful future and factors such as knowledge and use of contraception. Social progress in a nation is also create by enlightened political leadership and the committed leadership of individual citizens. The success of the English strategy to prevent teenage pregnancy is a testament to all of these. Alison Hadley, Venkratraman Chandra-Mouli and Roger Ingham tell an extraordinary tale of scientific understanding, visionary leadership, and long-term dedication to adolescent sexual and reproductive health. A story from which we all can learn.'

John Santelli, *MD, MPH, Professor, Population and Family Health and Pediatrics, Columbia University, New York City, USA*

'This book offers a valuable insight into the development and implementation of a long-term strategy to successfully address a complex public health priority. As well as documenting the important detail of the Teenage Pregnancy Strategy and its practical application at local level, it importantly includes the voices of those involved. This brings to life the reality of delivering the programme and illustrates the extraordinary commitment of so many people to improving young people's choices. As England continues to apply the lessons and make further progress, I am delighted the learning is being shared internationally in collaboration with the World Health Organisation.'

Duncan Selbie, *Public Health England*

Teenage Pregnancy and Young Parenthood

What happened next? This updated edition of Teenage Pregnancy and Young Parenthood examines the research and practice in this vital field since the end of the UK Government's highly successful Teenage Pregnancy Strategy (TPS) for England which contributed to reducing the under-18 pregnancy rate by well over 50%.

Alison Hadley, together with Roger Ingham, Joanna Nichols and Venkatraman Chandra-Mouli, summarise the latest research in the field, review the work of a wide range of local authorities, and provide insight from interviews with practitioners who are at the sharp end of delivering services both for young people seeking to prevent early pregnancy and for young parents. Providing a comprehensive overview of the original project, the book captures and shares the lessons from the TPS, documents the details of implementing a long-term strategy with its innovative approach to policy issues, and considers the implications of the study internationally.

Advocating a 'whole systems' multi-agency approach, it focusses on how to implement policy successfully, and demonstrates evidence for what is effective, both in helping young people avoid unplanned pregnancy and in improving outcomes for young parents. This edition also considers how to sustain the gains made by the original strategy. Key new topics covered include: an overview of the national context since 2016 through the pandemic; the introduction of Relationships and Sex Education (RSE); access to contraception and sexual health services; and addressing inequalities.

As in the first edition of the book, a chapter is devoted to efforts to reduce adolescent childbearing elsewhere in the world. It contains country case studies from Argentina, Ethiopia, Moldova and Thailand which illustrate what can be achieved with visionary leadership, rigorous science, and strong management in diverse contexts.

Teenage Pregnancy and Young Parenthood is essential reading for policy makers and practitioners dealing with young people's health, as well as undergraduate and postgraduate students in the fields of psychology, health studies, social work, youth work, education, social policy, sociology and related disciplines.

Alison Hadley OBE is the Director of the Teenage Pregnancy Knowledge Exchange at the University of Bedfordshire and previously led the implementation of the Labour Government's Teenage Pregnancy Strategy for England and was Teenage Pregnancy Advisor to Public Health England. **Roger Ingham** is Professor of Health and Community Psychology at the University of Southampton, **Joanna Nichols** is Associate Professor in the School of Nursing and Healthcare Leadership at the University of Bradford and **Venkatraman Chandra-Mouli** has recently retired after a 30-year career in the World Health Organisation.

Adolescence and Society
Series Editor: John C. Coleman
Department of Education, University of Oxford

In the 20 years since it began, this series has published some of the key texts in the field of adolescent studies. By publishing relatively short, readable books on topics of current interest to do with youth and society, the series makes people more aware of the relevance of the subject of adolescence to a wide range of social concerns. The books do not put forward any one theoretical viewpoint, the authors outline the most prominent theories in the field and include a balanced and critical assessment of each of these. The books summarise, review and place in context current work in the field to interest and engage both an undergraduate and a professional audience.

Teenage Pregnancy and Young Parenthood 2e
Effective Policy and Practice
Alison Hadley
with Roger Ingham and Joanna Nichols in collaboration with Venkatraman Chandra-Mouli

Wired Youth
The Online Social World of Adolescence
Ilan Talmud, Gustavo Mesch

Youth and Internet Pornography
The Impact and Influence on Adolescent Development
Richard Behun, Eric W. Owens

Mentoring Young People in Care and Leaving Care
Theory, Policy and Practice
Bernadine Brady, Pat Dolan and Caroline McGregor

Identity in Adolescence
The Balance between Self and Other
Laura Ferrer-Wreder and Jane Kroger

For more information about this series, please visit: https://www.routledge.com/Adolescence-and-Society/book-series/SE0238

Teenage Pregnancy and Young Parenthood

Effective Policy and Practice

Second Edition

Alison Hadley
with Roger Ingham and Joanna Nichols,
in collaboration with Venkatraman Chandra-Mouli

Routledge
Taylor & Francis Group
LONDON AND NEW YORK

Cover image: Rawpixel.com via Getty Images

Second edition published 2025
by Routledge
4 Park Square, Milton Park, Abingdon, Oxon, OX14 4RN

and by Routledge
605 Third Avenue, New York, NY 10158

Routledge is an imprint of the Taylor & Francis Group, an informa business

First edition published by Routledge 2018

British Library Cataloguing-in-Publication Data
A catalogue record for this book is available from the British Library

Library of Congress Cataloging-in-Publication Data
Names: Hadley, Alison, author.
Title: Teenage pregnancy and young parents : effective policy and practice / Alison Hadley, with Roger Ingham and Joanna Nichols, in collaboration with Venkatraman Chandra-Mouli.
Description: Second edition. | Abingdon, Oxon ; New York, NY : Routledge, 2024. | Includes bibliographical references and index.
Identifiers: LCCN 2024029233 (print) | LCCN 2024029234 (ebook) | ISBN 9781032525112 (hardback) | ISBN 9781032530871 (paperback) | ISBN 9781003410225 (ebook)
Subjects: LCSH: Teenage pregnancy—Government policy—Great Britain. | Teenage parents—Government policy—Great Britain.
Classification: LCC HQ759.64 .H33 2024 (print) | LCC HQ759.64 (ebook) | DDC 306.874/3—dc23/eng/20240716
LC record available at https://lccn.loc.gov/2024029233
LC ebook record available at https://lccn.loc.gov/2024029234

ISBN: 978-1-032-52511-2 (hbk)
ISBN: 978-1-032-53087-1 (pbk)
ISBN: 978-1-003-41022-5 (ebk)

DOI: 10.4324/9781003410225

Typeset in Times New Roman
by Apex CoVantage, LLC

For Jamie, for all his support and encouragement, and our children George and Lorna

Contents

Foreword *x*
Acknowledgements *xiv*

Introduction 1

1 Variation in teenage conception rates 7

2 Reducing rates of teenage conceptions 24

3 England's teenage pregnancy strategy: rationale, development and first phase implementation (1999–2005) 43

4 The second phase of implementation: reviewing, redoubling efforts and reaching the target (2005–18) 59

5 What happened next: a national and local perspective (2018–24) 81

6 Translating evidence into local action: continuing to embed the ten key factors for an effective strategy in a new and resource poor landscape 119

7 Improving the lives of young parents: developments and challenges since 2018 152

8 Adolescent childbearing globally: tangible progress made, but much more to be done – developments since 2018 193

Epilogue *212*
Index *215*

Foreword

We are delighted to contribute to a foreword to the updated edition of *Teenage Pregnancy and Young Parenthood: Effective Policy and Practice.*

Adolescent childbearing remains a significant public health challenge in high-, middle- and low-income countries. The majority of adolescent births occur in low and middle-income countries, where complications from pregnancy and childbirth are the leading cause of death among girls aged 15 to 19 globally. (WHO, 2023) However, young parents and their children in every country face disproportionately poor educational, health and economic outcomes contributing to cycles of inter-generational inequality.

While some adolescent pregnancies are planned and wanted, many of them are not. These unintended/unwanted pregnancies often result from consensual sexual activity where both partners are not motivated or equipped to make informed, safe choices. In many cases, unintended/unwanted pregnancies are the result of coercion or rape. While there are encouraging signs of declining motherhood in childhood and adolescence, the pace of change remains slow and uneven. There is an urgent need to accelerate efforts to protect girls' rights and choices, paying particular attention to families, communities and countries that are being left behind (WHO, 2023).

Prevention of adolescent childbearing is a high priority on the global agenda, as well as on the agendas of a growing number of countries. Three decades ago, the 1994 International Conference on Population and Development Programme of Action placed adolescent sexual and reproductive health on the map of international development. It highlighted the importance of reducing adolescent pregnancy and addressed the underlying factors contributing to it. The Programme recommended key actions for governments to take, focusing on reducing unintended pregnancies, unsafe abortions and sexually transmitted infections among adolescents (UNFPA, 2004).

Since then, evidence-based strategies to prevent adolescent childbearing have gained widespread support (Engel et al., 2019). They include ensuring access to high quality comprehensive sexuality education for all children and young people, alongside access to contraceptive and other sexual and reproductive health services that respond to the needs and preferences of adolescents and young people, with intensive support for adolescents at greater risk. Furthermore, when pregnancy has occurred in the context of coercion and abuse, medical care and support must be complemented with legal and social welfare measures. Efforts to prevent adolescent pregnancy and childbearing need to be part of broader efforts to create educational and employment opportunities for girls and boys, so that early childbearing within and outside marriage is not the only option available to them.

UNFPA's global Adolescent and Youth Strategy, "My Body, My Life, My World!", builds on this foundation. It identifies the unique needs of adolescents and the critical investments necessary to support their healthy transition into adulthood. Realising these goals requires the leadership and innovation of young people themselves (UNFPA, 2019).

A growing number of countries have used this knowledge to develop national policies and strategies to prevent adolescent pregnancy and are implementing them, more effectively in some places and less so in others. For example, as noted in a global stock-taking report on comprehensive sexuality education, while there has been substantial progress in policy adoption and curricular review, there are still gaps between policy and curricular implementation in many places (UNESCO, 2021). However, we are now beginning to see tangible results from some places.

England's ten-year Teenage Pregnancy Strategy (1999–2010) significantly reduced adolescent childbearing rates – a trend that has encouragingly continued in subsequent years since that Strategy ended. The experiences gained and the lessons learned were during the strategy period were documented in the first edition of this book. In the second edition of this book, Alison Hadley and her co-authors report on how the work to reduce adolescent pregnancy continued after the end of the Strategy, with a particular focus on the past five years, including the impact of the COVID-19 pandemic. Drawing on qualitative studies with local areas, they have identified some of the key features of success, as well as highlighted the challenges and the need for further government leadership. In addition, they describe and analyse efforts to respond to the health and social needs of pregnant and parenting adolescents, including young fathers, with examples of effective practice.

As in the first edition of the book, a chapter is devoted to efforts to reduce adolescent childbearing elsewhere. Dr Venkatraman Chandra-Mouli, who retired after a sterling 30-year career in the World Health Organization last year, reports on the progress made in reducing adolescent childbearing worldwide. With inputs from collaborators, he presents case studies from five global regions which illustrate what can be achieved with visionary leadership, rigorous science, and strong management in diverse contexts.

There are two take away messages that emerge from this book. First, concerted efforts to improve the provision of sexuality education, alongside access to contraception in England as in many other countries and creating educational and employment opportunities for adolescents and young people, have led to declining levels of adolescent pregnancy and childbearing. However, inequalities persist with a substantial minority being left behind. Second, while prevention has been a focus in England and in other countries, insufficient attention has been paid to responding to the needs of pregnant and parenting adolescents, including young fathers. It is encouraging to see this gap addressed through an increased focus on this issue in this edition, with examples of dedicated support programmes.

In 2024, the world commemorated the 30th anniversary of the International Conference on Population and Development. As we celebrate this milestone and look ahead towards the Sustainable Development Goals target date of 2030, it is important for us all to step up our efforts in these two areas, paying particular attention to ensure we reach those who are most vulnerable to the adverse health and social outcomes associated with adolescent pregnancy.

This updated edition aligns with the principles and objectives outlined in the recently published Accelerated Action for the Health of Adolescents (AA-HA!) 2.0 guidance by the World Health Organization (WHO, 2023), through its documentation of how the guidance has been operationalised at country level, as well as the role of rigorous monitoring and evaluation to understanding the impacts of comprehensive evidence-based strategies in promoting adolescent health and wellbeing. Moreover, the focus in the updated edition on evolving needs and contexts, for instance the implications of the COVID-19 pandemic on adolescent sexual and reproductive health, highlights the myriad threats and opportunities and the critical role of resilient, flexible and adaptive strategies and systems, as advocated by AA-HA! 2.0.

WHO's update of its *Guidelines on Preventing Early pregnancy and Poor Reproductive Outcomes in Adolescents*, which was first published in 2011 (WHO, 2011), is to be completed and published shortly. The Guidelines update has been informed by research evidence, as well as programmatic experiences from around the world, which are less likely to be documented than research studies are. That then is one of the vital contributions of this book – it represents a concerted effort to document what has been done to address adolescent pregnancy in England and elsewhere and what was achieved, so that these experiences may inform, inspire and challenge us to further improve and expand on our work for and with adolescents.

Sheri Bastien
Scientist
Department of Sexual and Reproductive Health and Research
(which includes the UNDP/UNFPA/UNICEF/WHO/
World Bank Human Reproductive Programme).
World Health Organization

Arushi Singh
Programme Specialist
Health and Education
UNESCO

Danielle Engel
Team Lead
Adolescents and Youth
Technical Division
UNFPA

References

Engel, D., Paul, M., Chalasani, S., Gonsalves, L., Ross, D.A., Chandra-Mouli, V., Cole, C.B., de Carvalho, E., Hayes, B., Philipose, A., Beadle, S. and Ferguson, J. A package of sexual and reproductive health and rights interventions – What does it mean for adolescents ? *Journal of Adolescent Health*, Vol. *65(6S)*, S41050, 2019.

UN. Programme of Action Adopted at the International Conference on Population and Development, Cairo, 5–13 September 1994. UNFPA, New York, 2004.

UNESCO, UNFPA, UNICEF, UN Women, WHO. *The journey towards CSE: A global status report*. UNESCO, Paris, 2021.

UNFPA. *My body, my life, my world. A global strategy for adolescents and youth.* UNFPA, New York, 2019.

WHO. *Guidelines on prevention early pregnancy and poor reproductive outcomes in adolescents in developing countries*. WHO, Geneva, 2011.

WHO. *Accelerated Action for the Health of Adolescents (AAHA!) 2.0*, WHO, Geneva, 2023.

WHO. *Adolescent pregnancy fact sheet* – online, 2023: www.who.int/news-room/fact-sheets/detail/adolescent-pregnancy.

Acknowledgements

I have so many people to thank for their help with writing this second edition. John Coleman OBE, the series editor, for recognising the importance of continuing to focus on this policy area. My original co-authors Professor Roger Ingham from the University of Southampton, Dr Venkatraman Chandra-Mouli who recently retired from the World Health Organisation and Dr Joanna Nichols from the University of Bradford, who has joined us as a co-author for this second edition. Roger for his expertise on the evidence and long-standing support for the strategy from the start; Chandra for his invaluable international perspective and enthusiasm for sharing England's experience globally; and Jo, whose passion for the work stems from her experience as a local and regional teenage pregnancy co-ordinator and member of the Teenage Pregnancy National Support Team. Her support in the qualitative research with local areas has been invaluable.

Special thanks too to Kate Thurland, for her help with data, and to those who contributed their specific expertise to Chapter 5. Lucy Emmerson from the Sex Education Forum, Catrin Hughes from the Faculty of Sexual and Reproductive Health, James Woolgar from the English HIV and Sexual Health Commissioners Group, Laura Hamzic from Brook, Laura Tantum on behalf of the Advisory Group on Contraception and Emma Rigby from the Association for Young People's Health.

Huge thanks also go to all those who provided insight from their local experience and provided case studies illustrating how the principles of the strategy can still be put into practice. Kate Adams Kerry Addison, Lindsay Andrews, Sarah Aston, Rachael Baker, Lisa Bartlett, Clare Blomley, Jacky Booth, Dougie Boyd, Erin Brennan-Douglas, Liz Bubbear, Sue Burridge, Ben Carr, Becky Clarke, Natalie Clark, Lucy Cooney, Helen Corteen, Jo Davies, Nick Dunne, Helen Earp, Steph Ebsworth, Simon Ford, Chris French, Helen Gregory, Lisa Hallgarten, Sam Hepworth, Joanne Hunt, Rattanaporn Ingham, Alice Jeavons, Kate Jennings, Irene Kakoulis, Beth Kelly, Lorraine King, Catherine Kirk, Toni Kittle, Linzi Ladlow, Stephanie Lamb, Carmen Lau Clayton, Kelly Lewington, Sarah Lyles, Sue Mann, Louise Marshall, Etty Martin, Jenny McLeish, Heather McKelvey, Debbie Mennim, James Moore, Bren Neale, Graeme Nicholson, Lemessa Oljira, Rebecca Pickerill, Cathryn Redfern-Light, Shelley Roberts, Dr Wiwat Rojanapithayaokorn, Tim Rumley, Rebecca Scott, Sarah Simons, Rachel Smith, Alex Stevenson, Dr Bunyarit Sukrat,

Anna Tarrant, Gail Teasdale, Diane Tinklin, Dimitrious Tourountsis, Sonia Walker, Carol Williams, Harriet Yudkin and Fernando Zingman.

And finally, all the original members of the Teenage Pregnancy Unit, the regional co-ordinators and the local co-ordinators who worked so hard to implement the strategy effectively – and to all the many hundreds who continue to do so because they know what a difference it makes to young people's lives.

Introduction

Why a Second Edition?

The final words of our first edition of *Teenage Pregnancy and Young Parents: effective policy and practice* were 'The journey continues' . . . and so it did! The teenage pregnancy strategy was a clearly defined ten-year programme, but it was never intended as a one-off strategy for one generation of young people. Rather, it was designed as a catalyst for change with the principles and actions of the strategy integrated into mainstream provision to support successive cohorts of young people. In the previous edition we described the actions taken to do that after 2010 (the calendar end of the strategy and the year that marked a change of government) up to 2017.

In the spirit of monitoring the continuing journey, in this edition we wanted to find out what happened next, from 2018 until 2023. What we found was a picture of passionate determination to support young people, in the face of a dramatically challenging landscape. Between the emergence of COVID-19 and the severely detrimental effects of long-term austerity things could not look bleaker for services supporting the teenage pregnancy strategy. However, the continued dedication of many in local areas championing young people's rights to healthy, happy, and productive lives, helped to mitigate some of the worst effects. Hope springs eternal and there is much optimism in local areas for teenage pregnancy work, which we hope we have reflected in this edition.

We looked at the national policy landscape relevant to teenage pregnancy and explored how local areas are trying to maintain the evidence-based approach of the strategy. Understanding the facilitators and barriers to sustaining change, without a defined government strategy, is essential for maintaining progress in England over the next decade. It also adds to the international learning on how to help ensure continuity of adolescent pregnancy programmes through changes of government and offers important lessons for other social policy and public health programmes focused on long term change. Documenting some – albeit a fraction – of the activity that has continued over the last five years also provides clear evidence to challenge the suggestion by some that as the strategy ended in 2010, it could not have contributed to any further declines in the conception rates.

DOI: 10.4324/9781003410225-1

The second, and arguably more important, reason for embarking on a revised edition was to shine a light on the need for continued focus and action. Although there has been a 72 per cent reduction in the under-18 conception rate from the start of the strategy to 2021 – a drop in numbers from 41,000 young women to 12,300 – stark inequalities persist between, and within, local areas and between individual young people. Worryingly, the outcomes for the diminishing cohort of young parents and their children remain disproportionately poor, with little improvement over the last five years. Of further concern is the increase in the most recent conception data. This may reflect lower rates during the pandemic lockdown periods in 2020/21 or mark the start of an upward trend, but it is an important caution against complacency, a risk highlighted by local areas.

An overriding concern voiced in the local area interviews, was the impact on young people from the fiscal choice of austerity and the cost-of-living crisis, which increased the prevalence of underlying risk factors for early pregnancy. These risks were further exacerbated by the COVID-19 pandemic. Resultant increases in family poverty, school absence and low educational attainment, young people's mental health and a sharp rise in the number of 15–16-year-olds going into local authority care have all added to a higher-risk environment for teenage conceptions. The risk of widening inequalities, and some young people and families being left behind, is also a global concern.

What did we find?

At a national level, we found a mixed picture. There have been some positive developments with potential to accelerate progress, notably: the long fought for achievement of legislation for statutory relationships and sex education in all schools; exciting digital and telemedicine developments to improve access to contraception, abortion and sexual health services; and an innovative reproductive health programme which, although not implemented, helped to inform the first ever women's health strategy with a ten-year implementation commitment.

Some of these national developments have clearly been supportive for local areas but other national aspects appear to have hindered progress. First, the lack of national leadership to signal why teenage pregnancy and young parents still matter, conveyed a sense of complacency that 'the job is done'. This has been reinforced somewhat by the delayed and much less regular publication of conception data, raising the concern that if it stops being counted, it will cease to count. Regular and reliable data at national, local and small geography areas was a key asset of the strategy and needs to continue to be published.

Second, inadequate funding at national and local level limited provision of essential prevention and support programmes. For example: the much reduced national investment to train and equip teachers to deliver high quality relationships and sex education, the potential route to universal primary prevention; the cuts to local authority budgets which not only squeezed funding of sexual health services but also caused a 70 per cent real term decline in funding for youth services since 2010–11, with severe impact on essential parts of local prevention eco-systems.

Thirdly, a marked shift away at a national level from advocating an integrated, public health multi-agency approach to prevention, and a notable lack of focus on a joined-up youth policy. This was key to the success of the strategy, sitting within the *Every Child Matters* policy context, alongside programmes addressing youth issues and embedding prevention and early intervention across all local services and settings, to ensure the strategy actions reach all young people (particularly those experiencing marginalisation).

Against this challenging backdrop the tenacity and resilience of local areas to maintain progress was even more notable. The case studies and our two qualitative studies found an extraordinary level of leadership in committed individuals determined to maintain a focus, re-establish partnership working and use local data and the views of young people to inform commissioning decisions that reflect the principles of the strategy. All faced the barriers mentioned above, and many reported staff burnout from the double impact of austerity and the COVID-19 pandemic, but optimism remained that the work would continue. That said, it was also clear that progress cannot and should not rely on individual champions. National actions are essential to sustain progress as is government investment to address the wider determinants of teenage pregnancy.

Exploring the national picture and collating the experiences of local areas, has provided a unique and fascinating insight into what has been happening over the last five years. It has identified the facilitators and barriers to progress, shone the light on examples of current effective practice, and helped inform recommendations for the much needed re-prioritising and scaling up of national support.

Chapter summaries

The first two chapters focus on research and evidence, and are written by Professor Roger Ingham, the research advisor on the Strategy's Independent Advisory Group and a long-time champion of young people's reproductive rights. **Chapter 1** considers different ways of understanding the term 'teenage pregnancy' and provides an overview of relevant research. Drawing on literature mainly from the UK and USA, issues discussed include why teenage pregnancy is of concern, the international, regional and local variations in rates, who is more likely to become pregnant and the likely outcomes, and the research challenges in understanding the causes and consequences of early pregnancy. **Chapter 2** explores some of the evidence of what contributes towards helping young people avoid unplanned conceptions – in particular the essential contribution of high quality sex and relationships education and access to effective contraception – but highlights that there is no easy answer to such a complex issue. The chapter concludes that the solution rests with a whole systems approach, with different agencies contributing what they can, with the interests of young people at the centre. This was the approach of the teenage pregnancy strategy in England and seems to encapsulate the situation in those countries that have adapted well to the changing circumstance of young people and society in general.

The next two chapters are from the first edition of the book and describe the journey of implementing the Labour Government's ten-year strategy. They have been included to provide the policy and organisational history to the ongoing journey described in this edition. The content also helps mitigate against the risk of time eroding the memory of such a well-developed and carefully implemented programme. **Chapter 3** sets out the rationale for prioritising teenage pregnancy, the analysis of why England had such high rates, the development of an evidence based action plan and the structures that were necessary for implementing a multi-agency long term programme. This is followed by an overview of the first phase of implementation from 1999 to 2005, describing specific actions of the strategy and how they were integrated into wider government programmes. **Chapter 4** describes the second phase of the strategy's implementation. Starting with the mid-course review, which confirmed the ten key factors for an effective strategy, the subsequent actions and ministerial involvement to accelerate progress, the strengthened focus on reaching young people most at risk, and the final push to improve sex and relationships education and young people's access to effective contraception. The chapter discusses how the priority was maintained over such a long period, and the importance of integrating teenage pregnancy into mainstream programmes to help sustain progress following the end of the ten-year strategy, and up to 2018.

Chapter 5: What happened next? is a new chapter exploring national and local developments since publication of the first edition. The first section focuses on the data and national landscape with an overview of how policy development and government decisions have helped or hindered progress. This is followed by more detailed contributions from leading Voluntary and Community Sector (VCS) organisations and professional and parliamentary collaborations[1], setting out the progress and challenges on the implementation of statutory RSE, improving access to contraception, and addressing some of the youth inequalities and wider determinants of pregnancy at a young age.

The second section focuses on the experience of those in local areas, working to develop and sustain whole systems approaches to reducing teenage pregnancy and support young parents, against a challenging background of loss of priority, austerity and the COVID-19 pandemic. It draws on two qualitative studies – one reporting in 2019 and one specifically conducted in 2023 to inform this revised edition – to understand the facilitators and barriers to sustaining change at a local level. The chapter ends with recommendations for national action to support further progress.

Chapter 6: Continuing to translate evidence into action describes thirty local case studies. In the previous edition, we described how the ten key factors for an effective strategy were translated into local practice to create the essential whole system approach, with illustrative case studies from over the course of the strategy. In this chapter we have collected a fresh set of current case studies from across the country, submitted by local areas in response to a request sent to the networks of the Teenage Pregnancy Knowledge Exchange[2] and the English Sexual Health and HIV Commissioners Group[3]. Despite the challenges and funding constraints reported in **Chapter 5**, they reflect the commitment of senior leaders, commissioners, practitioners and VCS organisations to continue implementing effective practice, to find new 'hooks' to integrate teenage pregnancy prevention into mainstream provision and to actively engage young people in the commissioning and monitoring of services.

Chapter 7: Improving the lives of young parents and their children, takes stock of developments and challenges since 2018. The chapter starts with updated national data on outcomes for young parents and their children, making a compelling case for further action. This is followed by findings and recommendations of recent reports investigating their needs; a summary of the evidence for effective approaches, with new developments and learning from the Family Nurse Partnership[4]; and an update on aspects of support initiated by the strategy – school and post-16 education of young parents, Care to Learn childcare funding and supported housing, with case studies demonstrating local efforts to maintain specific elements of support. The chapter includes a much expanded section on the lived experience of young fathers and initiatives to meet their needs, contributed by researchers who have championed a greater focus on support for young fathers. We end with four current local case studies illustrating NHS, Local Authority and Voluntary and Community Sector (VCS) examples of specialist support which reflect the principles of the national guidance, *A framework for supporting teenage mothers and young fathers.* We conclude by summarising the key themes of recent developments and recommend a set of actions to re-establish a system wide approach to young parents, scale up effective support and monitor progress.

Chapter 8 provides an international perspective and is written by Dr Venkatraman Chandra-Mouli, who until August 2023 led the work on adolescent sexual and reproductive health at the World Health Organisation. Dr Chandra-Mouli first saw the transferability of the strategy and has championed England's success internationally. Drawing from credible global surveys, the chapter begins by pointing to the progress that has been made globally in reducing levels of adolescent childbearing – slow and uneven, but tangible progress, nevertheless. Second, it describes the widely differing contexts in which adolescent childbearing occurs globally. Thirdly, it describes the evolution of global, regional and national responses to adolescent childbearing. It shines a spotlight on successful national government-led programmes in countries in four different world regions – Ethiopia (Sub-Saharan Africa), Thailand (South-East Asia), Argentina (Latin America), Moldova (Central Europe) and England (Western Europe) – which show what can and has been done with the application of wise and courageous leadership, good science, and strong management. It ends with data on countries, communities, families and individuals being left behind, and calls for tailored efforts to address these inequities, providing an example of a remarkable 40-year initiative from Jamaica to support adolescent parents to complete their education.

We end the book with a short epilogue, reminding us that this long continuing journey is all about making a difference to young people's lives; paying tribute to the tireless efforts and huge contributions made by individuals, the VCSs and political and organisation collaborations; but highlighting again that national action is needed urgently to maintain progress, halt and reverse the widening inequalities that risk blighting the lives of young people. Spending on young people now is investment for the future.

Notes

1 Relationships and Sex Education (Sex Education Forum, national VCS organisation); access to contraception (All-Party Parliamentary Group on Sexual and Reproductive Health, the Advisory Group on Contraception, the English HIV and Sexual Health Commissioners Group, and Brook, the national sexual health and well-being VCS organisation); and youth policy (Association for Young People's Health, national VCS organisation).

2 The Teenage Pregnancy Knowledge Exchange was established in 2013 at the University of Bedfordshire as the first national source of expert knowledge and advice on all aspects of teenage pregnancy.

3 The English HIV and Sexual Health Commissioners Group provides a strategic forum for commissioners of SRH services to meet, network and work together to improve the commissioning and delivery of local integrated services and strategies.

4 Family Nurse Partnership is an intensive home visiting programme for first-time young mothers and families.

1 Variation in teenage conception rates

1.1 Background

1.1.1 What is teenage pregnancy?

Although the phrase ‘teenage pregnancy’ is widely used and may sound straightforward, there is some confusion in the media and elsewhere as to what is actually covered. Strictly speaking, it should refer to a conception that occurs while a woman is still a teenager; that is, prior to her 20th birthday. However, such a definition would include births that occur up to about 20 years and eight to nine months of age, as well as abortions that take place either before the 20th birthday or some time afterwards. Such precise data are simply not readily available in the vast majority of countries.

Data on abortions by age are not routinely available in many countries. This is sometimes due to its illegality and/or the stigma attached to the process. In such countries, abortions still occur through women travelling to another country or US state for the purpose of obtaining one, or by obtaining medication for early medical abortion from the internet or through unofficial – and often unsafe – provision. These cases do not appear in routine official statistics – as well as being very risky in some cases.

What is important to clarify is how the phrase ‘teenage pregnancy’ is operationalised in practice. As mentioned above, strictly speaking it should cover all teen ages. However, countries use different age bands for various reasons, even within the United Kingdom[1]. In England, the main policy concern has focused on conceptions that occur under the age of 18, the statutory age for participation in education and training, with an additional focus on young women who conceive before 16, the legal age of sexual consent.

The England strategy, which is described in this book, set a target to halve conceptions among under-18s and establish a downward trend in conceptions among under-16s. What was of interest were the rates, not the absolute numbers, as an increase in age-specific population sizes will affect the actual numbers of cases. That said, calculating the rates based on the whole under-18 population would be misleading, mainly because most of the people captured within this group are not of reproductive age.

DOI: 10.4324/9781003410225-2

So, the pragmatic approach adopted in the UK for many years has been to use the age range 15 to 17 years as the denominator to calculate under-18 rates, and the age range 13 to 15 years to calculate under-16 rates. Data on conceptions are compiled by combining information from registrations of births, and notifications of legal abortions. Estimates are made for each birth and abortion as to the likely date of conception, and that date is linked to the age of the woman at the time. All such events that are estimated to have occurred between her 15th birthday and the day before her 18th birthday are counted as a case for under-18 conceptions, and the overall numbers are linked to the annual population size estimates of that age group in order to calculate rates. As an example, 60 conceptions among 2,000 women aged 15 to 17 years would be a rate of 30; 80 conceptions among 4,000 women aged 15 to 17 years would be a rate of 20. Clearly, some estimates are needed for these calculations regarding the actual dates of events, but the assumption is that these unavoidable misattributions are relatively consistent and so do not seriously affect data comparisons over time or place. Miscarriages are disregarded for the calculation of these rates, partly because their occurrence is assumed to be comparable across areas (and so do not affect comparative analyses), but also because some occur without a woman's knowledge, do not require clinical intervention, and so are not included in any official data.

A further figure that is of relevance is the proportion of those conceptions that do occur that end in abortion. This is important if the policy concern is more directed towards *births* that occur to young women, as opposed to *conceptions per se*. Out of every 100 conceptions a certain proportion will end in termination – this is called the *abortion proportion* (or *abortion ratio*).

These definitional distinctions are important since, among the various approaches to understanding the area of early conceptions, comparing data from different areas enables lessons to be learned as to how policy can be directed in more fruitful ways. For example, when the monitoring data for the England strategy showed that, within the overall reduction in conceptions, there was a steeper decline in births compared with abortions, additional attention was paid towards improving young people's access to, and uptake of, contraception. It is to some of these comparative data that focus is now directed.

1.1.2 International comparisons in teenage birth rates

Some of the earliest national comparative data analyses involved researchers from the Guttmacher Institute in the USA, which collected data from 37 industrialised countries in the mid-1980s; the data included teenage *birth* rates (not *conception* rates due to unavailability of abortion data in many countries) alongside a range of other indices that were thought could be related. These included the Gini coefficient (an index of income distribution within countries), levels of sex and relationships education in schools and the degree of openness regarding sexual issues including, for example, television advertising of contraception. In summary, they reported that countries with lower birth rates were characterised by a smaller gap between rich and poor, as well as having more 'open' cultures regarding sexual issues (Jones et al., 1985; 1986). A replication of this approach many years later focused on a smaller number of countries (five) in Europe and obtained very similar results (Darroch et al., 2001).

What had sparked these concerns in the USA was the country's very high birth rate compared with other rich nations. UNICEF carried out a similar comparative analysis in 2001, comparing data from 28 OECD countries (UNICEF, 2001). They pointed to the very wide range in teenage (under-20s) birth rates, with South Korea and Japan at one extreme (with around three per thousand), through Switzerland (5.5), the Netherlands (6.2) and Sweden (6.5) to the United Kingdom at 30.8 and the USA at 52.1. The proportions of these women who were married at the time varied from 86 per cent in Japan to two per cent in Iceland and about ten per cent in the UK, although no data are presented on cohabitation rates.

In attempting to account for these wide variations, the UNICEF report noted that there had been a general decline in teenage motherhood in most countries (probably linked to the increase in average age at marriage) but also large increases in sexual activity among young people. They argued that countries that have successfully reduced rates of teenage births are characterised by, among other features '. . . rising levels of education, more career choice for women, more effective contraception, and changing preferences . . .' (p. 2) and '. . . the widespread liberalisation of traditional sexual codes . . .' (p. 8). They also point out that, despite the general reduction over time in teenage birth rates, the perception of this being a problem in society has increased. In highlighting commonalities between countries in that birth rates are higher in the poorer areas, the authors proposed that rates can be understood in terms of both *means* and *motivation* to avoid early pregnancy. The *means* involves the availability of contraception and sex and relationships education that enables young people to make informed and mutually respectful choices; however, the expectation of inclusion in the benefits from education, employment and economic opportunities provides *motivation* to delay parenthood. It was these principles that underpinned the England strategy and the reason for its close links with other government programmes aimed at increasing educational attainment and narrowing inequalities of opportunity.

1.1.3 Regional variations in under-18 conception rates

As well as national variations, there are quite substantial regional variations in conception and birth rates within countries; here, the focus is on the situation in England.

In 1998 (the baseline year for the strategy) there were 41,089 conceptions to women aged under 18, with an overall rate per thousand of 46.6; using the government regions, the rates ranged from 66.7 in Inner London to 37.8 in the South East (ONS, 2017). At the local government level, rates ranged from 87.2 to 16.9. At the even lower geographical level of electoral wards (averaged over three years to avoid large year-by-year fluctuations due to small numbers) the rates for 2001 to 2003 ranged from 213.0 to 6.4.

Variation between countries, and regions within countries, indicates that research exploring why such variations occur will be fruitful, and should point towards potential foci for policy action. The importance of having accurate regional and local data to monitor progress and inform the England strategy is highlighted at several points in subsequent chapters.

1.1.4 Why is early conception an issue?

Whether or not early conception is regarded as a 'problem' is a matter for debate. In some countries (as in the UK going back some years), early marriage and child-bearing is (and was) the norm. There are other issues to be considered, however, such as 'forced' early marriage and societal pressures to be fertile, 'shotgun' marriages, gender inequalities and other factors impacting on individual choice; these are beyond the scope of the present volume.

In a rapidly changing world, however, where extended education, growing employment for women and smaller families are becoming the norm, an increasing number of countries regard teenage parenthood as carrying significant intergenerational disadvantage (for example dropping out of education as well as health problems), and are taking action to equip young people to avoid early conception (UNICEF, 2001; UNFPA, 2013a; 2013b; 2015). All the UK initiatives were developed with the aim of reducing social exclusion, poverty and inequalities, alongside improving young people's sexual health and wellbeing.

Meanwhile, however, it is worth noting variations in abortion proportions, which can be interpreted as indicating the degree of planning involved in the conceptions that do occur. Although circumstances can change between conception and birth (for example, partnership dissolution, housing and financial emergencies) most abortions arise from unplanned conceptions. In the same way that there are variations in conception rates across regions, so there are variations in abortion proportions.

Using the 1998 baseline data, and with an England overall figure of 42 per cent, across regions, the proportions of conceptions that ended in abortion ranged from 54.5 to 35.2 and, across local government areas, from 78.3 to 23.9. Lee et al. (2004) explored these variations using both qualitative and quantitative data and found that many of the statistical associates of variation in conception rates also applied to variations in conception outcomes, and that there are many attitudinal, community and societal factors that affect the choices that young women make when faced with a pregnancy. In brief, areas with high conception rates tend to have lower abortion proportions. Over the course of the strategy, the proportion of conceptions leading to abortion increased in all England regions (from 41.1 in 1998 to 53.3 in 2021)[2], including the most deprived areas. This trend may reflect an increase in the choice of outcome options offered by the wider availability of abortion services, described in Chapter 3, and subsequent ease of access through new legislation[3] in 2022 to allow provision of at home medical abortion. Greater awareness of the advantages of delaying early childbearing arising from the publicity surrounding the prevention strategy and/or other factors may also have contributed to the trend.

1.2 Research challenges

There are some important methodological challenges involved in the study of teenage pregnancy. These are briefly outlined now to avoid the need for repetition as the review progresses and different studies are described.

1.2.1 Distinguishing precursors from sequelae

There is interest in how teenage parents, especially mothers, may differ, as a consequence of being parents, from others who are not parents. Some research points to downward social mobility in the form of lower income, higher unemployment, increased likelihood of poor mental health, for example, postnatal depression and other negative outcomes. Studies generally obtain their samples after the event – that is, after parenthood has occurred – and compare young parents with similarly aged non-parents.

A major challenge with this research design is that it is very difficult to disentangle any factors, attributes, conditions or qualities that may have been present *prior to* the pregnancy from those that were brought about *as a result of* the pregnancy and birth. In other words, claims that the young age of the mother leads directly to negative outcomes need to be handled with great care. Attempting to ascertain factors that pertained prior to the birth from retrospective accounts are fraught with difficulties relating to memory, post-hoc justifications and other challenges.

Examples are provided later of studies that have to a large extent overcome these challenges by using longitudinal data obtained from large samples that provide relevant information before and after the transition to parenthood. Such studies, however, were not designed specifically in order to explore early childbearing so the level of relevant detail covered in the topics covered is limited. Further, some were commenced prior to early pregnancy being a particular focus of policy interest, so what we would now regard as highly relevant information was not collected from the outset.

Further, such studies do not necessarily capture information on young women who became pregnant but chose to have an abortion. Although this question may be asked, the stigma associated with abortion may lead to inaccurate responses. So, by just comparing young mothers with non-mothers, any potential differences between those who become pregnant from those who (perhaps) do not are hidden. A similar point can be made regarding young women who suffer miscarriages.

Even for studies that do have available data from before and after the event, confident attribution can be highly challenging. If, for example, an association is observed between a young woman's family structure at age 13 and the probability of childbearing before age 18, this does not indicate a direct causal relationship. It may provide clues as to where to search for explanatory links but does no more than this.

The so-called 'gold standard' approach to research involves randomly allocating people to different controlled conditions and then comparing outcomes subsequently. Such an approach is clearly inappropriate when considering teenage conception as an outcome, although some studies have adopted this method when looking at specific issues that may be relevant, such as different approaches to relationships and sex education. Some examples are considered later.

1.2.2 Variations in levels of sexual activity and/or levels of contraceptive use

It was mentioned earlier that teenage conception data are presented as rates per thousand women within specified age ranges. What this overlooks, of course, is that not all of these women will be sexually active. There is a strong case for presenting conception data as rates *per 1,000 sexually active women,* but the level of detail of local data that would enable this is not available and would take an extremely large and prohibitively expensive representative sample survey to obtain (even assuming accurate responses).

Consider an example: Area A has an under-18 conception rate of 50 per thousand while Area B's rate is 48 per thousand. If half of the young women in Area A have experienced penetrative heterosexual sexual activity, then the 'true' rate of conception among those at risk of conception is 50 per 500, which is 100 per thousand. In Area B, if three quarters have had penetrative heterosexual activity then the rate is 48 per 750, which is 64 per thousand. So, apparently similar conception rates (50 and 48) can arise from different areas' behavioural characteristics. Further, it is important to note that the category of 'sexually active' in this context simply means having experienced penetrative heterosexual activity but does not measure the *frequency* of such activity, an index that will clearly also affect the likelihood of conception.

Additionally, levels of correct and consistent contraceptive use will also affect outcomes. So, for example, in the two hypothetical areas outlined above, the seeming similarity in the traditionally expressed (per thousand women) rates conceal differences in levels of sexual activity (or status), but also reveal variations in effective contraceptive use. In the two examples above, it would appear that young women (or couples) in Area B are more effective users of contraception than those in Area A, as the conception rate among sexually active women is considerably lower (64 as compared with 100).

So, in accounting for variations in rates, as well as in devising suitable policy responses, it is important to gather more detail than the official published rates provide. As mentioned earlier, good data on area-level variations in sexual activity are not available, and nor are similar detailed data on contraceptive usage (the national survey – NATSAL – does involve a large sample across the country, but this is unsuitable for detailed age-related analysis once broken down into local levels). In England, local data on attendance at community contraceptive services is recorded by age and residence, but data are not available by age on other sources of contraception, nor on actual usage. Some studies do ask about *general* usage, or general properties or attributes, such as attitudes to risk, or sensation-seeking, as opposed to specific contextual factors that may account for risks occurring.

1.3 Who is more likely to get pregnant?

Bearing in mind the caveats outlined above regarding research in this complex area, this section provides an overview of key findings that have helped to identify some of the important factors that are associated with teenage conceptions. Consideration is given to variations at international, regional and individual levels. Finally, brief consideration is given to the issue of intentionality.

1.3.1 International variations

As mentioned earlier, because abortion is illegal or strongly proscribed and stigmatised in some countries, comparative data on conceptions from a wide range of countries are hard to access. Accordingly, emphasis is on birth rates and reference was made earlier to the initial (dated but still relevant) Guttmacher comparative studies, and the general societal characteristics that they reported were associated with variations in national rates (Jones et al., 1985, 1986). Similar general conclusions were reported by the UNICEF team based on a slightly different sample of countries. This also introduced the interesting notion of 'motive and means' as significant factors in accounting for variations in teenage birth rates between and within countries (UNICEF, 2001).

The UNICEF report draws attention to the reduced birth rates alongside higher abortion proportions in the Nordic countries and argues that these data represent a relative failure in relationships and sex education and/or service provision (on the grounds that abortion is unlikely to be a preferred choice). In identifying the Netherlands as a country with low birth *and* low abortion rates, the report calls this a 'remarkable achievement', the underlying reason for which is 'the combination of a relatively inclusive society with more open attitudes to sex and sexuality education, including contraception' (UNICEF, 2001, p. 23).

As well as interesting lessons that can be learned from comparative national birth rate data of this kind, focus can also be directed towards possible variations in levels of sexual activity and abortion proportions in different countries. In other words, are the birth rates higher in the USA and the UK just because more young people are engaging in sexual activity, and/or because more young people are making a positive choice of early parenthood, and are these affected by the cultural variations identified by the Guttmacher researchers and the UNICEF study?

Combining data on changes in levels of sexual activity across time in Europe reported by Bozon and Kontula (1998), and those reported by Singh and Darroch (2000), Ingham (2007) demonstrated that the large variations in birth rates across European countries was not accounted for by the proportions of women who reported heterosexual intercourse by the age of 20 years. What was also demonstrated was wide variation in the abortion proportions across countries. So, for example, across the ten European countries compared, Germany had a teenage abortion proportion of 29 per cent, compared with Sweden's 69 per cent. These variations suggest differing attitudes to abortion in the different countries, as well as, perhaps, different availability and efficient use of reliable contraception.

Relatively little is known about reported reasons for sexual activity among young people in comparative terms; such data would be immensely helpful in the attempts to account for national variation in rates of conceptions and outcomes. One such study was reported by Ingham and van Zessen (1997, 1998), albeit based on small samples in each country but derived from detailed interview data. They report that, whereas women provided broadly similar reasons in the two countries, men in the Netherlands were much more likely to report 'love', 'commitment', and similarly intimate reasons for first sex (around 60 per cent) than were men in the UK (around 15 per cent). Among the latter, 'opportunity', 'physical attraction' and 'peer pressure' were more frequently reported reasons. More intimate reasons (as seen in the Netherlands) are associated with longer length of relationship prior to first sex, higher levels of partner communication and more effective contraceptive use.

1.3.2 Regional variations

Close links between rates of teenage pregnancy and levels of social deprivation have been identified in a number of studies. One of the earliest in the United Kingdom was carried out in Scotland, with Smith (1993) demonstrating that young women living in the most deprived areas who became pregnant were considerably more likely to give birth while a teenager and to be less likely to have an abortion.

Using multi-level modelling (to account for shared characteristics at different levels of analysis) Diamond et al. (1999) found that specially developed (and directly relevant) indices of social deprivation predicted rates of teenage conception in local authority areas across the South West of England. These indices included (for urban areas) the proportion of under five-year-old children, the proportion of households without access to a car and the percentage of 17-year old children not in full-time education along with a measure of population mobility. In rural areas, significant predictors were 'non-car ownership, the proportion of children under five years old, overcrowding and lack of basic amenities' (Diamond et al., *op.cit.*, p. 283).

A more recent study (ONS, 2015) reported that child poverty and unemployment are the two area deprivation indicators with the strongest association with under-18 conception rates.

It needs to be borne in mind that this approach to the study of variations in conception rates runs the risk of falling into the 'ecological fallacy'; in other words, it should not be assumed that the characteristics of an area that relate to specific outcomes apply to *all* the individual people living in that area (although the chances are increased of course).

An illustration of this distinction comes from work by Smith and Elander (2006), who demonstrated that, in terms of early sexual activity and life expectations, levels of both family and area deprivation interacted. Although early sexual activity was associated with living in deprived areas, the effect was stronger among those in deprived families. Similarly, life expectations were higher in less deprived areas, but only among those in non-deprived families.

A more recent approach that explored recent changes in area teenage conception rates reported that some (but not all) of the change could be explained by different population ethnicity compositions, improved educational achievement and lower levels of youth unemployment; these patterns led to decreases in the gap between more and less deprived areas, as well as between different geographical regions (Heap et al., 2020).

1.3.3 Individual characteristics

Although national and regional variations, and their associated correlates, are of great interest in narrowing down the search for explanatory factors and developing policy interventions, they do not enable a level of understanding to identify individual level risk of, and/or vulnerability to, early pregnancy. As mentioned earlier, asking women after the event of a conception is not necessarily a reliable approach to the area.

A few studies in the UK have enabled a more thorough exploration of this issue. The first of these was carried out by Kiernan (1997) using data from the British Cohort Study that commenced in 1958 (BCS58). The study involved sending regular survey instruments to the parents of all children born within a specific week in 1958 and then subsequently to the children themselves as they became old enough to complete their own surveys. The clear advantage of this approach is that data are collected prior to key events occurring, and so challenges posed by (potentially misleading) retrospective accounting, are not pertinent.

However, as well as such studies not being designed specifically to explore teenage conception (as mentioned above), there is also the issue of attrition to consider. In other words, a certain number of the initial sample will drop out, through losing interest, moving house and becoming untraceable, or other significant life events. If these participants are more likely to be (or to have been) in one or other of the groups of interest, then bias will enter the analysis. Nevertheless, a considerable sample size remains, among which there was a sufficient number of teenage births to enable statistical comparisons to be made.

Kiernan identified a number of risk factors that predicted a teenage birth; these included reported 'emotional problems at ages 7 or 16', the 'teenager's own mother being a teenage mother', 'family experienced financial adversity when the child was 7 or 16', a 'preference towards being a teenage mother', and 'low educational attainment at age 16'. Women with all five of these characteristics had a 56 per cent chance of becoming a teenage mother, compared with 3 per cent for those with none of them.

Berrington et al. (2005a) carried out a similarly detailed analysis of data from the BCS70 survey (similar to BCS58 but using a cohort born in 1970). Key predictors of early parenthood were 'own mother was a teenage mother', 'no father figure at birth', 'father's social class 4 and 5 at birth', 'conduct disorder at age 10', and 'living in social housing at age 10'. The more of these risk factors that were present the higher were the odds of teenage childbearing.

More recently a study in an English region explored the impact of Adverse Childhood Experiences, defined as physical, sexual or emotional childhood abuse, family breakdown, exposure to domestic violence, and living in household affected by substance misuse, mental illness or where someone is incarcerated. Experiencing four or more ACEs was associated with a fourfold higher risk of having or causing an intended teenage pregnancy (Ford et al., 2016).

Berrington et al. (2005b) also considered the characteristics of fathers – these were included if their age at reported fatherhood was under 23 years (as most fathers of children born to young mothers are slightly older than the mother). Despite the risk that there is an element of under-reporting in these data, the characteristics that distinguished young fathers from others were remarkably similar to those obtained for young mothers. Again, the more risk factors that were present the higher the odds were of being a young father.

The reliance on parenthood as the outcome in these longitudinal cohort studies does not enable the factors associated with *conception* (including abortion) to be explored. Young women who conceive but then choose abortion will almost certainly differ from those who choose to give birth. A creative way of looking at this was devised by Ermisch and Pevalin (2003) who included in their analysis cases of teenage women who suffered a miscarriage as an additional comparison group for young mothers, the argument being that these had not opted for abortion. The analysis showed that, by age 30, the impact of early childrearing was strongest in terms of non-home ownership and, if partnered, the partner being unemployed.

A yet more recent study, using the large Millennium Cohort data set (Hawkes, 2010), reports that there are substantial differences in reported life circumstances, prior to the birth, between women who do and do not become young mothers; these include being '. . . more likely to have experienced the unemployment of a father at age 14, to have left school at the minimum school leaving age, to have experienced parental separation and to have lived away from home than all the other mothers' (p. 81). However, the study demonstrates that there are gradations of negative circumstances at the time of the birth itself, such that those associated with becoming a mother during the teenage years are not substantially different from those who become parents in their early twenties, in terms of partner presence, being an owner occupier, having a vehicle available and living in a disadvantaged area.

A 2013 study using an innovative design that became possible due to advances in data linkage cast further light on factors associated with susceptibility to early conception. One of the key questions in the broader research area is why some young women avoid early pregnancy despite sharing demographic and location data with some who do. By combining individual level data from conception and educational records, researchers from the Institute of Fiscal Studies were able to identify that educational progress between ages 11–14 and persistent school absence by the age of 14 were additional predictors of risk over and above all other known demographic aspects. However, it was notable that the individual data analysis found that the majority of young women conceiving before the age of 18 did not have specific risk factors. The study concluded that to achieve a significant reduction in conception rates, a strategy cannot solely concentrate on high-risk groups (Crawford et al., 2013).

In England, teenage births by ethnicity are not routinely published, so estimates need to be drawn from Census data, collected every ten years. In the data from the 2001 Census, motherhood under 19 was significantly higher among White British, Mixed White and Black Caribbean, other Black and Black Caribbean women, while all Asian groups were under-represented (Department for Education and Skills, 2006).

During the early days of the strategy, it was observed that areas in London with higher proportions of Black African and Caribbean young people tended to have higher rates of conceptions *and* higher abortion proportions, a different association from that found in most areas. Marked changes occurred, however, in the rates observed in these localities during the life of the strategy.

Aspinall and Hashem (2010) pointed out that, despite targeted work being a priority in the Public Service Agreement targets linked to the strategy, good quality locally coded ethnicity data on births and abortions were lacking, making specific targeted work very challenging.

Higher birth and/or abortion rates among some ethnic groups are likely to be influenced by the disproportionate impact of disadvantage on ethnic minorities – with young people in some groups over-represented in the care system or in school exclusions – as well as marked cultural variations in norms and behaviours. The consultation to develop the England strategy also highlighted that contraceptive services were frequently not designed in a way that would reach ethnic minority young people, an issue that was addressed in the strategy action plan.

1.3.4 Degrees of intentionality

One of the key challenges in the field of early pregnancy is to disentangle the various factors that have been associated with occurrence and outcomes and assess their relative importance. As mentioned already, designing studies to collect data that would enable clear distinctions to be made poses very real challenges.

Explanations for early pregnancy and childbearing raised in the studies cited above fall, to put it simply, into one of two (or both) categories. The first is historical; factors or contexts that occurred in the past are used to explain current risk behaviour and/or vulnerability. So, for example, living in a single parent family, having a mother who was herself an early child-bearer, receiving a poor level of sex education, lacking knowledge and understanding of fertility and contraception, acquiring gender normative behaviours that have restricted communication options, and so on. Wellings et al. (2013) on the basis of NATSAL3 data, reported that pregnancies among 16- to 19-year olds were most commonly unplanned, and were associated with lack of sexual competence at first sexual intercourse (see 2.6, Chapter 2), reporting higher frequency of sex in the previous four weeks, receiving sex education mainly from a non-school-based source, and current depression (Wellings et al., 2013, p. 1807).

The second group of factors relate to future orientations. So, the desire to have a baby to demonstrate capability in a non-academic or non-employment domain, or to have an object for one's affection, to cement a relationship (or attempt to maintain one), to demonstrate fertility, and so on. In practice, of course, the 'future-oriented' factors may well be a direct or indirect result of prior experiences and contexts.

Nevertheless, these different perspectives may affect the extent to which an early pregnancy is planned or unplanned. Pregnancies that are primarily driven by factors in the second category (future orientation) may well be planned, or not actively prevented, whereas those in the former category are more likely to be unplanned (which is not to say that they will not be wanted once a pregnancy is confirmed). Policy responses to these two groups of factors will vary – correcting or remediating past 'deficits' to enable more fully informed choices, and/or focusing on future orientations. A not uncommon expression in the field is that "ambition is the best form of contraception"; although it is of course the effective use of contraception that actually prevents pregnancy! In practice, all avenues should be covered, although the practical reality is that resources do not permit this coverage so priorities need to be selected. Achieving a suitable balance between targeted and universal interventions – proportionate universalism – was central to the ambition of the England strategy. As highlighted in Chapter 5 this continues to be a real challenge as need grows and resources diminish.

1.4 Impact of early conceptions

1.4.1 Impact on mothers

As mentioned earlier, distinguishing between the impacts of early motherhood from factors that predispose young women to early pregnancy is a major challenge. Some of the earlier studies that reported on negative outcomes for teenage parents were based on cross-sectional comparisons and so are rather restricted in what they can claim regarding the direct impact of parenthood. As mentioned above, all the British-based longitudinal cohort studies have pointed to teenage mothers having greater disadvantaged circumstances prior to the birth than those who did not become teenage mothers, but additional disadvantage appears to arise from early childbearing.

In presenting data in this – and other – areas it is crucial to note that the studies identify general statistical trends and not issues that are claimed to affect each and every young mother. Nor should any of the results presented be interpreted as casting any aspersions on young women's abilities to cope with early childbearing; obviously, as in any other walk of life, some will cope better than others. Indeed, it is an important aspect of work in the area that efforts are made to identify factors which assist young parents, and to enable improved support and provision for the families involved. This was an integral part of the England strategy and is discussed with an update on recent progress in Chapter 7.

The Berrington et al. (2005a) research (using the BCS70 data set) compared outcomes for mothers who had their first children at different ages. What this demonstrated was that the impact of age was incremental; in other words, the overall negative impact on parents who were teenagers at the time of the birth was somewhat more pronounced than the impact on women who were in their early twenties at the time of their first birth but was not qualitatively different. This result is similar to that found, using a different cohort and different data-collection methods, by Hawkes (2010).

However, the analysis by Berrington et al. revealed that it was not age *per se* that had an impact, but factors that are often associated with early childbearing but are not inevitable. Thus, a major negative outcome – depression – was associated with other independent factors at all ages but these are more likely to arise in the case of early childbearing. They include relative poverty, lack of partnered support and poor housing environment. The younger the mother at first birth, the more chance there is of her being un-partnered some years later; Chapter 7 discusses issues related to local support services for young parents.

1.4.2 Impact on fathers

Few studies have looked at the impact of early fathering on the young men involved. Again, Berrington et al. were able to do this (assuming that reports of being a father were fairly accurate). Key results were that, at age 30 years, men who fathered babies before the age of 22 years were more likely than matched non-fathers to be unemployed, to have separated from the mother, and to have re-partnered (Berrington et al., 2005b).

Contact with the mother and their child(ren) varied but was much lower, perhaps not surprisingly, when the primary relationship with the mother had broken down and the men had re-partnered. Although this might seem to be obvious, it is not an inevitable consequence and needs to be considered where continued contact between father and child is felt to be appropriate, as close involvement has shown to benefit young fathers and their children, even if the parental relationship ends (Fatherhood Institute, 2016). The experience of young fathers has been explored in more recent qualitative studies, which are discussed in Chapter 7.

1.4.3 Impact on children

Data on the impact on the children of teenage parents do show poorer outcomes compared with children born to older mothers. Again, however, few of these outcomes are a direct result of the age of the mother, but are influenced by pre-existing factors, circumstances and behaviours. For example, the higher risk of low birth weight, stillbirth and infant mortality for babies born to younger women is likely to be affected by poor nutrition and higher rates of smoking during pregnancy – the main modifiable risk factor for a range of child health outcomes (Chan and Sullivan, 2008).

Late booking of young parents with maternity services, alongside lack of accessible and trusted services, diminishes the protective benefits of antenatal care. Accessibility of antenatal classes may be restricted due to travel costs, as well as psychological barriers experienced by some young women due to feeling stigmatised when other members of such classes tend to be older. There are excellent examples of antenatal care specifically for teenage women, as illustrated in Chapter 7, but the ability to provide special antenatal classes may be constrained by funding limits and/or because there are insufficient numbers to justify this expenditure in many geographical areas. There are clear data from other countries on the beneficial effects of early ante-natal care among young mothers: see, for example, Nam et al. (2022) and Gardner et al. (2023).

So, some negative effects on children born to teenage mothers may reflect these differences. Premature birth and lower birth weight may make babies more prone to infection and other forms of ill-health and, if young parents have less money available, then visits to their doctors' surgeries may be more difficult and any required diagnosis and treatment may be delayed. Further, if young parents and their children are housed in poor and possibly overcrowded accommodation, then the probability of accidents may be higher, as well as the conditions impacting on their mental health and wellbeing.

Support for this interpretation arises from the analyses by Berrington and colleagues, using the ALSPAC data set, a longitudinal data set on all children born within a certain time in the Avon and Somerset areas (Golding et al., 2001). Analyses were carried out on children in over 9,000 families aged up to 42 months old, with comparisons being made between children born to women at different ages at the time of birth. On many measures (including vocabulary, gross and fine motor development), children of teenage parents were found to be no different from others. There were, however, adverse outcomes for the children in terms of behavioural adjustment including conduct, emotional behaviour and hyperactivity. These need to be considered as a whole, as they include factors that relate to family backgrounds of the mothers themselves, the adverse social circumstances or relationship breakdown experienced after the birth, and factors that might relate more directly to care provided by teenage mothers. Parental depression, for example, to which young mothers are particularly vulnerable, has been identified as the most prevalent risk factor overall for negative impact on child development outcomes (Sabates and Dex, 2012).

Hawkes (2010) reports on outcomes for children born to parents of different ages and, again, illustrates that some negative cognitive developmental indices are linked to age of the mother at birth in an incremental manner; these include vocabulary subscale and school readiness scores at age three, and some other cognitive measures at age five. Some behavioural outcomes show similar patterns, including hyperactivity, emotional difficulties conduct problems and peer problems. Morinis et al. (2013), based on the UK Millennium Cohort study found that, at age five, children born to mothers aged 18 years or under, when compared with children born to mothers aged between 25 and 34 years, were four months behind on spatial ability, seven months behind on non-verbal ability and 11 months behind on verbal ability; however, controlling for sociodemographic circumstances and perinatal risk removed these differences with the exception of verbal ability.

While the challenge remains in distinguishing the impacts of early motherhood from factors that predispose young women to early pregnancy, it is clear that many young women, and young men, enter parenthood with a disproportionate burden of disadvantage, which can affect outcomes for them and their children. The England strategy's approach to providing bespoke support for young parents was described in the previous edition. How support has progressed since the strategy ended is described in Chapter 7. Meanwhile, the next chapter describes some of what is known about means to reduce levels of unintended early conceptions.

Notes

1 In other countries in the UK, Northern Ireland focuses on under-20s and under-17s, Wales monitors under-18s but has a specific focus on under-16s, and Scotland focuses prevention on under-18s and support for parents up to age 26.
2 www.ons.gov.uk/peoplepopulationandcommunity/birthsdeathsandmarriages/conceptionandfertilityrates/bulletins/conceptionstatistics/2021#teenage-conceptions.
3 www.gov.uk/government/news/at-home-early-medical-abortions-made-permanent-in-england-and-wales.

References

Aspinall, P.J. and Hashem, F. (2010). Are our data on teenage pregnancy across ethnic groups in England fit for the purpose of policy formulation, implementation, and monitoring? *Critical Public Health*, 20(1), 47–70.

Atkins, D.N. and Bradford, W.D. (2021). The effect of state-level sex education policies on youth sexual behaviors. *Archives of Sexual Behavior*, 50, 2321–2333. 10.1007/s10508-020-01867-9.

Berrington, A.M., Diamond, I., Ingham, R. and Stevenson, J. (2005a). *Consequences of Teenage Parenthood; pathways which minimise the long-term negative impacts of teenage childbearing*. Final report submitted to the Department of Health, Social Sciences and Demography, University of Southampton.

Berrington, A.M., Cobos Hernandez, M.I., Ingham, R. and Stevenson, J. (2005b). *Antecedents and outcomes of young fatherhood: longitudinal evidence from the 1970 British Birth Cohort Study*. University of Southampton: S3RI Applications and Policy Working Papers, A05/09.

Bozon, M. and Kontula, O. (1998). Sexual initiation and gender in Europe; a cross-cultural analysis of trends in the twentieth century, in Hubert, M., Bajos, N. and Sandfort, Th. (Eds) *Sexual Behaviour and HIV/AIDS in Europe*. London: UCL Press, pp. 37–67.

Chan, D.L. and Sullivan, E.A. (2008). Teenage smoking in pregnancy and birthweight: a population study, 2001–2004. *Medical Journal of Australia*, 188(7), 392–396.

Crawford, C., Cribb, J and Kelly, E. (2013). *Teenage pregnancy in England, CAYT Impact Study, report number 6*. London: Centre for Analysis of Youth Transitions, NatCen, IoE, IFS.

Darroch, J.E., Singh, S., Frost, J.J. and the Study Team (2001). Differences in teenage pregnancy rates among five developed countries: The roles of sexual activity and contraceptive use. *Family Planning Perspectives*, 33(6), 244–281.

Department for Education and Skills (2006). *Teenage pregnancy: Accelerating the strategy to 2010*. London: DfES.

Diamond, I., Clements, S., Stone, N. and Ingham, R. (1999). Spatial variation in teenage conceptions in south and west England, *Journal of the Royal Statistical Society Series A (Statistics in Society)*, 162(3), 273–289.

Ermisch, J. and Pevalin, D.J. (2003). *Does a 'teen-birth' have longer-term impacts on the mother? Evidence from the 1970 British Cohort Study*. ISER University of Essex, ISER Working Papers, Number 2003–28.

Fatherhood Institute. (2016). *Research summary: Young fathers*. London: Fatherhood Institute.

Ford, K., Butler, N., Hughes, K., Quigg, Z. and Bellis, M. A. (2016). *Adverse childhood experiences (ACEs) in Hertfordshire, Luton and Northamptonshire*. Liverpool: Centre for Public Health, Liverpool John Moores University. www.cph.org.uk/wp-content/uploads/2016/05/Adverse-Childhood-Experiences-in-Hertfordshire-Luton-and-Northamptonshire-FINAL_compressed.pdf (accessed February 2017).

Gardner, M.M., Umer, A., Rudisill, T., Hendricks, B., Lefeber, C., John, C. and Lilly, C. (2023). Prenatal care and infant outcomes of teenage births: a Project WATCH study. *BMC Pregnancy Childbirth*. 23, 379. https://doi.org/10.1186/s12884-023-05662-x.

Golding, J., Pembrey, M., Jones, R. and the ALSPAC Study Team (2001). ALSPAC –5 The Avon longitudinal study of parents and children, *Pediatric and Perinatal Epidemiology*, 15(1), 74–87.

Hawkes, D. (2010). Just what difference does teenage motherhood make? Evidence from the Millennium Cohort Study, in Duncan, S., Edwards, R. and Alexander, C. (Eds), *Teenage parenthood: What's the problem?* London: the Tufnell Press, pp. 69–84.

Heap, K.L., Berrington, A. and Ingham, R. (2020). Understanding the decline in under-18 conception rates throughout England's local authorities between 1998 and 2017. *Health and Place*, 66. https://doi.org/10.1016/j.healthplace.2020.102467.

Ingham, R. (1998). Exploring interactional competence: Comparative data from the United Kingdom and the Netherlands on young people's sexual development. Paper presented at the 24th Meeting of the International Academy of Sex Research, 3–6 June, Sirmione, Italy.

Ingham, R. (2007). Variations across countries: the international perspective. In Baker, P., Guthrie, K., Hutchinson, C., Kane, R. and Wellings, K. (Eds), *Teenage Pregnancy and Reproductive Health*. London: Royal College of Obstetricians and Gynaecologists, pp. 17–29.

Jones E.F., Forrest J.D., Goldman, N., Henshaw, S.K., Lincoln, R., Rosoff, J.I., Westoff, C.F. and Wulf, D. (1985). Teenage pregnancy in developed countries: determinants and policy implications. *Family Planning Perspectives* 17(2), 53–63.

Jones, E.L. and Alan Guttmacher Institute Study Team (1986). *Teenage pregnancy in industrialized countries*. New Haven, CT: Yale University Press.

Kiernan, K. (1997). Becoming a young parent: a longitudinal study of associated factors, *British Journal of Sociology*, 48, 406–428.

Lee, E., Clements, S., Ingham, R. and Stone, N. (2004). *A matter of choice? Explaining national variation in teenage abortion and motherhood*. York: Joseph Rowntree Foundation.

Morinis, J., Carson, C. and Quigley, M.A. (2013). Effect of teenage motherhood on cognitive outcomes in children: a population-based cohort study. *Archives of Disease in Childhood*, 98, 959–964.

Nam, J.Y., Oh, S.S. and Park, E.-C. (2022). The association between adequate prenatal care and severe maternal morbidity among teenage pregnancies: A population-based cohort study. *Frontiers in Public Health*, 10 (31 May 2022). https://doi.org/10.3389/fpubh.2022.782143.

Office for National Statistics (2015). *Link between deprivation and teenage conceptions in England*. London: ONS.

Office for National Statistics (2017). *Conception statistics, England and Wales, 2015*. London: ONS.

Sabates, R. and Dex, S. (2012). *Multiple risk factors in young children's development*. CLS Working Paper 2012/1. London: IoE Centre for Longitudinal Studies.

Singh, S. and Darroch, J.E. (2000). Adolescent pregnancy and childbearing: levels and trends in developed countries. *Family Planning Perspectives*, 32(1), 14–23.
Smith, D.M. and Elander, J. (2006). Effects of area and family deprivation on risk factors for teenage pregnancy among 13–15-year-old girls. *Psychology, Health and Medicine*, 11(4), 399–410.
Smith, T. (1993). Influence of socio-economic factors on attaining targets for reducing teenage pregnancies. *British Medical Journal*, 306, 1232–1235.
UNFPA (2013a). *Adolescent pregnancy: A review of the evidence*. New York: UNFPA.
UNFPA (2013b). *Motherhood in childhood: Facing the challenge of adolescent pregnancy*. New York: UNFPA.
UNFPA (2015). *Girlhood, not motherhood: Preventing adolescent pregnancy*. New York: UNFPA.
UNICEF (2001). *A League Table of Teenage Births in Rich Nations*. Innocenti Report Card No. 3, Florence: UNICEF Innocenti Research Centre.
Wellings, K., Jones, K.G., Mercer, C.H., Tanton, C., Clifton, S., Datta, J., Copas, A.J., Erens, B., Gibson, L.J., Macdowall, W., Sonnenberg, P., Phelps, A. and Johnson, A.M. (2013). The prevalence of unplanned pregnancy and associated factors in Britain: findings from the third National Survey of Sexual Attitudes and Lifestyles (Natsal-3). *Lancet*, 382(9907), 1807–1816, 30 November 2013.

2 Reducing rates of teenage conceptions

2 Considerations regarding reducing rates of teenage conception

2.1 Overview

Much attention has been paid, especially in the USA and the UK, to whether and how levels of teenage pregnancies can be reduced. There is also major concern in many low and middle income countries. Although the detailed contextual features of these countries vary widely, the transferable success factors associated with the England strategy are summarised in Chapter 7 with examples of effective scaled up programmes in other countries.

In a nutshell, relatively high rates of teenage childbearing prior to the 1960s were accepted since most of them occurred within marriage. The degree of individual choice for early parenthood at that time is not possible to ascertain, but is likely to have been compromised by the illegality of abortion and the social pressures on some to arrange a marriage if pregnancy occurred. According to the UNICEF (2001) analysis, when age of marriage and the availability of contraception started to change in the 1960s, some countries adapted well to these changes and some did not. Those that did so experienced reductions in early childbearing; some primarily through increases in abortion proportions (the Nordic pattern) and some through reducing conception rates (the Netherlands being a prime example). Factors which are generally regarded as contributing to, or enabling, these reductions include macro-level social attributes such as greater gender equality and lower levels of income inequality, societal normative positions, such as assuming the need for, and delivering, sex and relationships education and accessible contraceptive and support services for young people, and acceptance of young people's sexual development and interests (not necessarily condoning, but being realistic and responding accordingly) which are linked to more open approaches to the whole area.

In the USA and the UK, however, these wider societal changes did not occur. There are various reasons for this that are beyond the scope of the current chapter, but it did mean that teenage conception and birth rates remained relatively high compared with many other higher-income countries. So, when policymakers eventually turned their attention to these figures, a variety of approaches were adopted

DOI: 10.4324/9781003410225-3

with the aim of reducing the levels (for one early overview of historic policy initiatives, see Wellings and Kane, 1999).

Basically, to reduce rates of teenage pregnancy, the levels of sexual activity need to be reduced, and/or the efficient usage of contraception by sexually active teenagers needs to be increased. Although this may sound relatively straightforward, in reality of course, both areas are highly complex. Across the board, different approaches to these challenges rest on quite different ideological positions with regard to intentions for intervening in this area. A major approach in the USA and in some other countries has been driven by the view that young people should not be engaging in sexual activity until they are married, or at least very close to it with a fully committed partner. So the emphasis is on encouraging abstinence by various means, of which abstinence-only sex education is a preferred option. An alternative view is that young people cannot be prevented from having sex, so resources are better directed towards equipping them to make safe and informed choices through comprehensive relationships and sex education and improved availability and use of contraception. Some selected issues involved in these endeavours are briefly reviewed.

2.2 School-based relationships and sex education

Since all young people in richer countries attend school up to the age of at least 16 years (or at least should do), great emphasis has been placed on the delivery of school-based sex education, albeit called by different names in different places. As mentioned above, successive US Governments encouraged states to adopt abstinence-only approaches, and for many years offered generous financial incentives to State legislatures to do so; few states declined the offer.

There were eight criteria that needed to be met to qualify for federal funding, including telling pupils that pre-marital sexual activity 'is likely to have harmful psychological and physical effects', and that 'bearing children out-of-wedlock is likely to have harmful consequences for the child, the child's parents and society', etc. (Advocates for Youth, 2007). Given that the median age of marriage is approaching 30 years in the USA, these teachings clearly place great demands on young people.

Part of the strict abstinence-only approach involves either the omission of any mention of contraception, or the inclusion of negative (and often false) information about its harmful effects. It is felt that, by mentioning that contraception is available and reasonably safe, many young people will find a ready alternative to the waiting that was required of them. This is despite clear evidence that teaching about contraception is not associated with increased risk of sexual activity or sexually transmitted infections in the teenage years (Kohler et al., 2008).

Alternative approaches in the USA include the so-called Abstinence Plus programmes, which are based on the desirability of abstinence until marriage, but do include (albeit seemingly reluctantly) some information on contraception – just in case some young people simply could not wait. The third approach is called Comprehensive Sexuality Education (CSE), with programmes being designed to provide full details, to improve communication skills, gender-related concerns, and other relevant topics. The aim is to equip young people with the knowledge, skills and confidence to make positive choices about relationships and sexual health (see, for example, Haberland and Rogow, 2015).

It is notoriously difficult to assess the impact of single programmes on teenage conception rates for a number of reasons. Factors affecting conception are complex and it is most unlikely that the impact of one single programme can be identified, quite apart from the very large numbers that would be required to demonstrate statistically significant results. Nevertheless, efforts have been made to evaluate programmes, with outcome measures ranging from the (very challenging) numbers of conceptions, or the more commonly reported self-reports of specific risk behaviours that increase the likelihood of a conception occurring, or measures of knowledge of sexual issues, and/or attitudes to risk.

Quite apart from issues of effectiveness, there have been serious questions raised about the medical accuracy of many of the abstinence-based programmes implemented (Santelli, 2008), the consequent breach to human rights by imparting false information (Santelli et al., 2006), as well as much broader issues regarding their impact on, for example, gender issues and self-esteem, (Fine and McClelland, 2006). So, in addition to the empirical assessments of the impact of sex and relationships education (SRE), there are powerful rights-based arguments for ensuring adequate provision to enable young people to make informed choices to protect their own, and others' health; these stem, in part, from the International Convention on the Rights of the Child (UNICEF, undated). From this perspective, provision of SRE is not about *whether* it should or should not happen, but *how* best to deliver it to enable the rights of all young people to be respected and protected. This indeed was the challenge made by the UN Special Rapporteur response to the British periodic review (UN, 2014).

Kirby was a leading researcher for many years, collecting data from large numbers of studies and reviewing published and unpublished material, some of which involved randomised allocations to conditions in different schools. In a series of reports and articles stretching over 20 years, he became more confident in asserting the lack of success of abstinence-only-based programmes, and started to identify the features of what the evidence pointed to as being essential for successful approaches to the area (Kirby, 2007, 2008). Many international agencies have drawn on his – and others' – work to develop their own guidelines (UNESCO, European Group, Advocates for Youth, SIECUS, etc.). Although specific details of these claimed key success factors vary across agencies, the UK's Sex Education Forum's identified reported characteristics of successful programmes derived from the work of Kirby, as well as Trivedi et al.'s NICE review update (2007), to produce the following list (Sex Education Forum, 2015, p. 5):

- a comprehensive range of topics is addressed, including contraception;
- trained educators are used;
- programmes begin before a young person first has sex;
- psychosocial factors which affect behaviour, including values, norms and self-efficacy, are addressed;
- participatory learning methods are used;

- children and young people are taught using small group work; and
- both school and home contribute to SRE.

The Sex Education Forum (SEF) updated its evidence summary in 2022 in the light of more recent research as well as guidance from the Department for Education regarding what should be covered at different levels of schooling (Sex Education Forum, 2022). Among the recommendations for inclusion during the primary years is the importance of correct naming of body parts; important in respect of coverage of safeguarding and reporting abuse, removal of shame and stigma and increasing empowerment regarding bodily boundaries.

The SEF has also reported the results of a reasonably large survey of young people designed and carried out in conjunction with young people themselves, including a series of discussions about the findings. Among the key results were that there was too little coverage of pleasure, pornography, power imbalances in relationships and issues linked to sexual orientation (Sex Education Forum, 2023). Similar results have been reported elsewhere (Pound et al., 2016).

In the UK, two large random control trials on SRE were funded in the 1990s. One (the SHARE programme) involved school-based delivery based in Scotland, with over 7,000 pupils being involved in 25 schools, randomly allocated to receive a specially designed (and theoretically based) 20-session programme delivered by specially trained teachers; the control group received their normal provision. Various measures were taken before and after the delivery (aged 13 and 14 years, as well as a longer term follow up to assess conception and abortion rates by age 20 years. Little impact of the intervention was found, although pupils reported higher enjoyment in the innovative programme (see Wight, 2011).

The other large UK programme (RIPPLE) involved the delivery of three sessions of peer-education in 29 schools in London and southern England, involving over 9,000 13- and 14-year-old pupils, with the schools being randomly allocated to receive the sessions or their normal provision. Minimal short-term or longer-term impact on the large number of outcome variables was observed (Stephenson et al., 2004, 2008; Parkes et al., 2011).

The lack of clear positive results from these two well-funded British studies led some critics to question the value of school-based SRE; indeed, one such example was provided when Baroness O'Loan cited the SHARE study in the House of Lords 'wash-up' late night debate on whether SRE should be made statutory in British schools:

> There was a project in Glasgow, of which I am sure noble Lords are aware. What was described as an ideal programme of PSHE was delivered. There was a follow-up across 25 schools, covering some, I think, 8,000 students, to see whether there was a reduced incidence of teenage pregnancy and abortion. The result was that there was not.
>
> Hansard, 7 April 2010, column 1589

This was, however, a quite inappropriate and unjustified reaction. All these studies show is that those specific programmes with that specific content and delivered to those specific school years did not show measurable impact on the selected outcome measure. The results certainly do not indicate that SRE is not worth delivering, or that efforts to increase its relevance and value should be reduced, or that longer-term and more sustained programmes starting much earlier in age would not be worthwhile developing.

A similar general critique can be made regarding the recent Cochrane Review on the effectiveness of school-based SRE on biological outcomes (pregnancy and HIV rates). Combining results from a large number of studies – including eight large random controlled trials (RCTs) involving over 55,000 students – the authors report that there is 'little evidence that educational programmes alone are effective . . .' in reducing these selected biological outcomes (Mason-Jones et al., 2016, p. 3). Quite apart from the immense challenges of carrying out RCTs, by combining simple outcome data from these studies (from across three continents) it can be argued to detract from the content of the programmes themselves and risks reducing SRE to little more than an injection! In any event, the conclusion refers to educational programmes alone, a policy that few would propose given the complexity of the issues involved.

Others have attempted to assess the impact of school-based SRE/RSE/CSE. One such example was reported by Paton et al. (2020) in which an attempt was made to assess the impact of sex education mandates in up to 45 countries; the authors claim that countries with laws that mandate SRE tend to have higher rates of teenage fertility. There are, however, a number of concerns regarding this study, including vague definitions of what is meant by 'sex education' in these 45 countries, what is covered and when, what ages the different materials are delivered, whether parents/carers can opt their children out of classes, how consistent policies are in countries across time, whether data include abortions (in many countries these data are hard to obtain), and the use of some rather superficial indices of outcomes. The other obvious issue – only briefly acknowledged by the authors – is that countries with higher rates of teenage fertility may be more likely to have mandated SRE as a response to this situation.

A further 'Global Research Review' that sought to assess the evidence of the effectiveness of CSE was published by the so-called Institute for Research and Evaluation' (Weed & Ericksen, 2019; Ericksen & Weed, 2019); this report – and other similar attacks on CSE – have, however, been heavily criticised on both methodologicl grounds (van Treeck et al., 2022) as well as in relation to their attacks on reproductive justice and human rights (IPAS, 2023).

A similar approach to the comparative study cited above – but just comparing states in the USA – was carried out by Atkins and Bradford (2021). Rather than using teenage pregnancy as the outcome measure (which is a relatively rare event despite the attention it receives) they looked at the association between mandated SRE programmes in 39 states and reported levels of sexual activity among young people. Using data from the Youth Risk Behavior Surveillance System in four waves between 2004 to 2010 and a range of standardised measures of state policies on SRE derived from the Guttmacher and SIECUS (2012) data bases, the authors conclude that, despite all the 'noise' in these data sets:

> Our findings suggest that laws requiring comprehensive sex education decrease sexual activity and raise contraceptive use for youth who are sexually active, while state policies that mandate abstinence only serve to increase sexual activity and decrease hormonal contraceptive use among youth who are sexually active.
>
> (op. cit. page 2331).

There are some indications that the quality of SRE in the UK may be increasing, despite the failure to get it established as a statutory subject (apart from the small very biological component in the Science National Curriculum subject) until the decision finally taken by government in March 2017 (Department for Education, 2017; and see Chapter 5 of this volume regarding some of the barriers faced). The most recent data from NATSAL (National Survey of Sexual Attitudes and Lifestyles – the most recent relates to NATSAL3, collected in 2010; data from NATSAL4 is anticipated being available in 2024–35) show that the reported importance of SRE received in school has increased over the past 20 years, although it should be noted that the increase in schools being cited as the 'most important source' could either imply an improvement in the actual quality of provision, or a reduction in the quality of other potential sources, or some of each. However, the young men and women who cited school as their main source were more likely to experience first sex at a later age and were less likely to report unsafe sex or to have a diagnosis of an STI; young women were less likely to be pregnant by 18 and less likely to have experienced sex against their will (Tanton et al., 2015; Macdowell et al., 2015). This positive association with consensual sex was also found in Lindberg and Maddow-Zimet (2012) where girls receiving comprehensive sexuality education were less likely to have a partner with a big age difference (associated with coercion and intimate partner violence) and were more likely to describe their first sex as wanted.

An overview of the international systematic review evidence on the impact of comprehesive sexuality education (citing over 150 papers) has recently been published by UNESCO and UNFPA.[1]

The authors conclude that:

> Overall, CSE is considered to be a right of the child, as well as an expressed need both from children/adolescents' perspectives and from the perspective of multi-lateral organisations, such as the WHO, UNESCO, UNFPA and others aimed at the improvement of education, health and wellbeing. These multi-lateral organisations have been judicious in citing benefits in terms of contributions to health and knowledge outcomes, while not overstating the case in terms of the effectiveness of CSE alone in shifting biological health outcomes, such as reductions in adolescent pregnancy and HIV. Nonetheless, as this report has shown there is growing evidence that CSE contributes to

> the reduction of adverse health outcomes such as intimate partner violence, HIV and unintended pregnancy by shifting knowledge, attitudes and sexual behaviours. There is also considerable evidence that CSE is more effective than other approaches, such as the AOUM approach.
>
> (p. 20)

2.3 *Provision of contraception*

Alongside improved sex and relationships education in schools, increased availability and usage of contraception has been strongly encouraged in the UK and in parts of the USA. In recent years, there has been much greater uptake of long-acting reversible contraception (LARCs) among young people in the UK (Connolly et al., 2014) and in the USA (Lindberg et al., 2016), although discontinuation for various reasons (mainly unwanted side-effects) remains a concern (Hoggart et al., 2013; Madden et al., 2014). However, although increased use of LARCs appears to have made a major contribution towards reductions in conception rates among young people, there are steady increases in new cases of sexually transmitted infections. Some of the increase is presumably due to an increase in screening leading to more detection, but it may also imply that regularity of condom use has declined. It does appear that increased usage of LARCs is associated with considerably lower rates of condom use among US high school students (Steiner et al., 2016). The England strategy tried to promote both effective contraception to prevent pregnancy and consistent condom use to avoid STIs, but achieving equal impact from both messages was a challenge. Efforts continue to ensure young people have accurate information and easy access to the full range of contraceptive options, and condoms, (see Chapters 5 and 6 – and endnote 2 below – for results from a recent Brook study on attitudes to contraception among young people which reflected some mistrust in hormonal methods).

2.4 *Reducing teenage conception rates in the USA*

There has been a decline in teenage pregnancy rates in the USA in recent years, although the reasons behind this change are disputed. The abstinence-only movement has claimed the success of their educational approach in reducing levels of sexual activity, while others have attributed success to the wider availability of contraception through school-based clinics and other opportunities for access. To help resolve this dispute, Santelli and colleagues analysed data from a number of large surveys between 1995 and 2002, developing measures termed *contraceptive risk index* and *overall pregnancy risk index*, which was calculated using the former index alongside the percentage of individuals reporting sexual activity.

Among 15- to 17-year-olds, rates of sexual activity declined by about ten per cent, but there was no decline among the 18- to 19-year-olds. In relation to the reduction in pregnancy risk among the younger age group, 77 per cent was attributable to improved contraceptive use, while this figure rose to 88 per cent across the whole age range. The authors conclude that ‘The current emphasis of US domestic and global policies, which stress abstinence-only sex education to the exclusion of accurate information on contraception, is misguided. Similar approaches should not be adopted by other nations.' (Santelli et al., 2007, p. 156). A more recent analysis using similar methods (Lindberg et al., 2016) reports that the decline over recent years in adolescent fertility is 'entirely attributable to improvements in contraceptive use' (p. 577). In a later paper, Lindberg et al. (2018) updated their earlier (2016) data analysis using more recent data and concluded that:

> Improvements in contraceptive use—including increases in use of long-acting reversible contraception and withdrawal in combination with another method—appear to be driving recent declines in adolescent birth and pregnancy rates.
>
> (2018, p. 253)

In any event, reductions in levels of sexual activity would not, in themselves, indicate any success for the abstinence-only approaches. Instead, reductions may arise, owing to increased awareness of risk among young people as a result of improved sex education in schools that have adopted comprehensive sex education programmes – which are associated with delayed age of first sex – from the media and within families. Greater sexual 'competence', discussed below, can include reduced gender power differentials (leading to reduced levels of coercive sexual activity), better knowledge of prevention, and other factors.

A comparative analysis between the USA and Britain looking at the trends in sexual activity, contraceptive use and pregnancy rates among young people used two rounds of data – roughly ten years apart – from the US National Survey of Family Growth and the British-based National Survey of Sexual Attitudes and Lifestyles. Higher proportions in Britain reported ever having 'had sex' and also reporting more effective use of contraception[2]. The authors conclude that:

> In both countries, improvements in contraceptive use have contributed substantially to declines in pregnancy rates; however, the steeper decline in the U.S. likely also reflects declines in recent sex occurring only in that country.
>
> (p. 582)

and:

> Contrasting the U.S. with Britain demonstrates that more sex among young people does not have to mean more pregnancies.
>
> (Scott et al., 2020, p. 587)

2.5 Other sources of sexual information

Apart from school and clinical services, young people learn a great deal about sex and relationships from other sources; these include families or carers, increasingly various media (including pornography and social media[3]) and friends or peers. Some of what is learned is specific (albeit correct or not) while other aspects are implicit and covert. So, for example, parents may answer specific questions about bodies, babies, and related issues in various ways and with different levels of accuracy (cf Stone et al., 2012; McGinn et al., 2016) but at the same time be modelling certain behaviours (for example, displays of affection or not, gender power, gender roles, reactions to television and other media stories', supposedly light-hearted 'throw-away' comments) that may well seriously affect the attitudes that their children develop as they get older, in a negative or positive way.

Other examples of less direct sources of information include the likely impact of media images of sexualised bodies, images and behaviours contained in pornographic material (although there is evidence that some young people actually learn a lot about bodies from such sources in the continued absence of any more reliable sources; cf McKee, 2007; McKee et al., 2022), what has become known as 'everyday sexism' (Bates, 2015, 2016), and many others. Young people's experiences of and views about online influences have been increasinglyimportant issues. How to effectively address these issues within RSE and equipping children and young people with the critical skills to maximise the benefits of the online world and minimise the risk is the is discussed in Chapter 5 and Chapter 6.

It is interesting to note from the NATSAL3 data that young people's preferred main source of information on sex and relationships is school, followed by parents and health professionals, suggesting a desire for support from trusted, authoritative sources. This contrasts with their current main sources which, after school, are friends and the media, with parents, particularly fathers, and health professionals playing an insignificant role (Macdowall et al., 2015). The importance of health professionals in providing young people with accurate information was highlighted by the American Academy of Pediatrics who called on their members to counter the gaps and misinformation from US abstinence programmes (Breuner et al., 2016).

2.6 Sexual competence

What all this points towards is that calls for *simple* solutions to the challenges posed by early unplanned pregnancy – through increased services for young people, and/or improved sex and relationships education, essential though they are – miss the point of the sheer complexity of the factors that affect early sex and contraceptive usage. Some years ago, Ingham and Van Zessen (1997), building on the earlier work of Rademakers (1991), pointed to the notion of 'sexual competence' as a way of accounting for the large differences between the UK and the Netherlands in aspects of sexual activity; for example reasons, protection and mutuality, and outcomes, notably early conception rates. They regarded this as being a cultural phenomenon, with various taken-for-granted assumptions (or discursive frameworks) guiding individual and policy-related decisions. Areas that are accompanied by division and debate within the UK (and USA, for that matter) – such as whether sex and relationships education should be offered in schools, whether contraception and sexual health services should be more widely available and less stigmatised – are not generally issues of dispute in the Netherlands. A fine illustration of how this general set of assumptions permeates societies is provided by Schalet's work comparing parental attitudes to their teenagers' sexual activity in the USA and the Netherlands (Schalet, 2000, 2011). A further example is provided by this summary of the underlying principles of sex education in schools in the Netherlands:

> Dutch sexuality education emerges from an understanding that young people are curious about sex and sexuality and that they need, want, and have a right to accurate and comprehensive information about sexual health . . . it encourages young people to think critically about their sexual health, including their desires and wishes . . . attention is paid on discussing values, establishing personal boundaries, communicating wishes and desires, and developing assertiveness.
>
> (quote from Ferguson et al., 2008, pp. 102–3)

Similar openness is observed in Nordic countries. This is how one leading commentator described the situation in Sweden regarding sex education in schools, a stark contrast with the typical US and British approaches and resistances:

> The guiding stars are knowledge instead of ignorance, openness with regards to facts instead of mystifying and an acceptance of young people's sexuality (or sexual emotions), relationships and love, with or without a partner. The idea is that the sex education should support and prepare young people for a responsible present and/or future sexual life . . . Sexual enjoyment is also regarded as a value in itself . . . There is no opposition to sex education in Sweden.
>
> (Sex Ed in Sweden; Katerina Lindahl, RFSU, personal communication)

These illustrations of 'competence' and how it can be instilled/enabled/encouraged make it easier to understand some of the likely reasons for the wide variations in levels of teenage conceptions between countries (alongside the economic and structural features). Note that for a broad-based sex education to be widely accepted requires the active co-operation of parents, teachers, school governors, the mainstream media, politicians and other policymakers and, of course, young people themselves. This is precisely why the notion of 'competence' can be regarded as a cultural phenomenon and not just an individual property (see also Hirst, 2012).

That said, however, some very useful work has been carried out in the UK by Wellings and colleagues using the NATSAL data. Operationally defining 'competence' at first ever sexual intercourse as comprising four elements – using a reliable form of contraception, the timing felt right, their reason for sex was an autonomous one, and both partners were equally willing – they demonstrated that higher levels of 'competence' were associated with higher age at first intercourse and lower risk of conception. This individual competence measure provides a potentially helpful set of 'assets' which SRE and targeted prevention programmes should aim to develop in young people (Wellings et al., 2013).

2.7 Is there a case for intervening?

There has been a steady series of critiques of the need for policy interventions in the area of teenage pregnancy, as well as in their implementation. Some argue that the negative health and social outcomes for young mothers and their children are exaggerated, or based on old data, or do not take sufficient account of the (often impoverished) living conditions after the birth. Others question what right the state has to intervene in personal decisions about family creation and development, whether setting targets to reduce rates simply serves to further stigmatise those already in vulnerable situations, or how the strategy is a modern-day form of eugenics since conception rates are higher in more deprived parts of the country so reductions will likely have unequal impact (see, for example, Arai, 2009 and various chapters in Duncan et al., 2010).

Other critiques came from ideological positions about the role of data in the context of religious teaching; a fine example is provided in an article from a (NHS-funded) consultant paediatrician in the north of England who, after reviewing the evidence as to whether abstinence-only education 'works' or not, concluded that:

> Proof of efficacy is not the predominant issue for the Christian as it is for the utilitarian secularist. We teach something because we understand it is right to do so.
>
> (Richards, 2005)

A regular critique of the strategy and those associated with its development queried their motives; this example comes from (at the time) a general practitioner:

> The vested commercial interests of contraceptive manufacturers and providers are as powerful as that of the tobacco industry in blinding their eyes to the evidence of the harm they are doing. Jesus had strong words to say both to those who led young people astray and those who rejected clear evidence because of ulterior motives.
>
> (Stammers, 2002)

The 'strong words' attributed to Jesus in this quote appear in the Bible:

> But if anyone causes one of these little ones who believe in me to sin, it would be better for him to have a large millstone hung around his neck and to be drowned in the depths of the sea.
>
> (Matthew, 18:6)

In a later issue of the Christian Medical Fellowship publication, the following exchange took place between Richards and Stammers debating the dangers (based on risk homeostasis) and merits (based on protecting the vulnerable) of the HPV vaccination given to early teenage girls:

> Richards – Second, young people will perceive that the consequences of fornication have been lessened and therefore fornicate more.
>
> Stammers – Wouldn't a good stoning have been a much better deterrent to casual sex than Jesus' gentle, 'Go now and leave your life of sin', spoken to the woman caught in adultery? Who are we to begrudge, let alone deny, young girls throughout the world being protected against a killer disease that many will otherwise die of as victims of predatory men?
>
> (Richards and Stammers, 2007)

Please note that we are not suggesting that Stammers would actually hang millstones around people's necks nor engage in stoning – but the use of such language is arguably dark, inflammatory and simply unnecessary.

The critiques of the TP Strategy (and other initiatives in the field of RSE and young people's sexual health) were and continue to be very concerning. They were at the time very active in media outlets and helped to cast doubts in the minds of those who may have felt uneasy about the direction of the Strategy. Similarly, they were active contributors to policy debates in Government and elsewhere, taking up a great deal of time of those who were required to address the issues with politicians and other policymakers; there can be few other areas of health and social care interventions that are so heavily infected by personal opinion, no matter what these are based upon.

Another consistent set of critiques of the TP Strategy comes from a researcher who uses an economic (and very statistical) approach to assess the impact of policies, such as mandated sex education, provision of contraception for young people, etc. Paton was skilled at casting doubt on the approaches adopted by the TP Strategy, be they providing more RSE or better access to contraception but is not so forthcoming when it comes to suggesting alternative ways forward. His close involvement with the Society for the Protection of Unborn Children provides some insight to his long-standing and persistent criticism of the TP Strategy; and a recent talk to the Family Education Trust[4] illustrates the ways in which he asserts that innovative policies *may* lead to increased rates of teenage pregnancy (what he calls 'unintended consequences') as well as the way that his and similar others' approaches tend to take extreme examples to argue their case against increasing provision for young people.

Baxter et al. (2021) analysed under-18 birth data from a range of high-income countries and concluded that the TP Strategy was not responsible for the reductions in rates in England since there were reductions in all the countries studied; but their conclusions are not as simple as they might appear. First, they compare rates in England with those in Scotland and Wales and find similar reductions even though the latter two countries did not have strategies nor the same level of financial backing. But what this overlooks is that during the whole period of the strategy, there was a great deal of contact between the countries, through mutual visits of key staff, joint conferences and other events,. Furthermore both Wales and Scotland implemented very similar policies to the Strategy, introducing RSE guidance and increasing access to contraception, including special initiatives to promote emergency contraception. Financial input is important in many ways but changes in awareness, attitudes, and motivation for change also count for a great deal. Second, and as regards the other countries in Baxter et al.'s comparisons, a number of quite questionable assumptions are made regarding the comparability of data across countries and the focus is on births rather than conceptions.

Their other point that the strategy was not important because reductions continued after the funding ceased is somewhat naïve; attitudes and ways of working that were established during the strategy's operation almost certainly continued after the 'official' ending of the initiative. This is illustrated in the qualitative research with local areas described in Chapter 5.

These critiques do raise some important questions (albeit some are more challenging than others) and are useful reminders for issues to be constantly borne in mind. But they were not reasons for governments not to develop strategies to address high rates. In England, for example, the fact that the target set in 1999 involved a 50 per cent reduction in under-18 conception rates is an indication that there was never any intention to try to prevent *all* teenage conceptions. Further, since around half of all under-18 and over 60 per cent of under-16 conceptions end in abortion, the majority of which were presumably not planned, efforts to reduce these can be justified on many grounds. It also needs to be fully recognised that beneath the headline rate data, a whole array of complex and dynamic processes are occurring that impact on early sexual activity and contraceptive use and pregnancy choices, some of which clearly indicate coercion, gender imbalances, and other features of sexually unhealthy societies.

Indeed, sometimes pregnancy choices and aspiration are shaped not by young people themselves, but by senior decision makers. As described in subsequent chapters, slow progress in reducing rates in some areas was influenced by those who believed early parenthood was an inevitable part of deprived communities and neglected to offer young people the knowledge, skills and opportunities to make different choices.

Even though targets for conceptions may have been the trigger, the introduction of the strategy encouraged a wide array of activities – based on learning from elsewhere and research evidence, as well as ideological positions based on gender equality, human rights, and the importance of the centrality of choice in determining futures. It was the opportunity to address these issues that contributed to the widespread support for the strategy from many NGOs and professional organisations, including those working with young parents.

Some of the critiques pointed out that negative outcomes are more likely to be linked to poor housing conditions, poverty, and lack of education and employment opportunity after the birth, than age *per se,* so efforts need to be directed towards respecting and supporting choices that young people make rather than trying to control their behaviours. The England strategy was intended to do both. Alongside the prevention target, there was a complementary target and programme of material and emotional support for young parents; these, and progress since, are described in Chapter 7.

2.8 Multi-pronged approaches

What becomes very apparent from consideration of the research in the area of early pregnancy is that there are no easy solutions. Although improving the extent and quality of sex and relationships education clearly seems to be of the utmost importance, on its own it will not achieve much in the absence of other enabling environments. To take a simple and obvious example; if young people in schools are educated about and advised to use condoms, but are then unable to access them, or if a young woman expresses a wish to use one but her male partner refuses, then the outcomes will not be positive. A whole systems approach is needed, with different agencies and concerned parties contributing what they can, with the interests of young people at the centre. This seems to be what encapsulates the situation in those countries that have adapted well to the changing circumstance of young people and society in general (UNICEF, 2001).

Within the UK, some support for this broad approach was received from research carried out when there was a national target (set by a previous government in 1990) to reduce rates of under-16 conceptions – one of the targets set in *The Health of the Nation* initiative established in 1992. Data were collected on the extent of change in under-16 conceptions rates during the 1990s. Those areas showing the twenty highest increases were compared with those showing the twenty highest reductions in relation to the extent of the provision of various initiatives. Data were collected through interviews with key agencies, close analysis of annual public health reports and other sources.

What emerged was that local government areas that showed the highest reductions (when compared with the 'increasing' sites) were characterised by a number of important features including better youth service provision, more targeted sexual health services for young people, improved sex education in schools, listening to young people's views and other initiatives (Ingham et al., 2001).

For these changes to be introduced in areas, a cultural change needed to have occurred in relation to young people and sexual health, along the lines of those changes that had occurred at national levels some years earlier in some countries. Further, what these early results demonstrated was that, while resources are genuinely required for change to occur, it is the cultural and attitudinal shifts that drive change; the finance facilitates and enables it. It was this comprehensive, whole systems approach to teenage pregnancy that underpinned the England strategy, the importance of which was confirmed during its implementation. The detail of how this was done and what has happened since is described in the following chapters.

2.9 *Finally . . .*

This chapter has provided an overview of some of the alternative ways of approaching the issue of early pregnancy, and why it is a worthwhile endeavour to attempt. It should be clear that, in introducing a public health approach to the many issues involved, the intention of the England strategy was not at all to moralise, or stigmatise, or direct, but to create contexts that would empower and support young people in managing the rapidly changing world around them so that whatever informed choices they make are respected and supported. Obviously, under the broad umbrella of the initiative, there will have been people who had their own agendas and reasons for feeling that action was (or was not) needed, and various sections of the media and the political world (and academia) raised regular questions and challenges along the way. But throughout, the strategy and its various amendments were informed by the latest research as opposed to ideologies or rhetoric. Anchoring the strategy in evidence secured the support of professional organisations and NGOs and, as described in the next chapters, gave government the confidence to pursue implementation even when early progress was slow. The detailed analysis by Wellings et al. (2016) indicates that this approach was well justified; in brief, areas that received higher strategy-related funding showed larger reductions in conception rates after controlling for deprivation levels, and the odds of young mothers being in education, work or training doubled between 2000 and 2010.

Finally, the initial Director of the Social Exclusion Unit has recently written a comprehensive report that demonstrates how closely integrated many of the disadvantages faced by young people are, and how there are dangers in isolating just one are of concern for attention. The report contrasts the 'first wave' between 1997 and 2010 under a Labour Government with the 'second wave' after 2010 under the Coalition and then Conservative Government. A range of indicators are discussed in some detail – including teenage pregnancy – and the importance of setting targets alongside cross-cutting approaches are stressed (Wallace, 2023).

Notes

1 UNESCO Office Montevideo and Regional Bureau for Science in Latin America and the Caribbean and United Nations Population Fund (2023). *Comprehensive sexuality education: an overview of the international systematic review evidence*. Document code: MTD/ED/2023/PI/03 (online, open access).

2 The data here are from NATSAL3 conducted in 2010, so are fairly dated now. A recent report based on the latest HBSC study suggests a slight decline in proportions reporting sexual intercourse among 15-year-old boys but a slight increase among girls between 2018 and 2022; however, declines since 2002 are fairly substantial. See p. 45 of the HBSC report: https://hbscengland.org/wp-content/uploads/2023/11/2022_FULL_REPORT_final_21.11.23-1.pdf.

3 See, for example, *Digital Romances:* www.brook.org.uk/wp-content/uploads/2020/03/DR_REPORT_FINAL.pdf; and the *Brook Conundrum Study*: www.brook.org.uk/blog/examining-attitudes-to-condoms-and-contraception.

4 Talk given to a meeting of the Family Education Trust in 2022: www.youtube.com/watch?v=FWRYokajCLc.

References

Advocates for Youth (2007). *The history of federal abstinence-only funding.* Washington DC: Advocates for Youth. www.advocatesforyouth.org/storage/advfy/documents/fshistoryabonly.pdf.

Arai, L. (2009). *Teenage Pregnancy: The making and unmaking of a problem.* Bristol: Policy Press.

Atkins, D.N. and Bradford, W.D. (2021). The effect of state-level sex education policies on youth sexual behaviors. *Archives of Sexual Behavior*, 50, 2321–2333.

Bates, L. (2015). *Everyday sexism.* London: Simon & Schuster.

Bates, L. (2016). *Girl up.* London: Simon & Schuster.

Baxter, A.J., Dundas, R., Popham, F. and Craig, P. (2021). How effective was England's teenage pregnancy strategy? A comparative analysis of high-income countries. *Social Science & Medicine*, 270, February, 113685.

Breuner, C.C., Mattson, G., AAP Committee on Adolescence and AAP Committee on Psychosocial Aspects of Child and Family Health (2016). Sexuality Education for Children and Adolescents. *Pediatrics*, 138(2), e20161348.

Connolly, A., Pietri, G., Yu, J. and Humphreys, S. (2014). Association between long-acting reversible contraceptive use, teenage pregnancy, and abortion rates in England. *International Journal of Women's Health*, 6, 961–974.

Department for Education (2017). *Policy statement: relationships education, relationships and sex education and Personal, Social, Health and Economic Education.* London: DfE.

Duncan, S., Edwards, R. and Alexander, C. (Eds) (2010). *Teenage parenthood: What's the problem?* London: Tufnell Press.

Ericksen, I.H. and Weed, S.E. (2019). Re-examining the evidence for school-based comprehensive sex education: A global research review. *Issues in Law and Medicine*, 34(2), 161–182.

Ferguson, R.M., Vanwesenbeeck, I. and Knijn, T. (2008). A matter of facts . . . and more: an exploratory analysis of the content of sexuality education in The Netherlands. *Sex Education: Sexuality, Society and Learning*, 8(1), 93–106.

Fine, M. and McClelland, S.I. (2006). Sexuality Education and Desire: Still Missing after All These Years. *Harvard Educational Review*, 76(3), 297–338.

Guttmacher Institute. (2012). *State policies in brief: Sex and HIV education.* New York: Guttmacher.

Haberland, N. and Rogow, D. (2015). Sexuality education: Emerging trends in evidence and practice, *Journal of Adolescent Health*, 56(1), S15–S21.

Hansard (2010). www.publications.parliament.uk/pa/ld200910/ldhansrd/text/100407-0018.htm (accessed 21 December 2015).

Hirst, J. (2012). 'It's got to be about enjoying yourself': Young people, sexual pleasure and sex and relationships education, *Sex Education: Sexuality, Society and Learning*, 13(4), 423–436.

Hoggart, L., Newton, V. and Dickson, J. (2013). *Understanding long-acting reversible contraception: An in-depth investigation into sub-dermal contraceptive implant removal amongst young women in London: a report for the London sexual health commissioning programme.* London: University of Greenwich School of Health and Social Care.

Ingham, R., Clements, S. and Gillibrand, R. (2001). *Factors affecting changes in rates of teenage conceptions.* unpublished report submitted to Department of Health, Southampton: Centre for Sexual Health Research, University of Southampton.

Ingham, R. and van Zessen, G. (1997). From individual properties to interactional processes. In Van Campenhoudt, L., Cohen, M., Guizzardi, G. and Hausser, D. (Eds), *Sexual Interactions and HIV Risk: New Conceptual Perspectives in European Research.* London: Taylor & Francis, pp. 83–99.

IPAS. (2023). *False pretenses: The anti-comprehensive sexuality education agenda weaponizing human rights.* Chapel Hill, NC: Ipas.

Kirby, D (2007). *Emerging answers 2007: Research findings on programs to reduce teen pregnancy and sexually transmitted diseases*. Washington, DC: National Campaign to Prevent Teen and Unplanned Pregnancy.

Kirby, D (2008). The impact of abstinence and comprehensive sex and STD/HIV education programmes on adolescent sexual behaviour. *Sexuality Research and Social Policy*, 5(3), 18–27.

Kohler, P.K., Manhart, L.E. and Lafferty, W.E. (2008). Abstinence-Only and Comprehensive Sex Education and the Initiation of Sexual Activity and Teen Pregnancy. *Journal of Adolescent Health*, 42, 344–351.

Lindberg, L and Maddow-Zimet, I (2012). Consequences of sex education on teen and young adult sexual behaviors and outcomes. *Journal of Adolescent Health*, 51, 332–338.

Lindberg, L., Santelli, J. and Desai, S. (2016). Understanding the decline in adolescent fertility in the United States, 2007–2012. *Journal of Adolescent Health*, 59, 577–583.

Lindberg, L.D., Santelli, J.S. and Desai, S. (2018). Changing patterns of contraceptive use and the decline in rates of pregnancy and birth among U.S. adolescents, 2007–2014. *Journal of Adolescent Health*, 63, 253–256.

Macdowall, W., Jones, K.G., Tanton, C., Clifton, S., Copas, A.J., Mercer, C.H., Palmer, M.J., Lewis, R., Datta, J., Mitchell, K.R., Field, N., Sonnenberg, P., Johnson, A.M. and Wellings, K. (2015). Associations between source of information about sex and sexual health outcomes in Britain: Findings from the third National Survey of Sexual Attitudes and Lifestyles (Natsal-3). *BMJ Open*, 5, e007837.

Madden, H., Eckley, L., Hughes, L., Lavin, R. and Timpson, H. (2014). *Long-acting reversible contraception; Young women and social norms*. Liverpool: Liverpool John Moores University, Centre for Public Health.

Mason-Jones, A.J., Sinclair, D., Mathews, C., Kagee, A., Hillman, A. and Lombard, C. (2016). School-based interventions for preventing HIV, sexually transmitted infections and pregnancy in adolescents (Review). *Cochrane Database of Systematic Reviews*, Issue 11, Art. No. CD006417.

McGinn, L., Stone, N., Ingham, R. and Bengry-Howell, A. (2016). Parental interpretations of "childhood innocence": Implications for early sexuality education. *Health Education*, 166(6), 580–594.

McKee, A. (2007). Positive and negative effects of pornography as attributed by consumers. *Australian Journal of Communication*, 34(1), 87–104.

McKee, A., Litsou, K., Byron, P. and Ingham, R. (2022). *What do we know about the effects of pornography after fifty years of academic research?* London: Routledge.

Parkes, A., Strange, V., Wight, D., Bonell, C., Copas, A., Henderson, M., Buston, K., Stephenson, J., Johnson, A., Allen, E. and Hart, G. (2011). Comparison of teenagers' early same-sex and heterosexual behavior: UK data from the SHARE and RIPPLE studies. *Journal of Adolescent Health*, 48, 27–35.

Paton, D., Bullivant, S. and Soto, J. (2020). The impact of sex education mandates on teenage pregnancy: International evidence. *Health Economics*, April 2020.

Pound, P., Langford, R. and Campbell, R. (2016). What do young people think about their school-based sex and relationship education? A qualitative synthesis of young people's views and experiences. *BMJ Open*, 6(9).

Public Health England (2015). *Reducing Infant Mortality in London: an evidence based resource*. London: Public Health England.

Rademakers, J. (1991). Contraception and interaction among Dutch boys and girls, *Planned parenthood in Europe (Planning familial en Europe)*, 19(3), 7–8.

Richards, C. (2005). Lovewise – Sex education in schools. *Nucleus*. Summer 2005. London: Christian Medical Fellowship.

Richards, C. and Stammers, T. (2007). HPV Vaccine (Letters). *Triple Helix*. Winter 2007. London Christian Medical Fellowship.

Santelli, J. (2007). Explaining recent declines in adolescent pregnancy in the United States: the contribution of abstinence and improved contraceptive use, *American Journal of Public Health*, 97(1), 150–156.

Santelli, J. (2008). Medical accuracy in sexuality education: Ideology and the scientific process. *American Journal of Public Health*, 98(10), 1786–1792.

Santelli, J., Ott, M.A., Lyon, M., Rogers, J., Summers, D. and Schleifer, R. (2006). Abstinence and abstinence-only education: A review of U.S. policies and programs. *Journal of Adolescent Health,* 38, 72–81.

Schalet, A. (2000). Raging hormones, regulated love: adolescent sexuality and the constitution of the modern individual in the United States and the Netherlands. *Body and Society,* 6(1), 75–105.

Schalet, A. (2011). *Not under my roof: Parents, teens and the culture of sex.* Chicago, IL: Chicago University Press.

Scott, R.H., Wellings, K. and Lindberg, L. (2020). Adolescent sexual activity, contraceptive use and pregnancy in Britain and the United States: a multi-decade comparison. *Journal of Adolescent Health*, 66, 582–588.

Sex Education Forum (2015). *SRE – the evidence.* London: Sex Education Forum, National Children's Bureau.

Sex Education Forum (2022). *Relationships and sex education: The evidence*. London, SEF.

Sex Education Forum (2023). *Young People's RSE Poll 2022*. London, SEF.

SIECUS. (2012). *SIECUS State Profiles: A portrait of sexuality education and abstinence-only-until-marriage programs in the states*. Sexuality Information and Education Council of the United States.

Stammers, T. (2002). Family planning services are ineffective – But when will those responsible admit it? *Triple Helix*, Summer 2002. London: Christian Medical Fellowship.

Steiner, R.J., Liddon, N., Swartzendruber, A.L., Rasberry, C.N. and Sales, J.M. (2016). Long-acting reversible contraception and condom use among female US high school students; Implications for sexually transmitted infection prevention. *JAMA Pediatrics*, 170(5), 428–434.

Stephenson, J.M., Strange, V., Forrest, S., Oakley, A., Copas, A., Allen, E., Babiker, A., Black, S., Ali, M., Monteiro, H., Johnson, A.M. and the RIPPLE study team. (2004). Pupil-led sex education in England (RIPPLE study): Cluster-randomised intervention trial. *Lancet*, 364, 338–346.

Stephenson, J., Strange, V., Allen, E., Copas, A., Johnson, A., Bonell, C., Babiker, A., Oakley, A. and the RIPPLE Study Team (2008). The long-term effects of a peer-led sex education programme (RIPPLE): A cluster randomised trial in schools in England. *PLoS Medicine*, 5, 1579–1590.

Stone, N., Ingham, R. and Gibbins, K. (2012). 'Where do babies come from?' Barriers to early sexuality communication between parents and young children. *Sex Education: Sexuality, Society and Learning*, 13(2), 228–240.

Tanton, C., Jones, K.G., Macdowall, W., Clifton, S., Mitchell, K.R., Datta, J., Lewis, R., Field, N., Sonnenberg, P., Stevens, A., Wellings, K., Johnson, A.M., Mercer and C.H. (2015). Patterns and trends in sources of information about sex among young people in Britain: Evidence from three National Surveys of Sexual Attitudes and Lifestyles, *BMJ Open,* 5, e007834.

Trivedi, D., Bunn, F., Graham, M. and Wentz, R. (2007). *Update on Review of Reviews on Teenage Pregnancy and Parenthood.* Submitted as an addendum to the first evidence briefing 2003. Hertfordshire: Centre for Research in Primary and Community Care, University of Hertfordshire, on behalf of National Institute for Health and Clinical Excellence.

UN (2014). Special Rapporteur on violence against women finalizes country mission to the United Kingdom and calls for urgent action to address the accountability deficit and also the adverse impacts of changes in funding and services. Statement accessed on 17 November 2014 from www.ohchr.org/EN/NewsEvents/Pages/DisplayNews.aspx?NewsID=14514&LangID=E.

UNESCO Office Montevideo and Regional Bureau for Science in Latin America and the Caribbean and United Nations Population Fund (2023) *Comprehensive sexuality education: an overview of the international systematic review evidence*.

UNICEF (undated). www.unicef.org.uk/what-we-do/un-convention-child-rights (accessed January 2017).

UNICEF (2001). *A League Table of Teenage Births in Rich Nations.* Innocenti Report Card No. 3, Florence: UNICEF Innocenti Research Centre.

Van Treeck, K., Elnakib, S. and Chandra-Mouli, V. (2022). Flaws and Errors Identified in the Institute for Research and Evaluation Report That Challenges Non-United States, School-Based Comprehensive Sexuality Education Evidence Base. *Journal of Adolescent Health*, 72(3), 332–333.

Wallace, M. (2023). *Trends in Adolescent Disadvantage Policy and Outcomes for Young People under Labour, the Coalition, and the Conservatives (1997 to 2019)*. SPDO Research Paper 15. London: LSE, Centre for Analysis of Social Exclusion.

Weed, S.E and Ericksen, I. (2019). *Re-examining the evidence for comprehensive sex education in schools: A global research review*. The Institute for Research and Evaluation, December 2019.

Wellings, K. and Kane, R. (1999). Trends in teenage pregnancy in England and Wales: how can we explain them? *Journal of the Royal Society of Medicine*, 92(6), 277–282.

Wellings, K., Jones, K.G., Mercer, C.H., Tanton, C., Clifton, S., Datta, J., Copas, A.J., Erens, B., Gibson, L.J., Macdowall, W., Sonnenberg, P., Phelps, A. and Johnson, A.M. (2013). The prevalence of unplanned pregnancy and associated factors in Britain: findings from the third National Survey of Sexual Attitudes and Lifestyles (Natsal-3). *Lancet*, 382(9907), 1807–1816, 30 November 2013.

Wellings, K., Palmer, M.J., Geary, R.S., Gibson, L.J., Copas, A., Datta, J., Glasier, A., Scott, R.H., Mercer, C.H., Erens, B., Macdowall, W., French, R.S., Jones, K., Johnson, A.M., Tanton, C. and Wilkinson, P. (2016). Changes in conceptions in women younger than 18 years and the circumstances of young mothers in England in 2000–12: an observational study. *Lancet*, 388(10044), 586–595, 6 August 2016.

Wight, D. (2011). The effectiveness of school-based sex education: what do rigorous evaluations in Britain tell us? *Education and Health,* 29, 67–73.

Winters J. (2024). *Education, access, stigma and young people: attitudes to contraception, condoms and sexual health.* (EASY). Brook.

3 England's teenage pregnancy strategy

Rationale, development and first phase implementation (1999–2005)

3 Where it began

3.1 The window of opportunity

The window of opportunity for England's Teenage Pregnancy Strategy was the incoming Labour Government in 1997, which had an explicit ambition to reduce intergenerational inequalities. Teenage pregnancy was seen as both a cause and consequence of poor health, education and economic outcomes affecting young parents and their children. Notably, British teenage birth rates were the highest in Western Europe and had shown no sustained downward trend. Although all countries, including the UK, had reduced rates during the 1970s, as the decline continued in other countries over the next two decades, British rates remained static. It was clear from comparative data that high rates were not inevitable and that young people in the UK were experiencing very different choices to their European peers.

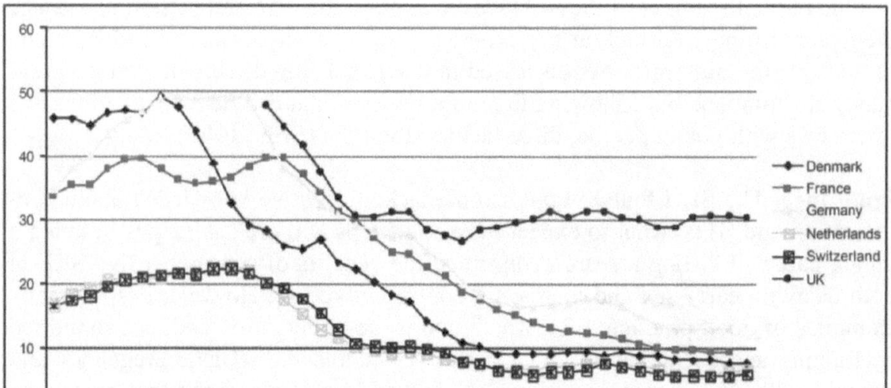

Figure 3.1 Comparative under-20 birth data.

DOI: 10.4324/9781003410225-4

The issue had not been entirely ignored by previous governments. In 1992, the Conservative Government's Health of the Nation strategy had included, with other health targets, a ten-year target to halve the rate of under-16 conceptions. The initiative saw an 83 per cent increase in the number of dedicated young people's contraceptive service sessions (London School of Hygiene and Tropical Medicine, UCL and BMRB, 2005) but lacked a clear action plan and failed to make a significant impact on the rates. It also omitted attention to 16- and 17-year-olds who experience 80 per cent of conceptions to the under-18 age group. Notably, an assessment of the overall policy found it was largely regarded as focusing only on the health sector, omitting other services involved with children, young people and their families. It also lacked the necessary horizontal and vertical structures for effective partnership working and failed to set out the tasks and responsibilities of different agencies (Universities of Leeds and Glamorgan and the London School of Hygiene and Tropical Medicine, 1998).

3.2 The development of the strategy

Recognising the need for a new approach, and responding to strong advocacy from the Voluntary and Community Sector (VCS) and professional organisations, the Labour government commissioned the newly formed Social Exclusion Unit (SEU) to do a thorough review of the evidence for the causes and potential solutions to the high rates, and develop a comprehensive ten-year strategy with a detailed implementation plan. The decision to commission the Social Exclusion Unit, rather than a government department, reflected the understanding that teenage pregnancy was a complex, cross-cutting issue. The SEU, established in 1997, was set up specifically to 'help government action to reduce social exclusion by producing joined-up solutions to joined-up problems'.

One of the first tasks of the SEU was to explore the data and pattern of teenage pregnancy in the UK, look at the experience of other countries, and identify the reasons for the high rates. As discussed in Chapter 1, the drivers of teenage pregnancy are complex, but following literature reviews, stakeholder consultations and interviews with young people, three factors stood out (SEU, 1999)

Ignorance. The SEU found young people lacked accurate knowledge about contraception and STIs, what to expect in relationships and the challenges of being a young parent. Existing research confirmed the benefits of comprehensive SRE in both delaying early sex and increasing contraceptive use. However despite many examples of good practice, SRE was found to be under resourced, not supported by training and not linked to wider initiatives addressing teenage pregnancy and sexual health. Young people and parents looked to schools as the preferred route for SRE but friends were as influential a source about sex as school. The universal message the SEU received from young people was that SRE fell far short of what they would like and what they need to equip themselves for developing healthy relationships, delaying pregnancy and looking after their sexual health. Friends, the media and magazine 'problem pages' were filling the gap.

Mixed messages. Young people's reporting of mixed messages appeared to be rooted in an unhelpful combination of exposure to widespread sexual imagery, but embarrassment in discussing personal issues and asking for advice. Young people consistently over-estimated the levels of teenage sexual activity and described peer pressure to fit in with the perceived, albeit inaccurate, social norm. However, they were missing accurate information and opportunities for discussion from inadequate SRE, finding it difficult to talk to their parents, and were apprehensive about accessing contraceptive advice. Fears about confidentiality, particularly for under-16s, and judgemental attitudes of staff were the major barriers. As one young person put it, 'it sometimes seems as if sex is compulsory but contraception is illegal'. There also seemed to be more embarrassment discussing or using contraception than about sex itself. In a comparative study, Dutch boys were 2.5 times more likely than their English peers to discuss contraception with their partners before first sex and, compared with many other countries, British teenagers were less likely to use contraception at first sex. The SEU review concluded that one of the results of mixed messages appeared to be that young people were not having less sex, but more unprotected sex.

Low expectations. Although data showed that teenage pregnancy affects all communities, young people with a history of disadvantage were at a significantly greater risk of becoming parents in their teens. Poverty and unemployment, low educational attainment, living in care, sexual abuse, mental health problems and crime were all found to be strongly associated with teenage parenthood. The effect of multiple risk factors (quantified in the 1958 birth cohort study) was particularly striking. Women with all the following characteristics had a 56 per cent chance of becoming a teenage mother, compared with a 3 per cent chance for those with none: emotional problems at ages seven and 16; having a mother who had been a teenage mother; families who experienced financial adversity when they were seven or 16; a preference for being a young mother; and low educational attainment at 16. Complex factors always influence individual decisions. For some, becoming a parent appeared to be motivated by a strong desire to provide a better experience for their child than they have had themselves. For others, with no expectation of employment or motivation to continue in education, early parenthood might seem to be the logical passport for making the transition from adolescence into adulthood.

3.3 Setting the goal and strategy themes

After eighteen months of analysing the issue, reviewing the international evidence, identifying existing good practice in England and consulting with a wide range of NGO and professional stakeholders, the Strategy was published in 1999 (SEU, 1999). It had two clear goals: a headline target of halving the under-18 conception rate in England by 2010, with 1998 as the baseline year; and a complementary target to increase the proportion of 16–19-year-old mothers in education, training or employment, to reduce the risk of intergenerational poverty and social exclusion.

The Strategy set out a 30-point action plan, framed around four themes:

Joined-up action with new mechanisms to co-ordinate action at both national, and local levels and ensure the strategy is on track.

Better prevention of teenage pregnancy: improving sex and relationships education in and out of school, and access to contraception for all young people, with targeted prevention for at risk groups and a new focus on reaching young men. Boys and young men were identified as half the solution to reducing early pregnancy but with contraception messages historically focused on girls and young women, had lacked advice and support to enable them to take responsibility.

A national campaign involving Government, media, NGOs and others to improve understanding and change behaviour.

Better support for pregnant teenagers and young parents, with a new focus on returning to education, with free childcare to enable participation; working to a position where no under-18 lone parent is put in a housing tenancy without support; and pilots around the country providing intensive support for young parents and their children. This chapter focuses on the prevention side of the strategy. Chapter 6 describes implementation of the support programme.

The action plan also included a commissioned research programme to explore issues identified in the SEU report as requiring more understanding (Teenage Pregnancy Unit, 2004–07).

Three features marked the difference in the Strategy from previous approaches. First, the recognition that the solution to teenage pregnancy was not in the gift of any one national government department or local agency. A multi-dimensional issue would require collective action, through successful collaboration across agencies at different levels. Second, that implementation of a complex programme needed to be anchored in robust structures and reliable resourcing. Third, that providing good support for young people who chose to become parents was an important contribution to the prevention strategy. In the short term by helping them prevent further unplanned pregnancies; in the long term by breaking inter-generational cycles of poverty and disadvantage and reducing the risk factors for teenage pregnancy among the next generation of young people. Notably, the new approach of the Strategy reflected the nine key characteristics of modern policymaking, identified by the National Audit Office (NAO, 2001).

3.2 The first phase of implementation: 1999–2005

Following a high-profile launch by the Prime Minister in June 1999, which helped signify its priority, the first phase of implementation began (Department of Health, 2001a; Teenage Pregnancy Unit, 2002a).

3.2.1 The structures, local targets and funding

A dedicated Teenage Pregnancy Unit (TPU) was set up in the Department of Health, to lead the strategy, with cross department funding. This was the engine room of the strategy and essential for leading such a large programme of work. The team of staff combined external experts and civil servants. Blending the unique skills of civil servants with specialist policy expertise was a new approach taken by the Labour Government and helped increase the credibility of the strategy with stakeholders. An inter-departmental Teenage Pregnancy Board was established to reflect the cross cutting nature of the policy challenge and the shared responsibility for implementation. A Teenage Pregnancy Independent Advisory Group (Advisory Group) was appointed, bringing together experts on all aspects of the strategy. The Group met every three months, with sub-groups formed to focus on specific aspects of the strategy, and had a remit to monitor implementation, advise and make recommendations to ministers and hold government to account for the strategy's progress. Regional Teenage Pregnancy Co-ordinators (regional co-ordinators) were appointed by the TPU for each of the nine Government Office regions. Locally every local government area and their health partner was asked to appoint a Teenage Pregnancy Co-ordinator (local co-ordinator) and a Teenage Pregnancy Partnership Board (partnership board) with representation from health, education, social services, youth services, housing and relevant voluntary sector organisations. A national VCS forum was established to harness additional expertise and involvement in the Strategy from organisations working closely with young people. An Inter-Faith Forum was set up to discuss and inform implementation of the Strategy in different faith contexts.

Local under-18 conception rate reduction targets for 2010 were agreed with each area: ranging from a 60 per cent target in high rate areas to 40 per cent in lower rate areas. The local targets were calculated on the progress needed to reach the national goal. If all areas achieved their local reductions, the 50 per cent goal for England would be met.

A Local Implementation Grant was provided to each area. The grant allocation was determined by the size of the local population of 15–17-year-old young women, and the baseline under-18 conception rate, which indicated the degree of challenge the local area would have in meeting the reduction target. Annual allocations ranged from £150,000 to £600,000, with most areas receiving around £300,000–400,000. The grant was ring fenced with conditions on how it was spent. This included appointing a co-ordinator, establishing a partnership board and providing the TPU with annual progress reports. In addition, the grant could be used for pump priming new initiatives or extending existing work, but was not intended to replace mainstream funding from other agencies. The total annual grant was around £25 million. A further £7 million was held centrally by TPU to support the national campaign and other strategy activity most efficiently commissioned at a national level.

Progress towards the strategy's goal was monitored through the quarterly and annual conception data. Independent academic researchers were commissioned to evaluate the first four years' of the strategy's implementation and report in 2005 (London School of Hygiene and Tropical Medicine, UCL and BMRB, 2005).

> I was appointed as the first Head of the Teenage Pregnancy Unit based on my experience as a former Chief Executive in successfully implementing health strategies in a number of local areas. In the early days I was encouraged by the then Permanent Secretary[1] to break all the normal rules to ensure a truly effective cross-government approach. The Unit as a mixture of civil servants and experts from the field was focused on ensuring that the strategy's detailed relevant policy was jointly developed across government departments, as well as having a significant outward face to ensure the right action was taken across every part of England. This outward focus continued when I set up some years later the Teenage Pregnancy National Support Team, referred to in the next chapter. It was an exciting time to develop from scratch the detailed implementation of the Social Exclusion Unit strategy and to start the see the impact across the country.
>
> Cathy Hamlyn, first head of the Teenage Pregnancy Unit and former senior civil servant in Department of Health.

3.2.2 National guidance and support for local strategies

Every local partnership board was asked to develop a local teenage pregnancy strategy, led by the co-ordinator. Guidance was provided by TPU with a template to complete. Each strategy was expected to a) reach all young people in the area, with additional focus in high rate areas or with groups of young people most at risk; b) be informed by the pattern of teenage pregnancy in the area and an audit of service provision to identify gaps; c) involve young people and local communities; and d) make links to other relevant local plans and initiatives. The regional co-ordinator and TPU assessed each strategy and provided feedback to the co-ordinator and partnership board.

3.2.3 National action to support local delivery

To assist local implementation, the action plan tasked the TPU with providing additional guidance and support across the different strands of the Strategy.

To improve the provision of sex and relationships education (SRE), the education department published new SRE statutory guidance for schools (Department for Education and Employment, 2000). To help dissemination and take up of the guidance TPU funded the Sex Education Forum to run regional seminars for local co-ordinators and their school and education colleagues. The Sex Education Forum is the leading NGO on SRE with a diverse membership including faith and parenting organisations, and is well respected by stakeholders. A video and training pack was provided for school governors to increase their understanding of SRE and strengthen school leadership. A new national Continuing Professional Development programme was established for teachers and school nurses on SRE and Personal Social and Health Education (PSHE), to increase the capacity of a skilled and confident workforce – identified as a key factor for delivering effective SRE. To help ensure SRE reached neglected or at risk groups, TPU funded the development by NGOs of targeted SRE; for example, resources to reach boys and young men (Davidson, 2003) and an accredited social and life skills module on SRE for young offenders.

To embed SRE within wider school programmes, there were strong links with the National Healthy Schools Programme (NHSP). Introduced in 1999, the NHSP aimed to support children and young people in developing healthy behaviours, and help raise pupil achievement, reduce health inequalities and promote social inclusion. Schools achieved National Healthy Schools Status (NHSS) if they met 41 criteria across four themes: PSHE, healthy eating, physical activity and emotional health and wellbeing (Department of Health and Department for Education, 2001). All areas were asked to have NHSP representation on their partnership board, and schools in the most deprived areas with high teenage pregnancy rates were encouraged to join the programme.

To help increase the provision of youth friendly contraception and sexual health services: the Department of Health published best practice guidance on youth friendly contraception services (Department of Health, 2000). The guidance drew on previous research with young people describing the ingredients of a service they would trust and find easy to use; in particular from a report by Brook, the leading young people's sexual health NGO, titled with advice from a young person, '*Someone with a smile would be your best bet*' (Brook, 1998). The guidance was disseminated to local areas through a series of regional seminars for co-ordinators, sexual health leads and commissioners. To see how well current services were meeting the criteria in the guidance, areas were asked to audit their community contraceptive services and general practices and use the results to improve their provision. To address young people's concerns about confidentiality, identified as a key barrier to accessing early advice, the Department of Health provided best practice guidance to health professionals on providing contraceptive and sexual health advice to under-16s (Department of Health, 2000, updated 2004).

TPU provided separate guidance to increase uptake of services by boys and young men (Teenage Pregnancy Unit 2000a)and young people from black and minority ethnic (BME) communities, which were also disseminated through regional and local networks (Teenage Pregnancy Unit, 2000b). To ensure young people were well informed about local services, each local strategy was required to produce credit card size publicity booklets and have a plan for effective dissemination.

To encourage young people to visit their general practice for contraceptive advice, TPU worked with the Royal College of General Practitioners (RCGP) to develop practical tips and a checklist for making general practice more young people friendly (RCGP and Royal College of Nursing, 2002). *Getting it right for young people in your practice* was sent to all general practices in England. As young people had particular concerns about the confidentiality of their 'family doctor', TPU funded regional events to promote training of practice staff using a *Confidentiality Toolkit*, developed by the RCGP, British Medical Association, General Practitioners Committee, Royal College of Nursing and the Medical Defence Union (RCGP et al., 2001). Accompanying confidentiality posters and leaflets for general practice were made available free to local areas.

Measures were taken through the Department of Health's Sexual Health and HIV Strategy to reduce later abortions among young people; in 2000, 16 per cent of under-20s had abortions at 13 weeks or later, compared with 10 per cent of women over 20. The Sexual Health and HIV Strategy, published in 2001 and implemented alongside the teenage pregnancy strategy, included a requirement that all women meeting the legal requirement for abortion should have access to an NHS funded abortion within three weeks of their first appointment. Partnership boards were asked to develop plans to increase early access for pregnant young women under 18 and to monitor numbers accessing abortion over 12 weeks' gestation. The Sexual Health Strategy also helped to hugely expand access to free emergency hormonal contraception through pharmacies, a health setting which is very local, open long hours and trusted by young women (Department of Health, 2001b).

To help build the capacity of a trained nursing workforce TPU funded the Royal College of Nursing, the UK's professional nursing organisation, to develop a distance learning course to help meet the staff needs of an increasing number of nurse led contraceptive and sexual health services and outreach work.

To strengthen links between SRE and services: TPU funded the Sex Education Forum to publish a guide for local areas, *Secondary Schools and Sexual Health Services: forging the links* (Sex Education Forum, 2003) and to run an email network to support schools with, or considering setting up, an on-site service. Government also published guidance on establishing on-site sexual health services as part of the Extended Schools programme (Department of Children, Schools and Families, 2006). Extended Schools, prioritised in poorer areas, provided a range of support services on one site, including access to health advice. Teenage pregnancy, sexual health and young parenthood were all identified as health priorities for school nursing, and a practice development resource pack highlighted the importance of school nurses providing confidential support to pupils. Resources to integrate school SRE and contraceptive services for young men were commissioned from Working with Men, a respected NGO. To help schools discuss abortion and ensure young people had accurate information, the NGO, Education for Choice, was funded to publish a cross curricula resource exploring the issue of abortion in a number of different subjects (Education for Choice, 2004).

> National evidence based guidance from the TPU made a huge difference, particularly on innovations that were seen as challenging. For example, guidance on the value of locating sexual health services in schools was enormously helpful as schools could see that this approach was being nationally

> endorsed and it certainly helped them to accept this as a new way of working. It opened doors for us, which might otherwise have been closed.
>
> Anne Colquhoun, Teenage Pregnancy Co-ordinator, Bristol

To engage the non-health wider workforce: TPU published guidance for youth support workers (Teenage Pregnancy Unit, 2002a, updated 2005) and social care practitioners (Teenage Pregnancy Unit, 2002a, updated 2004) on supporting young people to access contraception and sexual health advice. Specific resources were also commissioned to help local areas address the additional needs of young people in or leaving the care system (National Children's Bureau and Family Planning Association, 2002). The Connexions service, established in 2000, to provide information, advice and guidance for young people aged 13–19, included advice in their diploma training on linking young people into services. TPU also commissioned a diverse communities project to explore the faith and cultural influences on teenage pregnancy and sexual health issues and provide resources for local areas. This included a resource for practitioners, examples of multi-faith schools working with parents to develop a values framework for SRE, and a video and training materials for SRE in catholic schools (Teenage Pregnancy Unit, 2002c).

To involve young people, TPU published guidance for local areas on how to engage young people (young men and women), including teenage parents, in the development and monitoring of their strategies (Teenage Pregnancy Unit, 2002d) and later commissioned a practical guide with examples of effective practice (National Children's Bureau, 2006). A guide was also published on developing sex and relationships peer education projects (Teenage Pregnancy Unit, 2002b). Young men and young women were recruited onto the Advisory Group to contribute views from their constituency groups on the strategy implementation, and to inform annual recommendations to government. Recruited through NGOs and serving two-year terms, they were paired with an Advisory Group member and supported in preparing for, and contributing to, meetings.

The first young members of the Teenage Pregnancy Independent Advisory Group

> I've been working on a major project to find out the main barriers young mums face in getting back to work or training. I bring real experience and have already provided feedback to ministers.
>
> Rhoda Thomas, a young parent and advice worker for Connexions

> One of my driving concerns is that there are good accessible clinics and services so that teenagers can easily get the information and contraception they need. As a peer educator I was involved in mystery shopping of sexual health services, as well as delivering sexual health workshops in schools and

informal settings. This front line experience was invaluable for informing my contributions to the Advisory Group and enabled me to gather other young people's views on a range of issues and experiences.

Rhiannon Holder MBE, a sexual health peer worker and volunteer

3.2.4 *The national media campaign*

The media campaign aimed to improve knowledge, address mixed messages and encourage communication The design was informed by international desk research commissioned to identify which messages and advertising campaigns had worked best with young people (Eborall and Garmesomn, 2000). The findings shaped the aims of the campaign: to inform and support young people to take control; not feel pressured into having sex before they felt ready; and be confident in asking for contraception and sexual health advice. Importantly the messages needed to be delivered in a tone which neither scared nor lectured young people. Parents were identified as children and young people's preferred source of information, but caution and embarrassment appeared to block communication. Informed by the research, two campaigns were developed; one for young people, one for parents.

Sex. Are you thinking about it enough – 'ruthinking' – was launched in 2000, aimed at reaching all 13–17-year-old girls and boys. Running on radio and in teenage magazines, the campaign focused on resisting peer pressure, reassurance about the confidentiality of accessing advice and contraception, and using condoms to prevent pregnancy and STIs. Secondary messages about the full range of effective contraception were communicated through articles in magazines and websites.

To help maximise the impact of the campaign locally, regional road shows were organised to help local areas amplify the messages. Materials such as posters, leaflets, key rings and bus pass wallets, were free for local areas to distribute in

Figure 3.2 Example of ruthinking campaign message, 2001.

schools, colleges and other settings used by young people, as part of the media and communications plans required as part of their strategy. For efficiency some distribution of materials was organised nationally – for example, to general practices. Partnerships were developed with youth brands to place the campaign messages alongside popular products in retail outlets, including Superdrug, a leading high street pharmacist which ran an in-store campaign with radio and window displays.

To ensure the campaign had a targeted as well as universal reach, the messages and visuals were developed and adapted after testing with young people from ethnic minorities and vulnerable groups, such as looked after children and care leavers. Posters were distributed to shopping centre washrooms in high rate areas, partnerships were formed with relevant NGOs and local areas were encouraged to disseminate the materials through practitioners such as social workers, leaving care teams and youth offending teams. Popular BME radio stations, including the BBC Asian network, ran campaigns, supported with phone-ins providing advice from experts from NGOs and the Advisory Group.

The campaign was supported by the *ruthinking* website and a free telephone helpline, Sexwise, which was open from 7 am to midnight, seven days a week. The Sexwise helpline had been funded by the Department of Health since 1995, but calls increased by 58 per cent after the campaign was launched, with half the calls from boys and young men. Young people needing further advice or an urgent clinical service – such as emergency contraception – were referred on to their nearest local service from the helpline's database, which was regularly updated with information provided by local co-ordinators.

The campaign for parents – *Time to Talk* – encouraged parents to talk to their children about sex and relationships. To avoid being construed as 'nannying by government', and to use the expertise of parenting specialists, the campaign was delivered through Parentline Plus, the leading and well-trusted national NGO which provided support and a free helpline for parents on a wide range of issues. Posters, leaflets and booklets were again free for local areas to distribute through schools and other community settings and by practitioners trusted by parents. A set of *Time to Talk* materials was sent nationally to every general practice for display in waiting rooms. The campaign was also integrated with government's wider parents' communications strategy, enabling the *Time to Talk* leaflets to be widely distributed in community settings, including supermarkets. Parentline Plus helpline advisors received training on how to answer parents' specific questions on sex and relationships but also how to opportunistically raise the topic when parents called with concerns about potentially related issues; for example, queries about alcohol, peer pressure or staying out with friends.

3.3 Supporting the strategy through joint working

3.3.1 Establishing collaborative partnerships

By 2005 the strategy was regarded as a model for joint working, forging strong vertical links between national and local and strong horizontal links with relevant

Figure 3.3 Example of a *Time to Talk* poster, 2002.

partners. There had not previously been a strong tradition of successful collaboration between health, education, youth and social services, and the strategy was seen as succeeding in implementing joint working where others had not (London School of Hygiene and Tropical Medicine, UCL and BMRB, 2005). Key success ingredients were the near universal support for the strategy's aims and actions and the dynamism of the support structures.

Local partnership boards met regularly, often forming sub-groups to give detailed attention to specific aspects of the strategy. Partner agencies were keen to be involved, as one co-ordinator discovered when establishing their local board. *In the first few weeks I visited all the agencies that could possibly be involved in teenage pregnancy and invited them along to the group – my fault it got so big – because they all came – they were interested* (London School of Hygiene and Tropical Medicine, UCL and BMRB, 2005).

Regional co-ordinators facilitated regular network meetings for local co-ordinators to communicate policy information and share problems and solutions. TPU met regional co-ordinators bi-monthly to review progress and identify and address any barriers to implementation, and there was active engagement from the TPU with local areas. Annual conferences and policy events for co-ordinators were organised by TPU. Members of the Advisory Group visited local areas to inform their annual report and recommendations to government, as well as adding weight to local strategies by meeting local senior leaders. TPU hosted regular meetings with the NGOs and inter-faith forums to maintain a two-way exchange of information and discussion on strategy related issues.

> As a teenage pregnancy co-ordinator I never felt lonely. The local partnership board was always well attended with multi-agency commitment and interesting debate about the direction of our local strategy. There was a spirit of mutual support to spend the grant in the best way possible to get the best outcomes. The local meetings were supported by a fantastic regional and national network.
>
> Anne Colquhoun, Teenage Pregnancy Co-ordinator, Bristol

> The support provided nationally and regionally was invaluable to me as a local co-ordinator. It helped to be able to learn from other areas, especially statistical[2] neighbours, and developed a peer support network for local co-ordinators. The information shared by the TPU and regional co-ordinators helped the local strategy progress quicker, as if we hit a problem locally we could get advice from others tackling the same issues and find solutions quicker. It saved time and energy and was more efficient than each area developing policies and interventions in isolation.
>
> Gail Teasdale, Teenage Pregnancy Co-ordinator, Kingston-upon-Hull

> One of the key strengths of the strategy was the continuous feedback loop from local areas, via the regional co-ordinator to the TPU, with bi-monthly two day meetings giving sufficient time to discuss and address barriers. Having national government so close to the reality of local implementation, and being able to nimbly adapt the support provided, was crucial to success and totally unheard of before, or since.
>
> Kate Quail, Regional Teenage Pregnancy Co-ordinator and later Head of the Teenage Pregnancy National Support Team

3.3.2 . . . and integration into wider government programmes

During the first five years, much effort was put into maintaining the priority and embedding the strategy actions into relevant government policy and programmes. The teenage pregnancy target was included in the government's renewed national Public Service Agreement and as a performance indicator for local government and their health partners (Department for Education and Skills, 2004b). A Government Green Paper on Children – Every Child Matters (Department for Education and Skills, 2004a) – set out a new joined-up and holistic vision for children and young people, against five outcomes: being healthy, staying safe, enjoying and achieving, making a positive contribution and enjoying economic wellbeing. The under-18 and under-16 conception rates were included in the Be Healthy Outcome, alongside rates of STIs in under-20s to indicate the importance of addressing teenage pregnancy together with young people's sexual health. Joint working was strengthened by the Change for Children programme being enshrined in the Children Act (2004), which placed a duty on local authorities and their partners to co-operate towards meeting the five outcomes.

To reflect the more integrated approach, in 2003 the TPU was moved from the Department of Health to a new Children, Young People and Families Directorate in the Department of Education and Skills, with a new role of Children and Families Minister taking lead responsibility for the Strategy implementation. However, strong joint working continued with ministers and officials in the Department of Health and through the Teenage Pregnancy inter-departmental board.

Integrating SRE with the National Healthy Schools Standard programme helped to support improvements in SRE. In 2004, achievement of the NHSS required schools to deliver a planned SRE programme, informed by consultation with young people and parents. To help ensure good SRE reached more vulnerable young people excluded from or not able to be in mainstream school, a new definition of NHSS for pupil referral units included a requirement to provide a good quality PSHE programme. The increased priority of SRE and PSHE was reflected by 80 per cent of Local Authorities having a PSHE co-ordinator in place by 2004 (London School of Hygiene and Tropical Medicine, UCL and BMRB, 2005).

Efforts to increase provision of young people friendly contraceptive, sexual health and abortion services were bolstered by linking teenage pregnancy to the Sexual Health and HIV Strategy; a new public health programme, *Choosing Health* (Department of Health, 2004), which confirmed the importance of easily accessible contraception and sexual health services linked to improved SRE; and a new National Service Framework (NSF) for improving services for children, young people and maternity (Department of Health, 2004). Following a recommendation from the Advisory Group for a universally recognised symbol to denote young people friendly services, the principles of the strategy best practice guidance on contraceptive services and the NSF standards were translated into the Department of Health's *You're Welcome* criteria, later endorsed by the World Health Organisation (Department of Health, 2007, updated 2011).

Underpinning the first phase of implementation was government leadership, with explicit endorsement by ministers and an active and responsive national Unit. Locally, senior leaders brought agencies together to collaborate on joint action and maximise funding opportunities. The local implementation grant signalled the importance of the strategy, provided a reliable source of funding for the co-ordinator and helped attract matched funding from other agencies.

The role and seniority of the local co-ordinator was critical. The small number of areas where setting up the strategy was slower, were characterised by periods when there was no co-ordinator in post, the post was not full time or the role was not sufficiently senior to provide the necessary leadership.

> Local co-ordinators were described as the lynchpin of implementation. Their status in the community, their professional experience and the support they have received have been key to the success of their role.
>
> Teenage Pregnancy Strategy Evaluation, 2005

> In the first four years, the strategy has been implemented with energy and enthusiasm, in an atmosphere of co-operation and consensus of those involved.
>
> Teenage Pregnancy Strategy Evaluation 2005

> In 2000, during the early days of the Strategy, I was working in a local Teenage Pregnancy Team co-ordinating an SRE programme. It was an exciting time as it felt like an army was being mobilised all over the country. We were part of a network of individuals with a shared set of values and a deep commitment to see the Strategy succeed.
>
> Anna Martinez, later national co-ordinator of the Sex Education Forum

Notes

1 Permanent Secretaries are the most senior civil servants of British government ministries. They generally hold their position for a number of years at a ministry, as distinct from the changing political Secretaries of State to whom they report and provide advice.
2 Local government areas identified as having similar demographic characteristics.

References

Brook (1998). *Someone with a smile would be your best bet.* London: Brook.
Brook (2008; updated 2014). *C-Card condom distribution schemes: why, what and how.* London: Brook.
Brook (2008). *Sexual Health Outreach: why, what and how*. London: Brook.
Brook (2010). *Young Men, Sex and Pregnancy: practical guidance on effective approaches.* London: Brook.
Department for Children, Schools and Families (2006). *Extended Schools: improving access to sexual health services.* London: DCSF.
Department for Children, Schools and Families (2008). *Government Response to the 4th Annual Report of the Teenage Pregnancy Independent Advisory Group.* London: DCSF.
Department for Children, Schools and Families (2008). *Government Response to the Report by the Sex and Relationships Education (SRE) Review Steering Group.* London: DCSF.
Department for Children, Schools and Families (2008). *Review of Sex and Relationships Education (SRE) in Schools. A report by the External Steering Group.* Issues. London: DCSF.
Department for Children, Schools and Families (2009). *Government Response to the 5th Annual Report of the Teenage Pregnancy Independent Advisory Group.* London: DCSF.
Department for Children, Schools and Families and Department of Health (2009). *Teenage pregnancy prevention and support: a self-assessment toolkit for local performance management.* London: DCSF and Department of Health. Crown Copyright.
Department for Children, Schools and Families and Department of Health (2010). *Teenage Pregnancy Strategy: Beyond 2010.* London: DCSF and Department of Health.
Department for Education and Skills (2004). *Enabling Young People to access Contraception and Sexual Health Information and Advice: legal and policy framework for social workers, residential social workers, foster carers and other social care practitioners.* London: DfES. Updated from first edition published by Department of Health (2001).
Department for Education and Skills (2004a). *Every Child Matters: change for children.* London: DfES.
Department for Education and Skills (2004b). *Government Response to the Second Annual Report of the Independent Advisory Group on Teenage Pregnancy.* London: DfES.
Department for Education and Skills (2005). *Enabling Young People to Access Contraception and Sexual Health Advice: Guidance for Youth Support Workers.* London: DfES. Updated from first edition published by Department of Health (2001).
Department of Health (2000). *Best Practice Guidance on the Provision of Effective Contraceptive and Advice Services for Young People.* London: Department of Health.
Department of Health (2000; updated 2004). *Best practice guidance for doctors and other health professionals on the provision of advice and treatment to young people under 16 on contraception, sexual and reproductive health.* London: Department of Health.
Department of Health (2001a) *Independent Advisory Group on Teenage Pregnancy. First Annual Report.* Crown Copyright.
Department of Health (2001b). *The national strategy for sexual health and HIV.* London: Department of Health.
Department of Health (2004a). *Choosing Health: making healthy choices easier.* London: Department of Health.

Department of Health (2004b). *National Service Framework for children, young people and maternity*. London: Department of Health.
Department of Health (2007; updated 2011). *You're Welcome: quality criteria for young people friendly health services.* London: Department of Health.
Department of Health and Department of Children, Schools and Families (2009). *Teenage Pregnancy and Sexual Health Marketing Strategy.* London: Department of Health and DCSF.
Eborall C. and Garmesomn G. (2000). *Teenage Pregnancy In England: Desk Research to Inform the National Campaign.* London. Teenage Pregnancy Unit.
Education for Choice (2004). *Abortion: Rights, Responsibilities and Reason – a cross curricula resource.* London. Education for Choice.
London School of Hygiene and Tropical Medicine, UCL and BMRB International (2005). Teenage Pregnancy Strategy Evaluation. Final Report Synthesis. London: LSHTM.
National Audit Office (2001). *Modern Policy Making: ensuring policies deliver value for money.* Report by the Comptroller and Auditor General. HC 289 Session 2001–02. London: NAO.
National Children's Bureau (2006). Involving Young People in Teenage Pregnancy and Sexual Health Work: a practical guide. London: NCB.
Sex Education Forum (2003). *Secondary schools and sexual health services: forging the links.* London: National Children's Bureau.
Social Exclusion Unit (1999). *Teenage Pregnancy.* London: SEU, Cmnd 4342.
Teenage Pregnancy Unit (2000a). *Guidance for Developing Contraception and Sexual Health Advice Services to reach Boys and Young men.* London: Teenage Pregnancy Unit.
Teenage Pregnancy Unit (2000b). *Guidance for Developing Contraception and Sexual Health Advice Services to reach Young People from Black and Minority Ethnic Communities.* London: Teenage Pregnancy Unit.
Teenage Pregnancy Unit (2002a). *A Guide to Involving Young People in Teenage Pregnancy Work.* London: Teenage Pregnancy Unit.
Teenage Pregnancy Unit (2002b). *Diverse Communities: Identity and Teenage Pregnancy.* London: Teenage Pregnancy Unit.
Teenage Pregnancy Unit (2002c). *Government Response to the First Annual Report of the Independent Advisory Group on Teenage Pregnancy.* London: Teenage Pregnancy Unit.
Teenage Pregnancy Unit (2002d). *Involving young people in peer education: a guide for establishing sex and relationships peer education projects.* London: TPU.
Teenage Pregnancy Unit. (2004–07). *Teenage Pregnancy Research Briefings 1–8.* London: Department of Health.
Universities of Leeds and Glamorgan and the London School of Hygiene and Tropical Medicine (1998). Health of the Nation: a policy assessed. London: Department of Health.

4 The second phase of implementation

Reviewing, redoubling efforts and reaching the target (2005–18)

4.1 The mid-course review

4.1.1 Taking stock of progress

In 2005 the independent evaluation of the first phase of the strategy (London School of Hygiene and Tropical Medicine, UCL, BRMB, 2005) and monitoring of the data prompted a mid-course review (Department for Education and Skills, 2006). Although there had been a fairly steady decline in the national under-18 conception rate of 11 per cent, the reduction was significantly behind the trajectory needed to meet the target. It also masked a very wide variation in progress between local areas. The majority of areas had achieved declines but at one end of the spectrum rates had fallen by 42 per cent and, at the other end, increased by 43 per cent. If all local areas had achieved the reductions of the top quarter, the fall in the national rate would have more than doubled.

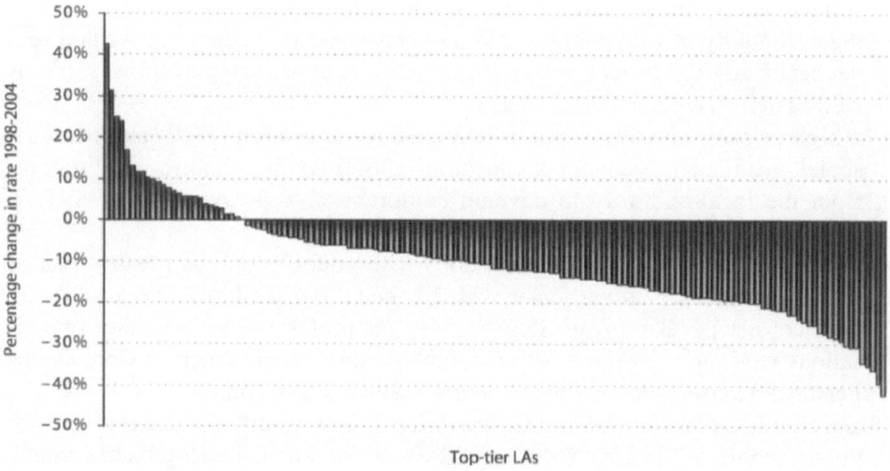

Figure 4.1 Illustrating variation in progress between 1998 and 2004.

DOI: 10.4324/9781003410225-5

4.2 Comparing areas with varying performance

This variation in performance prompted two 'deep dive' in-depth reviews; the first led by the TPU, and the second carried out in partnership with the Prime Minister's Delivery Unit (PMDU). The PMDU was a high-profile unit established in 2001 to strengthen government's capacity to deliver its key priorities, and to monitor performance of indicators in the Public Service Agreements.

The reviews compared three local areas with declining rates and three areas – with similar populations and levels of deprivation – where rates were static or increasing. The review team, including members of the Unit, the Advisory Group and the regional co-ordinators, visited each area for two days. Interviews were conducted with all partner agencies from senior managers through to front line practitioners and young people. Questions focused on how the area had implemented the strategy actions, including the establishment of joint working, leadership and accountability. Detailed interview notes were compiled and the results compared.

The findings clearly identified that the high-performing areas were implementing all aspects of the strategy effectively, supported by senior leadership with a strong co-ordinating function. Areas with slower progress had certainly not been idle, but they had only implemented some actions, or had focused on small geographical areas and at risk groups, rather than combining a universal and targeted approach. Notably, they lacked senior leadership.

The key factors evident in the areas showing progress were:

- a strong senior champion who was accountable for and took the lead in driving the local strategy and co-ordinating the contribution of partner agencies
- active engagement in joint working of all of the key mainstream delivery partners who have a role in reducing teenage pregnancies – health, education, social services and youth support services and the voluntary sector;
- the availability of well publicised young people-centred contraceptive and sexual health advice services, with a strong remit to undertake preventive work, as well as delivering reactive services;
- a high priority given to sex and relationships education (SRE) and personal social, health and economic education (PSHEE) in schools, with support from the local authority to develop comprehensive programmes of SRE in all schools;
- a strong focus on targeted interventions with young people at greatest risk of teenage pregnancy, in particular with Looked After Children; the availability (and consistent take-up) of SRE training for professionals in partner organisations working with the most vulnerable young people (such as Connexions Personal Advisers, youth workers and social workers); and
- a well-resourced Youth Service, providing things to do and places to go for young people, with a clear focus on addressing key social issues affecting young people, such as sexual health and substance misuse.

4.2 Actions following the mid-course review

4.2.1 The critical importance of a 'whole systems' approach

The mid-course review was an important milestone for the strategy. First, the contrasting progress of very similar areas made it clear that continuing high rates were not inevitable. With leadership and the right actions, rates could be reduced, even in the most deprived areas. This was an important message for areas where some senior leaders believed the high rates of teenage parenthood were an intractable part of the local culture and impermeable to prevention. Second, it confirmed the underlining principle of the strategy that the complex issue of teenage pregnancy has to be addressed through a collaborative 'whole systems' approach. The benefits of youth friendly contraceptive services would only be realised if other agencies and practitioners in touch with young people were part of the prevention pathway and linked them into services; and specific teenage pregnancy actions needed to be integrated into wider programmes addressing underlying risk factors of low aspirations and poor educational attainment. In essence, teenage pregnancy needed to be everybody's business; but if the right actions were taken, everybody benefitted.

2.2 New more prescriptive guidance and self-assessment toolkit for local areas

To provide a more detailed road map for local areas, ministers published new and more prescriptive guidance setting out more clearly the practical actions for all relevant partner organisations (Department for Education and Skills, 2006).

The two diagrams below were used to illustrate how to translate the complex issue of teenage pregnancy into a whole systems approach, with every agency understanding their contribution. Senior leadership was at the centre to signal the critical importance of commitment and accountability. How the ten key factors were implemented locally is described in the next chapter (5).

To strengthen local performance management, TPU developed a self-assessment toolkit to enable areas to review their strategy against the ten key factors and to identify and address gaps. To underline the importance of joint working and strategic leadership, the toolkit was jointly published by DfES and DH (Teenage Pregnancy Unit, 2006; updated 2009).

Local self-assessments were led by the co-ordinator working with the partnership board, and moderated by the regional co-ordinator. Results were shared with local senior strategic leaders to provide summaries of local performance and informed commissioning decisions to address any gaps and weaknesses. TPU and regional co-ordinators used the self-assessments to gain a better understanding of the problems in under-performing areas, identify common themes, and provide additional support.

TPU also provided detailed data analysis sheets for each local area showing their conception trend, broken down by conceptions leading to maternity and

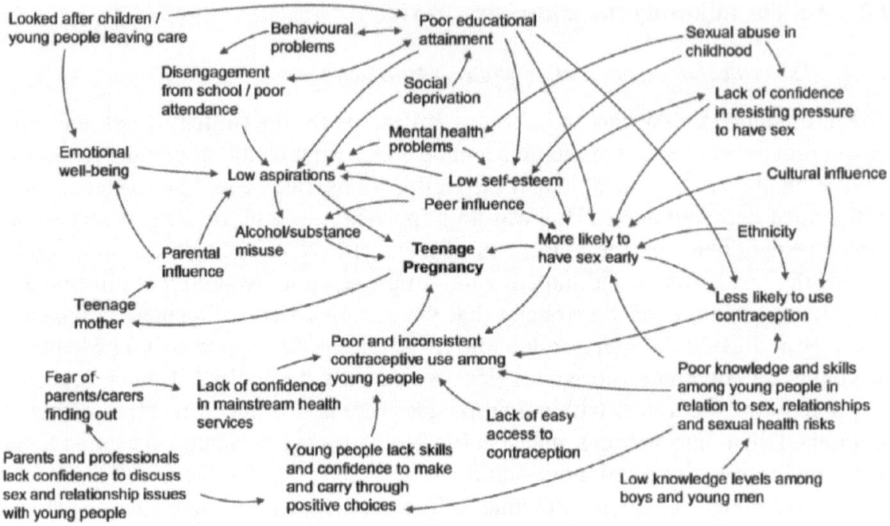

Figure 4.2 Translating the complex issue of teenage pregnancy with a range of risk factors . . .

Source: Acknowledgement Dilwyn Sheers et al., Teenage Pregnancy Unit

. . . into a collaborative 'whole systems' approach with clear actions for each agency

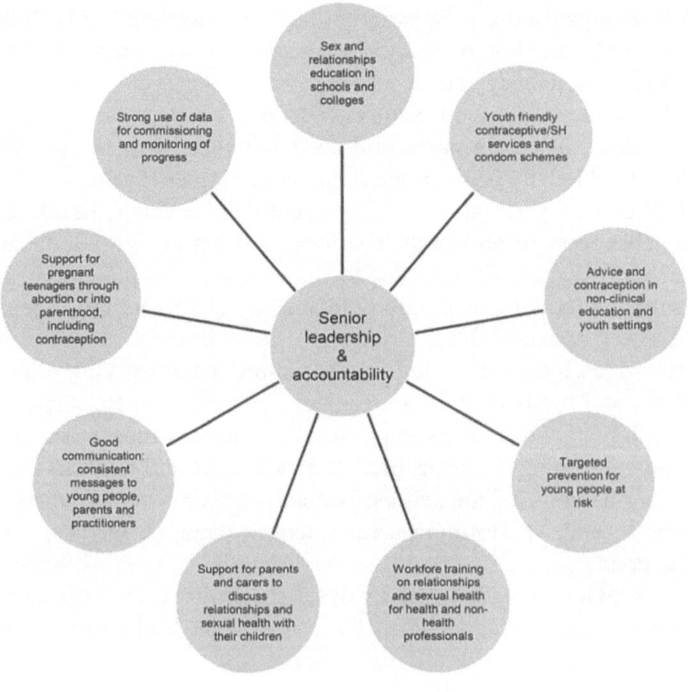

Figure 4.3 The ten key factors for effective local strategies.

conceptions leading to abortions. The analysis also included other relevant data on education attainment and data from local areas, identified by a recognised set of criteria as 'statistical neighbours', to allow like with like comparisons (Department for Education and Skills, 2006).

4.2.3 Direct ministerial contact with local areas

Recognising that improving progress in the poor performing areas was essential for accelerating the national downward trend, DfES and DH ministers decided to establish direct communication with the 21 local areas with high and increasing rates. Senior leaders of local government and their health partners were requested to submit progress reports three times a year, setting out the actions they were taking, which received joint ministerial feedback. They were also invited, with an elected councillor, the Director of Public Health and the local co-ordinator, to attend an annual ministerial meeting to discuss and share effective practice.

> There was tension between the desire to support local areas but at the same time to push the poorest performers closer to the achievements of the best. The key to progress, I was convinced, was having a dedicated senior person at local level who was committed to driving the necessary change across key agencies. This was supported by having Ministerial meetings with the key local players to examine with them their progress, or lack or if, and agreeing what needed to happen next. We expected very senior people, including Chief Executives, to attend these meetings. The sharing of good practice from successful areas was important encouragement that change was possible.
>
> Baroness Hughes of Stretford (Beverley Hughes, former Minister of State for Children and Young People)

The areas were provided with additional support from the regional co-ordinators, supplemented by more intensive in-depth reviews and recommendations from a newly appointed Teenage Pregnancy National Support Team (TPNST). The National Support Teams were established by the Department of Health in 2006 to work directly with health and local government to support them to deliver their public health priorities (including teenage conceptions, sexual health, obesity, mental health and infant mortality). The TPNST was made up of highly respected experts from across the country and headed up by a previous regional co-ordinator with extensive experience of implementation. Visits involved members of the Advisory Group, the Unit and the regional co-ordinator and took a similar approach to the mid-course deep dives, interviewing key informants, analysing local data and exploring how the ten key factors were being implemented. Feedback was rapid with constructive recommendations and the offer of further support if needed (Department of Health, 2011).

4.2.4 Strengthening targeted prevention to reach young people most at risk

In response to the findings of the mid-course review and recommendations from the first phase evaluation, TPU carried out further evidence reviews and data analysis to help all areas strengthen their targeted prevention work (Department for Education and Skills, 2007b).

Investigation into the very small area data found that 50 per cent of the under-18 conceptions occurred in 20 per cent of wards, with almost all local government areas having at least one very high-rate ward. This was a particularly important message for senior leaders in areas where, because rates were at or below the national average, teenage pregnancy was not necessarily identified as a priority.

Local areas were also given updated evidence briefings on the characteristics of young people most at risk of early pregnancy, to help them identify the practitioners, services and relevant programmes that needed to be part of the

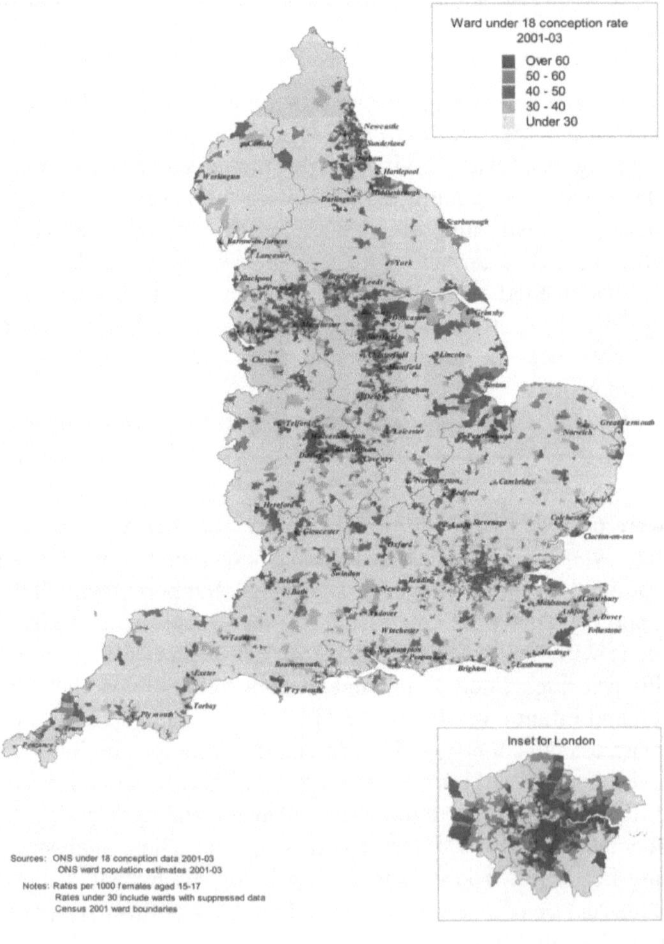

Figure 4.4 Map showing high-rate wards in England.

prevention pathway. Divided into different categories, the following risk factors had the strongest association.

- **Risky behaviour:** early onset of sexual activity; poor contraceptive use; mental health, conduct disorder or involvement in crime; and alcohol and substance misuse.
- **Education-related factors:** low educational attainment; disengagement from, and dislike of school; and leaving school at 16 with no qualifications.
- **Family and background factors:** low parental aspirations; living in care; being the daughter of a teenage mother; and
- **Ethnicity:** having a Mixed White and Black Caribbean, Black Caribbean or Other Black ethnicity.

Data also showed that teenagers with a previous pregnancy were at greater risk. An estimated 20 per cent of births to under-18s were to young women who were already teenage mothers. Of abortions among under 19-year-olds, 11 per cent were to young women who had one or more previous abortions, but the percentage varied significantly between local areas, ranging from 5 per cent to 39 per cent.

4.2.5 Reviewing and revising the national campaign

To support the next phase of the strategy and include a more targeted approach, TPU also reviewed and revised the national campaign, A new look *RUthinking* continued to provide universal messages for younger teenagers on delaying sex until they felt ready, challenging myths about the proportion of young people having sex under 16, and encouraging early uptake of confidential contraception and sexual health advice from local services. Partnerships continued with popular youth brands. Collaboration with the commercial sector not only helped to carry the campaign messages into retail outlets, but also secured additional advertising exposure at no cost. Materials were free for local areas to use in relevant settings and to support targeted work. They were also made available to schools in areas with high and increasing rates and in schools serving high-rate wards.

To complement *Ruthinking*, messages targeting slightly older sexually active teenagers were delivered through a new campaign. *Want Respect: Use a Condom* was based on the principle of gaining peer respect from practising safer sex, and shifting the social norms around carrying and using condoms. The campaign adverts included a focus on condom negotiation and empowering women as well as men to carry condoms with confidence. *Want Respect* was communicated through media channels popular with the target audience and in conjunction with youth brands that lent credibility to the message, particularly with young men. Partnerships with condom manufacturers and retailers helped to improve easy access to condoms, which was identified as key to increasing use (Department for Children, Schools and Families, 2008a). The Sexwise helpline answered calls from around 1.4 million young people – 50 per cent of whom continued to be boys and young men.

The *Time to Talk* campaign for parents continued with advice provided through the Parentline Plus helpline and website, with materials free for local areas. To

Figure 4.5 Example of a Want Respect ad, 2006.

amplify local dissemination, there was national distribution of the *Time to Talk* materials through both the National Healthy Schools and Extended Schools Programmes. National funding was provided for the Family Planning Association *Speakeasy* programme, which had been commissioned by many areas to support parents and carers in discussing sex and relationships with their children. Speakeasy is an eight week course, run one evening a week in small groups, which aims to equip parents and carers with an understanding of the physical and emotional changes taking place at puberty, awareness of what sex and relationships education means in the context of family life, confidence and skills in identifying and responding to the needs of their own children, awareness of societal and cultural attitudes towards sex and sexuality as it relates to children, knowledge of the different kinds of contraception that are available, information on sex and relationships education in schools, and information and knowledge on child protection strategies. The funding enabled local areas to sustain the programme by training their own practitioners to become Speakeasy facilitators.

TPU led regional seminars for co-ordinators and sexual health leads, to ensure they understood the new campaign approach and were supported to extend it effectively at a local level. The self-assessment toolkit included a media and communications strategy checklist and TPU provided an additional Communications Guide for local areas.

4.2.6 Maintaining the priority, joint working and integration into wider government programmes

Government's sustained priority and leadership were signalled by continuing to include the teenage pregnancy target in the new joint DfES and DH Public Service Agreement to 2008, and as an indicator in the performance frameworks for health and local government (Department for Children, Schools and Families, 2008a). Increasing recognition of the importance of teenage pregnancy was reflected in the high numbers of local government areas choosing teenage pregnancy as a priority in their local plans. To help ensure all areas maintained a focus, TPU provided guidance showing how progress on teenage pregnancy helps support achievement of other local priorities, such as reducing child poverty and increasing the proportion of young people in education and training.

Implementation of the new guidance and actions following the mid-strategy review was supported by wider government initiatives to promote a more joined-up and holistic approach to improving outcomes for children and young people.

Notably, the further embedding of *Every Child Matters*, the expectation of local areas to integrate their teenage pregnancy strategies into the new requirement to develop a Children and Young People's Plan to meet the five Every Child Matters outcomes, and a new Targeted Youth Support (TYS) programme aimed at addressing the underlying risk factors that can result in a range of poor outcomes (Department for Education and Skills, 2007a). To have the maximum impact on reducing teenage pregnancy, TYS practitioners were given guidance on providing young people with the knowledge and skills they need to develop positive relationships and good sexual health and to promote access to contraception when they need it (Department of Education and Skills, 2007a). A strengthened National Healthy Schools Standard programme continued to reinforce the links between SRE and sexual health services, and through the Extended Schools programme, schools were encouraged to offer on-site contraception and sexual health advice as part of a range of services. New guidance was published on establishing on-site services in Further Education colleges to provide easy access to contraceptive advice for large numbers of 16–17-year-olds (Department for Education and Skills and Department of Health, 2007).

The joint departmental guidance highlighted the mutual benefits of collaboration. Reductions in pregnancy would contribute to local health targets but also helped improve student retention rates, one of the FE college inspection criteria, by reducing numbers of young women dropping out of courses, owing to pregnancy. The drive to increase the provision of young people friendly services was strengthened by national funding to help areas implement the *You're Welcome* quality criteria. This included recruiting and training young people to 'mystery shop' local services to assess whether or not they met the quality criteria, with a feedback report and constructive recommendations provided to services to help shape improvements.

The local implementation grant funding continued at same level, but in 2006 the ring fence was removed to encourage joint planning and collaborative funding. The location of the Unit in the newly named Department of Children, Schools and Families (DCSF) continued to foster integration of the strategy actions into relevant programmes aimed at reducing underlying risk factors, building aspiration and increasing education attainment. However, strong joint working with the Department of Health ensured improvements in access to contraception, STI screening and pregnancy options were complemented and strengthened by the National Strategy for Sexual Health and HIV. Integrated working was supported and reinforced by the very strong and visible joint ministerial team from the two departments.

> Strong Ministerial engagement was crucial to the effective implementation of the strategy, as well the knowledge that the Teenage Pregnancy Strategy was but one strand of a much wider government commitment to ending child poverty.
>
> It also helped that my position as Minister of State for Children and Young people was deliberately a cross-departmental brief. However, the personal commitment of another female Minister of Health was equally important especially in forging the collaboration needed both between government departments and at local level.
>
> Baroness Hughes of Stretford (Beverley Hughes, former Minister of State for Children and Young People)

4.3 2008–10: a further review of progress

4.3.1 A strengthened focus on SRE and effective contraception

Over the next two years, there was close monitoring of local progress, with an updated self-assessment toolkit for all areas to complete (Department for Children, Schools and Families and Department of Health, 2009b). Local areas under ministerial focus were taken off the list when data showed evidence of improvement, and new high-rate areas added if the pace of change was slow. The regional co-ordinators, complemented by the National Support Team, provided expert support. By 2010 a total of 68 areas had received a NST in-depth review and bespoke recommendations for further actions, with local areas strongly welcoming the specialist advice and constructive support model.

> The National Support Team visit played a vital part in embedding local work and ensuring the strategy left a legacy in the quality of the services for young people. The thorough review of our strategy by a highly regarded national team helped to validate the investment of commitment and resources by celebrating our good practice, but also highlighted gaps and the need for multi-agency collaboration. The NST engagement with senior officials opened doors and led to strengthened partnership working.
>
> Claire Whiteley, Teenage Pregnancy Co-ordinator, Bradford

> We gained a better understanding of the scale of the issue in our area . . . For us 'a light came on'!"
>
> Local Authority Chief Executive, NorthWest

In addition to supporting improved local performance, further thought was given to what national action would help accelerate progress. An updated international research review, commissioned by the TPU, confirmed the original evidence base for the Strategy: that the provision of high-quality comprehensive sex and relationships education and improved use of contraception were the areas with the strongest empirical evidence for reducing teenage pregnancy rates. Furthermore, within the overall reduction in the conception rate, the data showed that conceptions leading to birth were declining faster than those leading to abortion. In other words, fewer young people were getting pregnant but, of those who did, an increasing proportion was deciding against teenage parenthood and choosing abortion instead. These were clearly unwanted pregnancies, underlining the need to strengthen the prevention programme. Some step changes were needed to further improve SRE and access to effective contraception.

4.3.2 A concerted push for statutory sex and relationships education

From the start of the Strategy there had been a sustained call to Government from the Advisory Group, the Sex Education Forum and other NGOs and stakeholders, to make SRE within PSHE education a statutory part of the curriculum; a recommendation reiterated in the independent evaluation of the strategy's first phase. This was considered essential to increase the priority in schools and address the unacceptable variability between young people in relation to the amount and quality of SRE they received (Ofsted, 2007). While statutory status alone would not guarantee quality, it would secure a place for SRE/PSHE in the curriculum, require training of specialist teachers and continuing professional development, and ensure inspection of school provision. Following a survey of 20,000 young people from the UK Youth Parliament (UK Youth Parliament, 2007), which showed that 40 per cent rated their SRE poor or inadequate, and a campaign – *Beyond Biology* – from the Sex Education Forum (Sex Education Forum, 2006), Government accepted the need for change and commissioned an external review of SRE and PSHE (Department for Children, Schools and Families, 2008c). In 2008, at a national Sex Education Forum conference Jim Knight, the schools minister, announced that government intended to make PSHE, including SRE, statutory (Department for Children, Schools and Families, 2008b), receiving a standing ovation from delighted stakeholders!

To determine the most effective ways of achieving this, government commissioned an independent review. Led by Sir Alastair Macdonald, a prominent education leader, the review confirmed that statutory SRE and PSHE, at both primary and secondary levels, was key to raising the status and improving the provision and made recommendations for government to take forward into legislation (Department for Children, Schools and Families, 2009a). However, to widespread dismay and strong criticism by the Advisory Group and stakeholders, the Bill failed to get passed in the final legislative session before the general election in May 2010.

Nevertheless, during the preparation for the Bill important progress was made in improving the understanding of SRE and building consensus for universal provision. Once myths were dispelled about the sexual content of SRE at primary level, and parents understood that good SRE delayed rather than lowered age of first sex, opinion polls and focus groups demonstrated strong support for provision in all schools.

> We are not talking about five-year-old kids being taught sex. What we're talking about for key stage 1 is children knowing about themselves, their differences, their friendships and how to manage their feelings.
>
> Jim Knight, Schools Minister (*The Guardian*, 23 October 2008)

Similarly, discussions with faith communities and organisations also elicited support for statutory status. The Advisory Group and NGOs played a critical role in calmly making the case for the benefits of SRE, and supporting ministers to explicitly support the move to statutory status. The expectation of statutory status also prompted some local areas to raise the priority of SRE and develop programmes and training to prepare schools.

> It was hugely disappointing that the legislation fell at the final hurdle. However, the review which led to the decision for statutory status demonstrated that when evidence and testimonies are presented from those affected by poor provision, and the content of SRE is explained, fears and misconceptions fall away and a consensus emerges that SRE is essential to protect and promote the health and wellbeing of children and young people.
>
> Jane Lees, Chair of Sex Education Forum 2008–2017

4.3.3 ***Improving young people's knowledge and access to effective contraception***

The importance of improving young people's access to and use of contraception was highlighted by new research attributing 86 per cent of the recent decline in US teenage pregnancy rates to better contraceptive use (Santelli et al., 2007). To support local areas in improving access to effective contraception, the Department of Health secured £33 million additional funding from the Government Spending Review settlement for 2008–11 (Department for Children, Schools and Families, 2009a). The primary aim was to increase access for all women, including young people under-18s, to all types of contraception and particularly to ensure that the choice of Long Acting Reversible Contraceptive (LARC) methods was easily available in all areas. Expanding availability of LARC methods had also been a recommendation of the first phase evaluation.

Funds were distributed through the regional network of Strategic Health Authorities[1], which were asked to ensure investment was made on activities that would be sustainable beyond the three-year lifetime of the funding. A proportion of funding was ear-marked to support local areas expand the collaboration with Further Education colleges to set up on-site services. To continue the important promotion of condoms to protect against STIs, Brook was funded to develop guidance for local areas on condom distribution schemes. TPU also funded Brook to develop guidance on sexual health outreach to help local areas take services to young people who might be wary of accessing other settings (Brook, 2008), and to provide updated guidance and best practice examples of engaging with boys and young men (Brook, 2010).

4.3.4 A new national campaign to normalise discussion about contraception

As part of the drive to improve awareness and uptake of contraception, there was a rethink of the national campaign and the Department of Health commissioned an evidence review to identify the most effective role of communications (Department of Health and Department for Children, Schools and Families, 2009a). The review found that while there were multiple influences on behaviour, the strongest predictors of young people practising safer sex was not their attitudes or stated behavioural intention, but their 'preparatory' behaviours – accessing condoms, carrying condoms, and discussion about condom use. Discussion about condom use prior to sex had the strongest overall influence. The biggest impact of a communications campaign would be through normalising everyday discussion about contraception and sexual health to reduce the stigma and embarrassment, which young people reported as deterrents to seeking early advice.

Developed in close consultation with stakeholders and NGOs, a new campaign was launched in November 2009, aimed at young people up to the age of 25. *Sex. Worth Talking About* – a notable shift of emphasis from the earlier teenage pregnancy strategy campaign, sex, are you *thinking* about it enough? – ran TV, radio, cinema and online ads showing conversations about contraception and chlamydia between young people, with parents and with health professionals in a range of everyday scenarios. For the first time, government ads about the range of contraceptive choices and the importance of STI testing were brought into the living room, before the 9 pm 'watershed'. The notable absence of complaints from the public was a further reflection of the growing consensus that providing young people with good information was important in helping them prevent early pregnancy and to look after their sexual health.

Young people seeking further information were directed to a new *Sex. Worth Talking About* website and the Sexwise helpline was rebranded, *Worth Talking About*. To help extend the messages into local settings, a separate campaign website was developed for co-ordinators and sexual health professionals, with a campaign toolkit, free posters and resources to disseminate to young people and health professionals. A new guide for parents – *Talking to your teenager about sex and relationships,* co-branded with the NHS logo and Parentline Plus, was also distributed to all independent pharmacies in England. Pharmacies were chosen as a

Figure 4.6 Sex. Worth Talking About campaign logo, 2009.

frequently visited and trusted source of health advice with a presence in all local communities, including the most deprived.

As a result of the election and change of government in May 2010, and although materials continued to be available for local areas, the national campaign activity only ran for four months, significantly limiting its impact. Nevertheless, there were some encouraging signs. Despite the short duration, follow up evaluation found there was very high recognition of both the contraception and chlamydia adverts, and increased awareness of long acting reversible contraception, particularly the implant. Interestingly, the chlamydia messages appeared to particularly increase parents' intention to talk to their teenagers about sexual health. Service data also suggested some positive impact, with a 10 per cent increase in chlamydia screening between 2009 and 2010 and a rise in the proportion of young people choosing a LARC method from 24 per cent in 2008/09, (HSCIC, 2009) to 26 per cent in 2009/10 (HSCIC, 2010) and 28 per cent in 2010/11 (HSCIC, 2011). Although it is not possible to attribute to the campaign, the under-18 conception rate showed the largest single year decline of 8 per cent between 2009 and 2010.

4.3.5 Maintaining the priority, joint working and integration into wider government programmes

As well as these specific actions and the close monitoring of local progress, Government signalled the continuing priority of teenage pregnancy in the new Public Service Agreements. To further integrate the strategy into wider programmes, teenage pregnancy was included as one of five leading indicators in a new Youth PSA – increasing the number of young people on the path to success. Each PSA was underpinned by a cross-department delivery agreement. Although DCSF led on the Youth PSA, all departments, including DH, shared responsibility for the PSA and progress on the under-18 conception rate. The indicator also continued to be included as a priority in the NHS Operating Framework. Locally, the under-18 conception rate was now chosen by 106/150 areas as a priority indicator, second only to the proportion of young people not in education, employment or training (Department for Children, Schools and Families, 2009a). To support local areas strengthen the monitoring of progress and accountability, TPU provided a revised self-assessment toolkit and a local monitoring dataset, with suggested indicators to measure the delivery and impact of the different strategy actions. To help ensure the self-assessment was part of the overall commissioning cycle, the toolkit included a one-page summary of progress and further required actions for sign off by senior leaders (Department for Children, Schools and Families and Department of Health, 2009b).

The importance of joining up teenage pregnancy work was reinforced by a strong ministerial presence. The Children's and Health ministers spoke together at regional conferences for co-ordinators and senior leaders; ministers responsible for healthy schools, extended schools and further education spoke publicly about the benefits of on-site contraception and sexual health services; and ministerial promotion of a new Child Health Strategy reinforced the benefits of SRE, easy access to confidential services, early targeted help and support for parents (Department for Children, Schools and Families, 2009a).

Improvements in SRE were supported by a new statutory duty on schools to improve pupil wellbeing, and continuing inclusion in the National Healthy Schools Programme and in a new Enhanced Healthy Schools Programme. In addition to the contraceptive investment, the drive for increased youth friendly services was strengthened by a new Healthy Child Programme for five- to 19-year-olds and continued funding for the *You're Welcome* accreditation programme. Early help for young people most at risk was extended through the Targeted Youth Support programme.

By 2010 the strategy was regarded by many as being the vanguard of joint working between government departments, local partners and professionals and, in particular, a catalyst for partnership working between health and education.

> The Teenage Pregnancy Strategy wasn't just successful in reducing teenage conceptions and supporting young parents, it also rewrote the book on how to effectively deliver complex, often believed impossible, changes within society. The model of integrating national policy with local implementation created strong vertical links through national, regional and local co-ordinators, but also wove together diverse services across local areas. One of the lasting impacts of the strategy has been to engender a new way of joint working.
>
> Jo Nichols, Local and regional teenage pregnancy co-ordinator, and Associate National Delivery Manager Teenage Pregnancy National Support Team

> *The strategy forged the way for improved joint working on addressing other young people's risk taking, such as alcohol. Partner agencies saw the benefits of collaboration between services and practitioners.*
>
> Gail Teasdale, Teenage Pregnancy Co-ordinator, Kingston-upon-Hull

4.4 2010 and beyond

4.4.1 Keeping the focus beyond the end of the strategy

In 2010 the Government published new guidance for local areas for two key reasons (Department for Children, Schools and Families and Department of Health, 2010). First, this was the final year in which local areas could take action to influence the original target. Second, the guidance made an important statement that the strategy was not ending. The original reasons for the strategy remained, and although the downward trend was starting to accelerate, there was much more to do. It was clear that with the right actions rates could be reduced but the priority needed to continue. *Teenage Pregnancy Strategy: Beyond 2010*, was informed by an updated evidence review, summarised the progress and learning so far, illustrated by a range of local case studies, and set out proposals for further national actions.

In May 2010 a new Coalition Government was elected, marking the end of thirteen years continuous Labour administration. Ministers from the renamed Department for Education and the Department of Health decided against publishing a further standalone strategy or setting new national and local targets. Instead they made clear they wanted teenage pregnancy to remain a priority but for the actions to be integrated into wider programmes to narrow inequalities and address child poverty. Local areas were asked to continue to prioritise reducing teenage pregnancy rates, using the international evidence and lessons from the areas where rates have fallen fastest to accelerate progress. The Advisory Group published its final report and recommendations to new ministers in December 2010. *Past successes – future challenges,* stressed the importance of a continued focus from the new administration and the economic, as well as human costs of disinvestment (Teenage Pregnancy Independent Advisory Group, 2010):

> The reduction in the teenage pregnancy rate over the past decade – to the point where it is at the lowest level for over 20 years – is very welcome and reflects the hard work of people working at a local level to help young people make safe and healthy choices about sex and relationships. But we still have very high rates compared to many other countries and clearly there is still much more to be done. I want local areas to maintain their efforts to reduce teenage pregnancy rates further, making a vital contribution to their strategies to reduce child poverty and health inequalities.
>
> Sarah Teather, Minister for Children and Families, 2010

To signal an on-going national focus on teenage pregnancy, reducing the under-18 conception rate was one of eight ambitions in the Department of Health's new policy guidance on improving sexual health (Department of Health, 2013a), and the under-18 conception rate was included as one of three sexual health indicators in a new Public Health Outcomes Framework, designed to monitor national and local progress (Department of Health, 2013b). The benefits of SRE were highlighted in a new Schools White Paper (Department for Education, 2010), and the importance of youth friendly services underlined by revised *You're Welcome* quality criteria (Department of Health, 2011). A cross-government youth policy, *Positive for Youth* (HM Government, 2011), emphasised the importance of building young people's knowledge and confidence to delay early pregnancy and look after their sexual health. Notably, the policy included a case study of Brook's Sex Positive Campaign, a marker of progress in government's ease in discussing sexual health.

The Sex Positive Campaign was developed by Brook young volunteers, as part of 'V talent year', a national full time volunteering programme for young people. The campaign was prompted by their personal experiences of poor sex and relationships education, overwhelmingly negative attitudes to young people's sexuality and a lack of information about sexual health services. Recognising that many young people had the same experiences, the young volunteers were inspired to start a campaign to encourage societal attitudes to be sex positive, making it easier for young people to talk about and make well-informed and positive choices about sex, and remove the stigma about asking for advice on sexual health. The campaign evolved into a Sex Positive movement, as subsequent cohorts of young volunteers took ownership, leading their own social action projects at national and local level, meeting with MPs and ministers and promoting awareness and discussion online.

However, national funding for the strategy, including the media campaign stopped, visible government leadership ceased and the structures for strategy implementation began to be dismantled. The regional co-ordinator posts, government offices and National Support Teams ended in 2011 and the Teenage Pregnancy Unit closed in 2012. So too did the national and regional structures for supporting local implementation of the *National Healthy Schools Programme* and the *You're Welcome* standards. Decisions about co-ordinators, partnership boards and accountability arrangements were left to local government, which, following the Health and Social Care Act, now had responsibility for public health, including the commissioning of clinical sexual and reproductive health services. However, a study in 2011 found one third of the dedicated co-ordinator posts had been cut (Nichols, 2011). In 2013, the previous head of TPU established a new independent Teenage Pregnancy Knowledge Exchange at the University of Bedfordshire, to ensure a national source of expertise continued, and shortly after became teenage pregnancy advisor to Public Health England to develop further national guidance and provide support to local areas.

A teenage pregnancy briefing was published for elected councillors highlighting the need for continued attention and further development, and illustrating effective local practice (Local Government Association and Public Health England, 2016, updated 2017). Guidance was published for local areas, which restated the principles for implementing the ten key factors and provided a self-assessment checklist for reviewing progress and addressing gaps (Public Health England and Local Government Association, 2017). A framework for supporting teenage mothers and young fathers set out the evidence and multi-agency contribution for improving outcomes (Public Health England and Local Government Association, 2016). These, and other new policy and guidance documents which include teenage pregnancy strategy actions, are referenced in Chapter 7 of the first edition in the discussion on sustaining momentum beyond the end of the strategy.

4.4.2 Reaching the target!

The original reduction target of the strategy was finally achieved in 2014. The under-18 conception rate of 22.8 per 1,000 15–17-year-olds marked a 51 per cent reduction from 1998, with the number of conceptions dropping from 41,089 to 21,282. The under-16 conception rate also fell by over 50 per cent. Both had reached the lowest levels since 1969 when conception data collection began. All

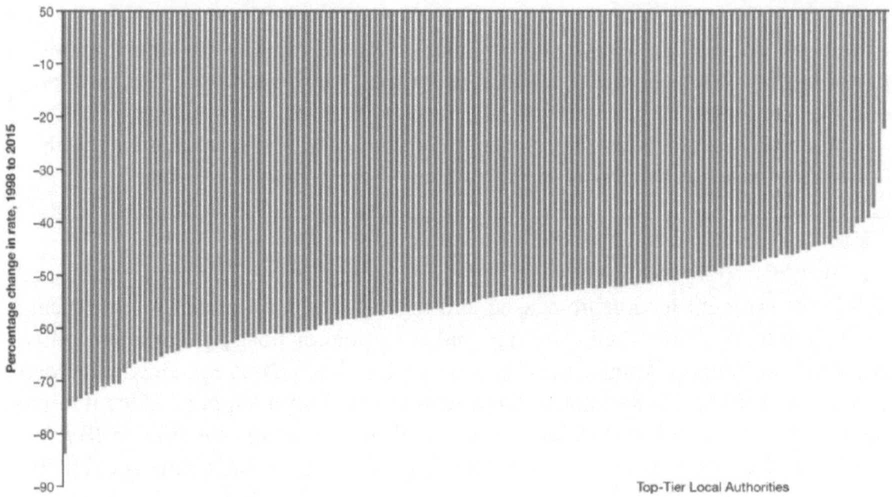

Figure 4.7 Under 18 conception rates: Change in conception rate per 1,000 girls aged 15–17: 1998–2015.

areas had seen reductions, including those with previously slow progress, (see Figure 4.7) and abortions and maternity rates were declining in parallel (Figure 4.8). The impact of the strategy was also explored in an independent observational study. Routinely collected area level conception data, deprivation and local implementation grant expenditures were combined with individual level risk factor information from the three waves of the National Surveys of Sexual Attitudes and Lifestyle (Natsal) to describe changes in conceptions, abortions and maternities to under-18s in England. The study reported a marked decline in conceptions, which was greater in areas of higher deprivation and also in areas of higher teenage pregnancy strategy investment (Wellings et al., 2016).

National data on monitoring indices of the strategy implementation are limited. However, there was a doubling in the number of youth specific community contraceptive clinic sessions between 1997/98 and 2009/10, a large increase in the use of LARCs by under-18s accessing contraceptive clinics (Health and Social Care Information Centre, 2008/09 and 2009/10), a significant expansion in the number of school (Sex Education Forum, 2008a) and college-based clinics providing reproductive and sexual health advice (Sex Education Forum, 2008b) and an upward trend in the proportion of young people reporting school as their main source of SRE, which is associated with lower under-18 conception rates and STI diagnoses (Tanton, Jones and Macdowall, 2015).

As Figure 4.8 illustrates, the decline accelerated after 2008, with a 39 per cent reduction between 2010 and 2015. As teenage pregnancy is a complex issue requiring a multi-faceted approach, it is unlikely that one factor drove the steeper decline in the later stages of the strategy. More probable is a combination of factors, including the increasing priority given to teenage pregnancy by local areas after

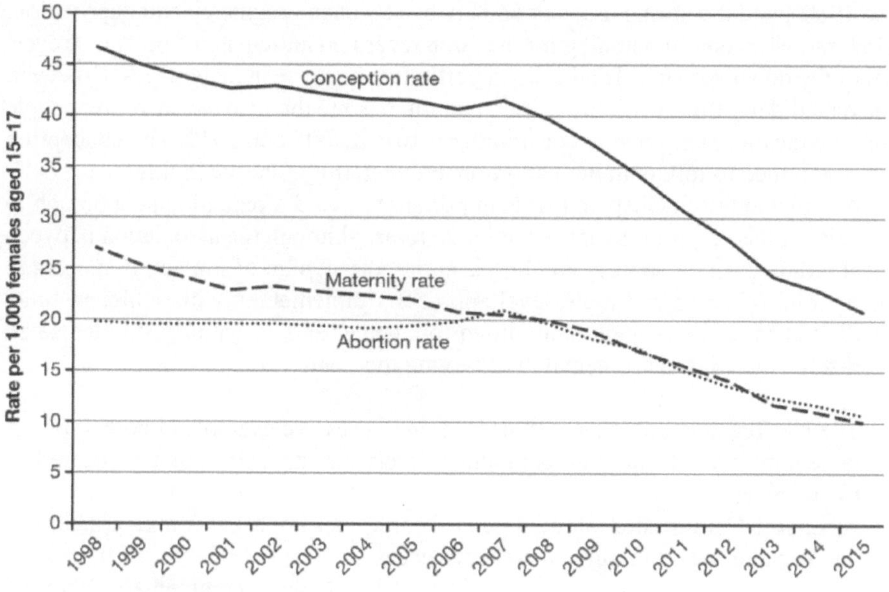

Figure 4.8 The national trend in under-18 conceptions, maternities and abortions: 1998–2015.

the mid-strategy review in 2006, with increased ministerial focus and additional support, the cumulative impact of a long term programme of prevention work through service improvements, workforce training and wider government initiatives to strengthen partnership working and improve wider outcomes for children and young people, an increase in under-18s choosing one of the LARC methods, and the benefits of time in changing the culture of strategic leaders and service providers that, when young people are given choices, high rates are not inevitable.

> I have been a Teenage Pregnancy Co-ordinator since the beginning of the strategy and now have a lead commissioning role for young people's health in Public Health.
>
> I have never since experienced the enormous benefits of the strong vertical communications between national, regional and local. The strengths in collaborative working and true partnerships were evident for local young people – teenage pregnancy wasn't inevitable and it was part of everyone's responsibility to support young people.
>
> Kerry Clarke, Teenage Pregnancy Co-ordinator, Brighton & Hove

This last point is particularly important given that the downward trend continued despite the impact of the recession. During the British recession in the early 1980s, there was a marked increase in the under-20s conception rate, mainly accounted for by a rise in conceptions leading to maternity (Brook, 2014). Based on the trend in the 1980s, and the strong association between teenage pregnancy and deprivation, Government scenario planning for the 2008 recession anticipated a potential reversal of the downward trend and a disproportionate increase in maternities. However, the data did not follow the anticipated pattern, despite the increase in young people not in education, employment or training between 2008 and 2012. The conception rate continued to fall, with both abortion and maternity rates declining.

As pointed out in Chapter 1, it is important to avoid a reductionist approach to explaining the very significant reduction in rates, although the association between local reductions and strategy funding is an important sign of impact. It appears to be the multi-faceted and multi-level approach, implemented with sufficient time, facilitated by a Government committed to change, and an enthusiastic dedicated workforce that was instrumental in achieving the goal.

> The UK Teenage Pregnancy Strategy is an impressive example of how a sustained, multilevel, and multicomponent intervention, such as that advocated by the recent
>
> Lancet Commission on adolescent health, can impact a complex health and social issue, with high cost-effectiveness.
>
> (*Lancet* commentary, 2016)

4.4.3 What were the success factors and what might have been done differently?

Understanding the success factors is important for maintaining the downward trend in the UK and for other countries seeking to address high rates. So too is reflecting on what might have been done differently to strengthen the strategy. The points summarised below are explored in more detail in Chapter 7 of the first edition, described under the WHO criteria for effective national adolescent sexual and reproductive health programmes.

Features of success

- Creating and maximising the opportunity for collaborative action
- Developing a credible, evidence-based strategy with national and local targets
- Establishing the structures and support for effective strategy implementation
- Regularly reviewing the strategy and tailoring actions to address the findings
- Embedding the strategy in wider government programmes aimed at improving health, education and economic outcomes
- Maintaining leadership and accountability throughout the strategy, with sufficient time to bring about change

What might have been done differently to strengthen the strategy?

- Making SRE statutory as an action of the strategy
- Issuing more prescriptive guidance from the start, with stronger performance management of strategy inputs
- A stronger campaign focus on effective contraception, with condom use as a secondary rather than primary message
- An annual national survey of young people to monitor impact of strategy actions, which could be used by local areas
- More proactive work with the media from the start of the strategy to highlight consensus and counter misleading media reports

Note

1 Strategic health authorities (SHA) were part of the NHS structure in England between 2002 and 2013. Each SHA was responsible for implementing policies of the Department of Health at a regional level.

References

Brook (2008; updated 2014). *C-Card condom distribution schemes: why, what and how*. London: Brook.

Brook (2008). *Sexual Health Outreach: why, what and how*. London: Brook.

Brook (2010). *Young Men, Sex and Pregnancy: practical guidance on effective approaches*. London: Brook.

Brook (2014). *Teenage conceptions: statistics and trends*. London: Brook.

Department for Children, Schools and Families (2008a). *Government Response to the 4th Annual Report of the Teenage Pregnancy Independent Advisory Group*. London: DCSF.

Department for Children, Schools and Families (2008b). *Government Response to the Report by the Sex and Relationships Education (SRE) Review Steering Group*. London: DCSF.

Department for Children, Schools and Families (2008c). *Review of Sex and Relationships Education (SRE) in Schools. A report by the External Steering Group*. Issues. London: DCSF.

Department for Children, Schools and Families (2009a). *Government Response to the 5th Annual Report of the Teenage Pregnancy Independent Advisory Group*. London: DCSF.

Department for Children, Schools and Families and Department of Health (2009b). *Teenage pregnancy prevention and support: a self-assessment toolkit for local performance management*. London: DCSF and Department of Health. Crown Copyright.

Department for Children, Schools and Families and Department of Health (2010). *Teenage Pregnancy Strategy: Beyond 2010*. London: DCSF and Department of Health.

Department for Education (2010). *The Importance of Teaching. The Schools White Paper 2010*. London. DfE.

Department for Education and Skills (2006). *Teenage Pregnancy Next Steps: Guidance for Local Authorities and Primary Care Trusts on Effective Delivery of Local Strategies*. London: DfES.

Department for Education and Skills and Department of Health (2007). *Teenage Pregnancy: working towards 2010. Good practice and self-assessment toolkit*. London: DfES and Department of Health.

Department for Education and Skills (2007a). *Targeted Youth Support: a guide*. London: DfES.
Department for Education and Skills (2007b). *Teenage Pregnancy: Accelerating the Strategy to 2010.* London: DfES.
Department of Health (2007; updated 2011). *You're Welcome: quality criteria for young people friendly health services.* London: Department of Health.
Department of Health (2011). Teenage Pregnancy National Support Team: evaluation of impact. London: Department of Health.
Department of Health (2013a). *A Framework for Sexual Health Improvement in England.* London: Department of Health.
Department of Health (2013b). *Public Health Outcomes Framework 2013–2016.* London: Department of Health.
Department of Health and Department of Children, Schools and Families (2009). *Teenage Pregnancy and Sexual Health Marketing Strategy.* London: Department of Health and DCSF.
Department of Health and Department for Education and Employment (2001). *National Healthy School Standard: Sex and Relationships Education.* London: Department of Health and DfEE.
Local Government Association and Public Health England (2016). *Good progress but more to do: teenage pregnancy and young parents.* London. LGA and PHE.
London School of Hygiene and Tropical Medicine, UCL and BMRB International (2005). Teenage Pregnancy Strategy Evaluation. Final Report Synthesis. London: LSHTM.
Nichols, J. (2011). *Reducing Teenage Pregnancy Rates in England Post-2010; The Challenge of Changing Times*, MSc Dissertation, University of Bradford.
Public Health England and Local Government Association (2016). *A Framework for supporting teenage mothers and young fathers.* London: PHE and LGA.
Public Health England and Local Government Association (2017). *A Framework to support young people to prevent unplanned pregnancy and develop healthy relationships.* London: PHE and LGA.
Santelli, J.S., Lindberg, L.D., Finer, L.B. and Singh, S. (2007). Explaining recent declines in adolescent pregnancy in the United States: The contribution of abstinence and improved contraceptive use. *American Journal of Public Health* 2007, 97(1), 150–6.
Sex Education Forum (2006). *Beyond Biology.* London: National Children's Bureau.
Sex Education Forum (2008a). *Are you getting it right? A toolkit for consulting young people on sex and relationships education.* London: National Children's Bureau.
Sex Education Forum (2008b). *National mapping of On-site Sexual Health Services in Education Settings: Provision in schools and pupil referral units in England.* London: National Children's Bureau.
Tanton, C., Jones, K.G. and Macdowall, W. (2015). Patterns and trends in sources of information about sex among young people in Britain: evidence from three National Surveys of Sexual Attitudes and Lifestyles. *BMJ Open*.
Teenage Pregnancy Unit (2006; updated 2009). *Teenage Pregnancy: working towards 2010. Good Practice and Self-Assessment Toolkit.* London: Teenage Pregnancy Unit.
Teenage Pregnancy Independent Advisory Group (2010). *Final report. Teenage pregnancy: past successes – future challenges.* London. TPIAG.
UK Youth Parliament (2007). *SRE: are you getting it? A report by the UK Youth Parliament.* London: UKYP.
Wellings, K., Palmer, M.J., Geary, R.S., Gibson, L.J., Copas, A., Datta, J., Glasier, A., Scott, R.H., Mercer, C.H., Erens, B., Macdowall, W., French, R.S., Jones, K., Johnson, A.M., Tanton, C. and Wilkinson, P. (2016). Changes in conceptions in women younger than 18 years and the circumstances of young mothers in England in 2000–12: an observational study, *Lancet,* 388(10044), 586–595, 6 August 2016.

5 What happened next

A national and local perspective (2018–24)

5 Overview

This chapter explores what has happened since publication of the first edition, focusing on both the national policy landscape and the local experience of trying to maintain the evidence-based approach of the strategy. Understanding the facilitators and barriers to sustaining change without a defined strategy or target is important learning for other social policy and public health programmes. It is also important evidence for some who suggest that the strategy ended in 2010, so could not have contributed to any further declines.

In the previous chapter we noted the accelerated decline in the under-18 conception rate after 2008 and concluded the most probable reason was the cumulative impact of local prioritisation, a long-term programme of prevention, an increase in uptake of Long Acting Reversible Contraception (LARC) methods and, with the benefits of time, a recognition that high rates are not inevitable if the right actions are put in place.

The further reduction of 39 per cent between 2010 and 2015 happened during a period of political change, with the incoming coalition Government of 2010 making new fiscal, policy and structural choices. Although Ministers asked local areas to continue prioritising teenage pregnancy using the evidence from the strategy, key local and regional structures which had supported implementation were dismantled; the local area co-ordinator role became something of a rarity and the choice of austerity resulted in significant cuts to national and local funding. Against this challenging backdrop, it might have been reasonable to expect a stalling of the downward trend. However, qualitative research in 2019, conducted with local areas that achieved the largest reductions between 2010 and 15, identified some clear supportive factors. A subsequent study conducted in 2023 identified the same factors at play. The findings of both studies are introduced and discussed from section 5.4 onwards in this chapter.

5.1 What do the data say? 2015–22

To return to the national context, after 2015 the downward trend continued albeit at an uneven rate (see Figure 5.1). This was particularly notable in 2020 which saw a

DOI: 10.4324/9781003410225-6

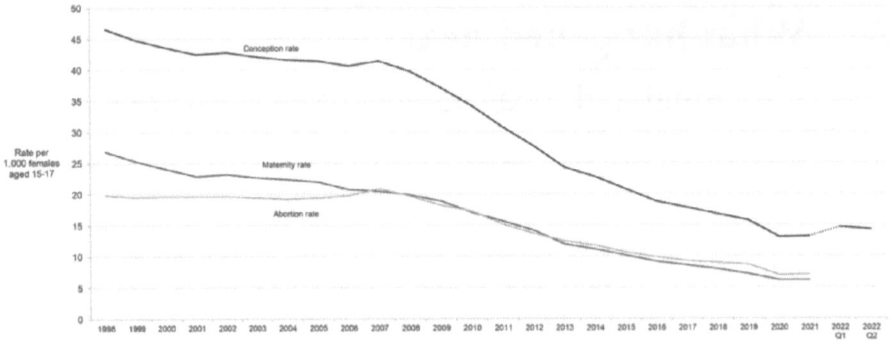

Figure 5.1 The national trend in under-18 conception, maternity and abortion rates. 1998–2022.

much larger reduction. This was influenced by a drop of 33 per cent in the conception rate during April-June, the period of the first COVID-19 pandemic lockdown (Office for National Statistics, 2022). As access to contraception was much reduced during lockdown, this was most probably due to a significant decrease in young people's sexual activity. Interestingly, while rates dropped in most areas, a small minority saw rates rise – an anomaly that has not yet been explored. The under-18 conception rate then returned to the previous downward trajectory. However the 2021 conception data showed a small 0.8 per cent increase – the first for 14 years – with the rate increase continuing into the first six months of 2022. This reversal of the downward trend affected all regions, with significant changes in some local areas (Office for National Statistics, 2024). With delays to the Office for National Statistics publication of the full 2022 data, owing to a lack of resources, it is not possible to judge whether the increases in the first two quarters of 2022 reflect lower rates during lockdown periods in 2021, or mark the start of an upward trend. It is, however, an important caution against complacency that the 'job is done', a risk highlighted by local areas later in this chapter.

The persistent inequalities evident in the data from 2015–21 also signal the need for a continued focus. Despite the 72 per cent reduction in the under-18 conception rate England's teenage birth rate remains higher than comparable Western countries (Eurostat, 2017); teenagers are at highest risk of unplanned pregnancy (Wellings et al., 2013) with over half of under-18 conceptions and almost two thirds of under-16 conceptions ending in abortion (Office for National Statistics, 2023); there are wide variations in the under-18 conception rate persist between local areas (see Figure 5.2); and within local areas 60 per cent of local authorities have at least one high-rate ward[1]. Individual young people also face unequal risks, with those who have experienced four or more adverse childhood experiences being between three and seven times more likely to experience an accidental teenage pregnancy, become a teenage parent and have a lifetime diagnosis of a sexually transmitted infection (Wood et al., 2022). And although the maternity rate to under-18s has fallen by 77 per cent

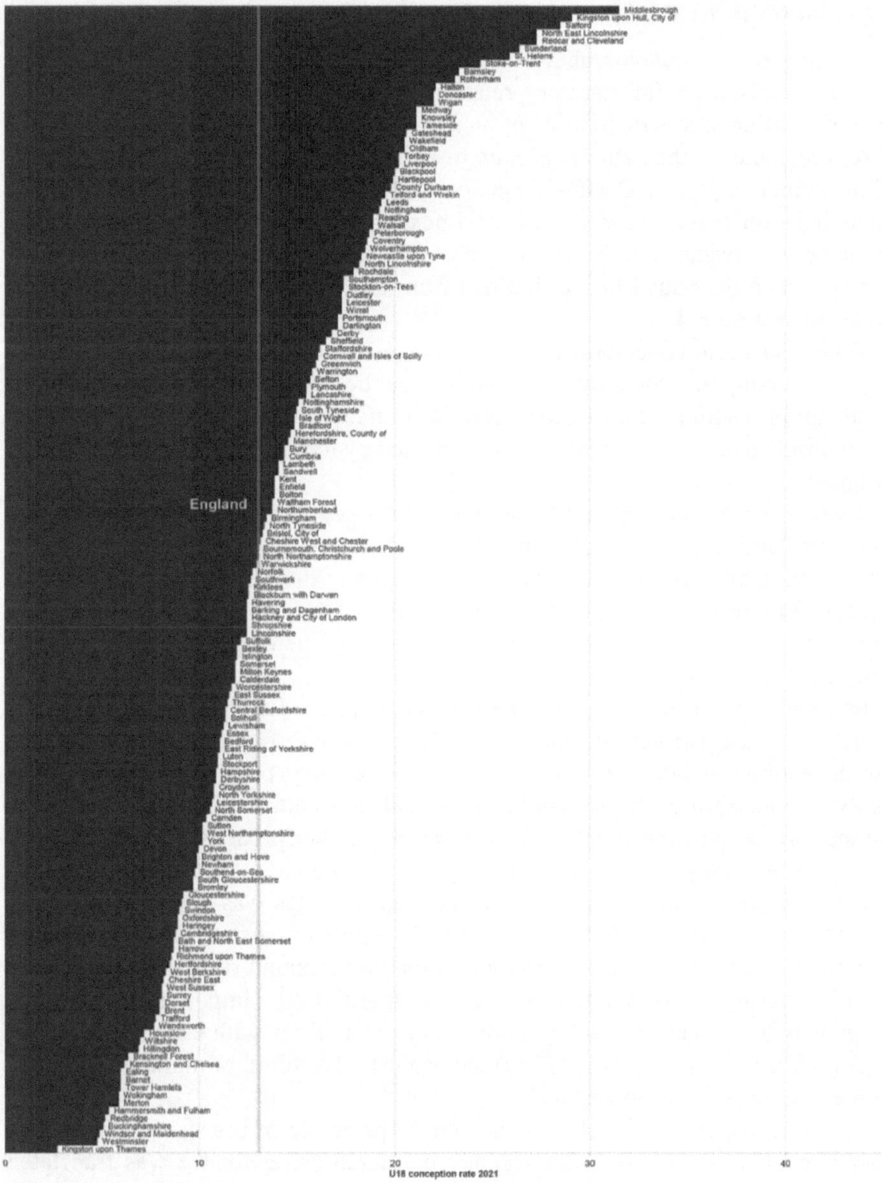

Figure 5.2 The variation in under-18 conception rates between local authorities in England. 2021.

(1998–2021), with numbers of young mothers under 18 falling from 23,600 to 5,700 (Office for National Statistics, 2023), the outcomes for them and their children remain disproportionately poor with little improvement over the past six years (see Chapter 7).

5.2 National policy development 2018–23: progress and challenges

Regarding policy development which is likely to facilitate further progress – securing legislation for statutory relationships and sex education (RSE) in all schools, easier access to contraception and addressing the wider determinants of early pregnancy – the national picture over the past six years is mixed, with lack of investment and the COVID-19 pandemic impacting all three. The progress and challenges on these issues are covered next in the more detailed contributions from national organisations. The way the wider context affected local implementation is then described in the findings from the qualitative research with local areas, in section 5.4.

Two other national factors have also influenced progress: the absence of government leadership and the move away from a public health, whole system focus on upstream prevention. Both factors were instrumental in effective implementation of the original strategy, and their loss often cited by local areas as hindering further progress.

Leadership at national and local level was a key factor in the strategy's success, explaining why teenage pregnancy mattered and its intergenerational impact on health and educational outcomes. While the Teenage Pregnancy Prevention Framework (Public Health England and Local Government Association 2018) remains the government guidance, after the closure of Public Health England there has been no teenage pregnancy policy lead in any government department. Office for National Statistics conception data releases are disseminated by the Department of Health and Social Care through regional networks, but the additional data analysis and the bespoke teenage pregnancy reports previously provided for each local authority by Public Health England have stopped. So too have any government media responses – either proactive or reactive – to teenage pregnancy data or related issues. The need to address the inequalities behind the significant fall in under-18 conception rates was highlighted in the[2] Health and Social Care Select Committee's report on sexual health (House of Commons, 2019) but is not mentioned in the Government response (2019). The Local Government Association continues to highlight the importance of teenage pregnancy and young parents in addressing inequalities with case studies illustrating effective action (LGA, 2022a) but against a backdrop of minimal prioritisation at national government level.

A whole system approach was the central principle of the strategy with success dependent on strong multi-agency partnerships. Evidence was translated into clear actions with each agency contributing to a collective aim of equipping young people to prevent unplanned pregnancy and of improving outcomes for young parents and their children. This approach embeds prevention and early intervention across all services and settings and helps ensure the strategy actions reach all young people, particularly those experiencing marginalisation. While partnership working is promoted in the teenage pregnancy frameworks on both prevention and young parent support, neither framework has been updated in the past six years. Nor are they referenced in other relevant policy guidance, for example the guidance for local authorities on reducing numbers of 16–17-year-olds not in education or training (Department for Education, 2016), a cohort of young people more likely to have associated risk factors for early pregnancy or in the guidance for Family Hubs (HM Government, 2022). As described later in this chapter and illustrated in the case studies in Chapter 6, local areas are trying hard to maintain or re-establish partnerships but are hampered by the lack of a national strategic messaging about the benefits of an integrated approach to prevention and clear hooks in the relevant policies to engage agencies.

At a broader strategic level, there has been shift away from a public health approach to integrated upstream prevention. There was a consultation on *Advancing our Health: prevention in the 2020s* (Cabinet Office and Department of Health and Social Care, 2019), albeit largely focused on prevention of NHS-related outcomes, but this was not followed up. In 2021, following the closure of Public Health England, the new Office for Health Improvement and Disparities was established in the Department of Health and Social Care to 'drive the prevention agenda across government to reduce health disparities, many of which have been exacerbated by the COVID-19 pandemic and improve the public's health'. However, the vision set out of cross-departmental integrated approach to tackling the wider determinants of health and inequality (Department of Health and Social Care and Office for Health Improvement and Disparities) is yet to materialise. The *Integration and Innovation White Paper* (Department for Health and Social Care, 2021) and subsequent statutory Integrated Care Systems and Integrated Care Boards (Department of Health and Social Care 2022) were welcomed for the ambition for collaboration and partnership but focused largely on the NHS. The statutory guidance for Integrated Care Boards requires inclusion of a lead Board member with explicit responsibility for children and young people aged 0–25 (NHS England, 2022) and there are signs from the case studies in Chapter 6 that some teenage pregnancy work is being included in Integrated Care Board planning. However as noted later in this chapter, the potential for positive whole system change will depend on leadership, youth engagement, join up with other relevant agencies, staff training and service investment. The decision was also taken not to publish a promised white paper on health inequalities (re-titled health disparities), feeding the issues instead into a *Major Conditions Strategy* focusing more on treatment than prevention (Department of Health and Social Care, 2023a). These are missed opportunities to address the factors that shape health and create inequality (Health Foundation, 2023), which for young people had been further widened by the pandemic with significant concerns on the longer-term impact on their health and wellbeing.

More positively, an innovative Reproductive Health Programme, developed by Public Health England (Public Health England, 2021) promoted an integrated system-wide approach, explicitly drawing on the teenage pregnancy framework's ten key factors. With insufficient investment, and the closure of Public Health England, the programme was not implemented. However, the model helped inform the development of the first Women's Health Strategy for England (Department of Health and Social Care, 2022b) which incorporates the importance of prevention across the lifecourse, highlighting the importance of RSE, de-stigmatising menstrual and reproductive health, and improving access to the full range of contraceptive options. With the appointment of a Women's Health Ambassador for England (UK Parliament, 2022b) implementation of the ten-year strategy has the potential to re-establish cross-government working and strengthen partnerships at a local level through the development of Women's Health Hubs (Department of Health and Social Care, 2023b) (UK Parliament, 2022). But the plan will need a clear focus on young people and reaching marginalised groups through joint working with relevant statutory and voluntary sector services.

A further opportunity to promote joined-up working, strengthen prevention and to bring teenage pregnancy back into focus would be the development of a new sexual and reproductive health strategy. With the existing strategy ten years old (Department of Health, 2013) this was called for by the Health and Social Care Select Committee in their 2019 report on sexual health. The Government response made a commitment to a new strategy and held initial consultation workshops on its content, but progress was halted by the pandemic and not re-started. Further development will depend on decisions of the Labour Government elected in 2024.

5.3 RSE, contraception and youth policy: progress and challenges since 2018

The following contributions provide detail on the progress and challenges on the implementation of statutory RSE, improving access to contraception, and addressing some of the youth inequalities and wider determinants of early pregnancy. They have been written by leading VSOs and professional and parliamentary collaborations. The perspective on RSE is provided by the Sex Education Forum, on access to contraception from the All-Party Parliamentary Group on Sexual and Reproductive Health, the Advisory Group on Contraception, the English HIV and Sexual Health Commissioners Group and Brook, and on youth policy from the Association for Young People's Health.

They provide an expert view from a national perspective, but they have also been included to highlight the critical advocacy role of the voluntary sector and professional and parliamentary collaborations in maintaining a focus and holding government to account. As described in earlier chapters (3 and 4), they played a key role during the implementation of the original strategy, but their work has been particularly important during this recent period of policy drift and lack of prioritisation and commitment.

5.3.1 Relationships and Sex Education: a milestone achieved but the benefits not yet realised

SEX EDUCATION FORUM: STATUTORY RSE – THE JOURNEY TO CONTINUES[3]

Throughout the course of the Teenage Pregnancy Strategy, the Independent Advisory Group had made recommendations for statutory RSE to embed primary prevention in all schools. After a failed attempt at the end of the Labour administration (2010), history was finally made in 2017 when the Children and Social Work Act made Relationships and Sex Education statutory. The positive political mood and public support that surrounded the passing of the Act set the scene for Parliamentarians and officials to navigate the detailed process of drawing up new guidance for schools.

This statutory guidance was to replace the non-statutory sex and relationship education guidance published in 2000 at the start of the Teenage Pregnancy Strategy. It would set out what exactly should be taught and clarify for schools how recent laws such as The Equality Act 2010 and Marriage (Same Sex Couples) Act 2013 affected the provision of RSE. It would explain how policies such as the parental right to withdraw from non-statutory sex education would be enacted.

Ministers were interested to hear directly from young people themselves about what they hoped for from statutory RSE, and in November 2017, in a packed Committee room in the Houses of Parliament, the Sex Education Forum brought MPs, young people, teachers, voluntary sector organisations and the then Secretary of State (Rt Hon Justine Greening) together to discuss what was needed. Signatures were added to a Sex Education Forum banner displaying the '12 principles of good RSE', which was a joint initiative involving six education unions and four national children's charities (Sex Education Forum, 2017).

Relationships, Sex and Health Education is born

The Department for Education held a series of roundtable meetings with stakeholders to inform the development of the guidance, which was published in draft for public consultation in 2018. The new guidance introduced Health Education, which would sit alongside RSE, to form 'RSHE'. Unlike sex education, Health Education would have no parental opt out. Health Education includes a wide range of curriculum content including mental health and emotional wellbeing, drugs and alcohol, sleep, vaccinations, first aid, menstrual wellbeing and the changing adolescent body including puberty. This was a big win for campaigners, though it fell short of mandating the full breadth of personal, social, health and economic (PSHE) education, because economic education was absent.

The RSHE guidance was debated in Parliament and was followed by a watershed vote in the Commons on 27 March 2019, resulting in 538 'Ayes' and 21 'Noes' (UK), and 482 'Ayes' and 14 'Noes' (MPs representing constituencies in England), providing overwhelming support for the new guidance.

Parent voice

At the same time, a minority of parents protested against the changes, with particular focus on the LGBT+ inclusive aspects of Relationships Education – and the absence of parental opt out from Relationships Education. Protests were held outside schools, initially in Birmingham. A High Court judge permanently banned protesters from outside the gates of one primary school.

A pivotal requirement of the new guidance was that schools must consult with their parent community about aspects of how they would provide RSE. Schools approached this in very different ways, whether by holding parent evenings in the school hall or sending out a questionnaire. Initially there was little guidance about how to design and manage the consultation process and for some schools this became a stressful and resource intensive activity. Others reported productive dialogue that resulted, over a period of time, in greater understanding about the aims and content of RSHE, for example the parent and community engagement case study described in Chapter 6.

Delays to the start of statutory RSE

Schools were originally to follow the RSHE guidance fully from 1 September 2020, but primarily because of the disruption of the COVID-19 lockdowns, were given leeway to phase in the guidance if they had not completed their preparations in time. All schools were expected to follow the guidance from 1 September 2021, four years after the Children and Social Work Act 2017 was passed.

The implementation of the legislation got off to a bumpy start. Not only did schools have different start dates but approaches to parental consultation varied greatly and schools allocated different amounts of time to teaching the subject. Notably, Government investment in implementation was minimal (UK Parliament, 2022a) Far less was spent on training teachers than was promised, and only an estimated 15 per cent of schools accessing the Government-funded training (UK Parliament, 2021, 2022).

Monitoring statutory RSE

For those involved in the campaign for statutory RSE, the focus shifted to monitoring the quality of implementation and calling out the gaps. It was in 2021 that the Sex Education Forum moved from its original home within the National Children's Bureau and established as an independent charity. Later in that year the Sex Education Forum commissioned an independent poll of 1,000 young people aged 16 and 17 years old. Findings from the poll showed only 35 per cent rated their RSE as very good or good and worryingly almost half had received no RSE at school or at home during the COVID-19 lockdowns in 2020. It was also clear that some RSE topics were seriously neglected, for example 37 per cent had learnt nothing about 'power imbalances in relationships', 36 per cent had learnt nothing about pornography, and 33 per cent had not learnt about how to access local contraceptive and sexual health services, despite it being a mandatory part of the curriculum (Sex Education Forum, 2022).

A focus on sexual harassment in schools further highlighted the inadequacy of RSE in meeting young people's needs. The campaign 'Everyone's Invited', founded in 2020 collected and published thousands of anonymous testimonials from survivors of sexual violence, abuse and harassment alongside a list of the schools, colleges and universities where incidents had taken place. The campaign triggered a special review of sexual abuse in schools and colleges, which was carried out by Ofsted and added to the evidence from 'Everyone's Invited' that sexual harassment is widespread in schools (Ofsted, 2021).

However, since the start of statutory RSE, the previous Government was almost completely silent on monitoring the quality of provision in schools and did not publish findings from evaluations that they commissioned. Meanwhile, the voluntary sector has been active in producing specialist training and resources to support schools in addressing topics that are 'difficult' and neglected. The Sex Education Forum has held events addressing themes such as engaging boys and young people, faith and RSE, and parental engagement, and inviting researchers, educators and policymakers to come together and share evidence and practice solutions.

Statutory status has impacted the organisation of RSE in schools

Through Sex Education Forum's regular contact with schools and organisations who support them, there is encouraging anecdotal evidence that statutory RSHE has prompted change in how RSE is prioritised, organised and provided in schools. Many secondary schools have made adjustments to give RSHE regular space on their timetable, and it is now commonplace to have a lead teacher for RSHE or PSHE education. However, there is also concern about a lack of stability in the staffing of RSHE. Some secondary schools rely on form tutors to deliver RSHE in 20-minute blocks, others change the staff involved in delivering RSHE every year. An optimist view is that schools are heading in the right direction, some faster than others. However, there are few university courses in RSHE and therefore a lack of specialist RSHE teachers fresh out of teacher-training colleges. A system wide vision is needed that considers the RSE training needs of all prospective and existing teachers.

No Government plan to professionalise the teaching of RSE

With trained educators a key factor in effective delivery of RSE, (UNESCO, 2018) the lack of any plan for how to professionalise the teaching of RSE is a major flaw in the implementation of statutory provision. A survey by NSPCC and the teaching union (NSPCC & NASUWT, 2022) found that 46 per cent of secondary school teachers say they don't feel confident teaching RSE. Young people say that increasing open discussion would improve their RSE, but facilitating this takes skill and confidence. The poll evidence shows that young people often experience RSE lessons that lack the level of interaction that they need; 29 per cent of the 1,000 young people surveyed had had opportunities to ask their questions and get answers as part of their school RSE (Sex Education Forum, 2023). As one young person said: "Allow lessons where questions are asked and answered and to gather student perspectives". The urgent need for training was also starkly highlighted in the Ofsted review on sexual abuse, with a recommendation for high-quality training for teachers delivering RSHE, well sequenced curricula, and allowing 'time for open discussion in RSE lessons of topics that children and young people tell us they find particularly difficult, such as consent and the sending of 'nudes''. The previous Government responded by promising to produce guidance for schools on teaching about sexual harassment and abuse but this was not published before the 2024 election.

Young people's voices

While the statutory guidance encourages schools to consult with pupils, there is no obligation to do so. This contrasts with the priority given to parental consultation as a legal requirement. There is much to be gained from pupil consultation, as their views and experiences can then be shared (anonymously) with the parent community, enabling a much more localised understanding of the needs of their children. Sex Education Forum continues to advocate for children and young people's views to be centred in RSE and for parent and pupil involvement to go hand in hand.

The statutory guidance sets out high expectations for RSHE akin to other curriculum subjects and requires that learning is assessed, and pupil progress monitored. This gives an invaluable signal about the rigour and level of resourcing needed to deliver high-quality RSHE and cannot be done without active pupil engagement.

Backlash and challenge

Against a backdrop of little communication about RSE coming from Government, a small minority of anti-RSE campaigners have pushed forward their agenda with a dual focus on parent rights around access to RSE materials used in schools and the anti-trans movement, which focuses on gender identity within RSE and uses RSE within schools as a flashpoint for 'culture war' debates.

Since RSHE became statutory, organisations supporting schools, and schools themselves have received numerous communications from parents which have often focused on seeking clarity around aspects of the RSHE guidance that are vague. Often there is productive and mutual dialogue and matters are satisfactorily resolved, but there have been high-profile legal cases such as Clare Page vs The Information Commissioner and the School of Sexuality Education (2023) combined with the support of a small number of influential Parliamentarians, for example the Westminster Hall Debate sponsored by Miriam Cates MP in June 2022 (UK Parliament, 2022c).

2023 – RSE is politicised

Despite the lack of credible evidence of any widespread poor practice in RSE teaching, political pressure has fomented around a need to regulate and 'control' RSE. When the RSHE guidance was updated in 2019 regular reviews were promised, and a review in 2023 was expected. However, the rhetoric of restriction and age-limits on RSE content has been threaded through the Government Review of RSHE announced by the former Prime Minister Rishi Sunak in March 2023 (Department for Education, 2023b), signalling that politics is driving the review rather than the expressed needs of young people. Public support for sex education remains widespread, as reflected in the YouGov tracking poll, but is often a 'silent majority' in media and political debate.

Dealing with anti-RSE backlash has been very time-consuming for voluntary sector and statutory organisations. In its role as sector leader, Sex Education Forum has provided a safe space for our Partners to meet and share common issues and solutions. Interventions from Government, such as letters from the Secretary of State for Education to schools emphasising the rights of parents (Department for Education, 2023a) are fed the intense politicisation of school RSE in the lead up to the general election in 2024. The fallout lands on schools and those who support them with RSE, such as local authorities and the voluntary sector.

What next?

Improving RSE is an urgent task. The views of young people make this clear. So too does the data. Teenagers remain at highest risk of unplanned pregnancy (Wellings et al., 2013), rates of STIs among young people are increasing (UK Health Security Agency, 2023), sexual harassment is widespread in schools, 10 per cent of children aged nine have accessed pornography (Children's Commissioner, 2023b), with 'digital influencer culture' impacting on young people's attitudes towards harmful gender norms and behaviours. In 2022 the British Government reported to the United Nations Convention on the Rights of the Child that 'In England, mandatory RSHE for secondary pupils, including sexual orientation and gender identity introduced in 2020, was informed by a consultation, including children' (Convention on the Rights of the Child, 2022). This confident portrayal of universal entitlement will need to be monitored and protected. The 2024 Sex Education Forum poll of 1,000 young people (Sex Education Forum, 2024) shows promise, with 50 per cent of young people rating their RSE at school as good or very good – a 15-percentage-point increase on the 2021 poll.

Follow through on statutory RSE remains the key challenge. Securing the legislation was a milestone achievement but we know the benefits of RSE will only reach all children young people if implementation meets the criteria for effective delivery clearly set out in UNESCO's International Guidance (UNESCO, 2018). It is also possible to push the limits of the legislation and go further. *Make it Mandatory* is a grass-roots youth-led social action movement calling for statutory RSE to be extended up to age 18. The campaign recognises the relevance of ongoing RSE for 16- and 17-year-olds, and is supported by over 95,000 petition signatories. After the UK's general election in 2024, it's time to call on the new Labour Government to show leadership in their support for RSE, be outspoken about explaining the health and safeguarding benefits and crucially be prepared to invest in resourcing a preventative measure that makes economic sense and contributes significantly to preventing unplanned pregnancies and STIs, as well as to the health and happiness of future generations. As the Chief Medical Officer for England explains, information about sexual health is a safeguard for children, and not a threat, normalising prevention messages depends on starting well before sexual debut and 'schools have a huge part to play' (House of Commons, Women's and Equalities Committee, 2024).

5.3.2 Improving access to contraception: the case for greater investment

5.3.2.1 THE ALL-PARTY PARLIAMENTARY GROUP ON SEXUAL AND REPRODUCTIVE HEALTH[4]: *AN INQUIRY INTO CONTRACEPTION ACCESS AND A FOCUS ON RSE*

The All-Party Parliamentary Group on Sexual and Reproductive Health (APPG SRH) was established to promote awareness and understanding in Parliament of a range of issues relating to sexual and reproductive health (SRH) across the life course. The APPG has identified access to contraception as a human right with the ability to decide whether and when to have children fundamental to the physical, psychological and social wellbeing of women. This is reflected in the UN Sustainable Development Goals, where universal access to contraception and other sexual and reproductive healthcare underpins Goal 3 of Good Health and Wellbeing (United Nations, 2015).

Since the passage of the 2012 Health and Social Care Act, the APPG became increasingly concerned that cuts to budgets, fragmented commissioning and workforce issues were affecting women's ability to access contraception in a way that meets their holistic sexual and reproductive health needs. In 2019 an inquiry was launched in response to these concerns and re-launched in 2020 to include the impact of the pandemic on women's access to contraception.

The report, *Women's Lives, Women's Rights* (September 2020) collated over 70 submissions of oral and written evidence from the Minister for Women's Health, the Department of Health and Social Care, Public Health England (now the Office for Health Improvement and Disparities), the Faculty of Sexual and Reproductive Healthcare, the Royal College of Obstetricians and Gynaecologists and other relevant bodies.

The inquiry found that women in England are facing difficulty in accessing contraception, with many being bounced from service to service, putting them at risk of unplanned pregnancy and increasing the demand for maternity and abortion care. It also found that the COVID-19 pandemic exacerbated many of these issues, especially for the most marginalised communities. Specialist services for young people were particularly vulnerable from funding cuts and pandemic pressures. This has led to reduced opening hours, the defunding of roles, the reduction in the age range catered for or the closure of the service altogether. In some cases youth provision was subsumed into an all-age integrated service, raising SRH and safeguarding concerns that young people may be deterred from seeking early advice. The report made five overarching recommendations including 'maximising the potential of statutory Relationships, Sex and Health Education (RSHE) to equip young people with an understanding of fertility and contraception and support easy access to services'.

The critical importance of RSE and improving young people's access to contraception has been central to other APPG activities including, in 2022, a parliamentary roundtable event to discuss the publication of the Government's Women's Health Strategy and the launch of the Faculty of Sexual and Reproductive Health's Hatfield Vision – a framework to improve reproductive health outcomes, which includes a specific action on monitoring implementation of statutory RSE guidance (Faculty of Sexual and Reproductive Health, 2022).

5.3.2.2 THE ADVISORY GROUP ON CONTRACEPTION[5]: INTERROGATING FUNDING CUTS TO PUBLIC HEALTH AND THE CONSEQUENCES FOR SEXUAL AND REPRODUCTIVE HEALTH SERVICES

The Advisory Group on Contraception (AGC) was formed in 2010 and works to ensure that all women[6] across England have comprehensive and open access to a full choice of contraceptive methods, from a range of settings. Through a blend of parliamentary and policy engagement and research-based work, the AGC aims to shine a light on the challenges many women face conveniently accessing their preferred method, and advocates for a life-course approach to contraceptive provision. Supporting young people to access services that are designed around their unique needs is critical to this, as is ensuring every young person's navigation of the system is informed by robust RSE that equips them with knowledge about their fertility and their contraception options.

AGC research paints a stark picture of the impact of national public health funding cuts, first implemented in England in 2015/16, on local authority spending on SRH. Government data shows that between 2015 and 2020, local authority contraceptive spend saw 20 per cent real-terms cut (Ministry of Housing, Communities and Local Government, 2023), while a 2018 Freedom of Information request audit conducted by the AGC found that 8 million women of reproductive age were living in an area where SRH spend had been cut. A total of 66 per cent of councils reported reducing or planning to reduce their budget for SRH over the three-year period from 2016/17 to 2018/19 (Advisory Group on Contraception, 2018). These funding challenges, alongside both a highly stretched health and care system and deeply fragmented commissioning arrangements for women's reproductive health – which sees responsibility split between the NHS and local authorities – have had a material impact on women's access to contraception (Advisory Group on Contraception, 2020).

- The proportion of local authorities reducing the number of sites commissioned to provide contraception increased from 9 per cent in 2015/16 to 26 per cent in 2018/19, with a further 18 per cent of councils planning closures in 2019/20, prior to the outbreak of COVID-19.
- Overall, 39 per cent of councils commissioned fewer sites to deliver contraceptive services in 2018/19 than they did in 2015/16.
- In 2019 a total of 17 per cent of responding local authorities reported that they did not commission any outreach contraception services to more vulnerable

groups and 10 per cent reported either having stopped, or planning to stop, commissioning standalone services for under-25s.

The COVID-19 pandemic threw these challenges into even sharper focus. Local authority contraceptive spend dropped even more steeply during 2020/21, as systems scrambled to tackle the pandemic, and the repercussions for contraceptive access continue to reverberate: NHS data shows that even in 2022/23, contacts with SRH services for contraception were down 43 per cent compared with 2014/15 (NHS Digital, 2023).

The launch of the Women's Health Strategy in 2022 indicates a welcome, and unprecedented, commitment to women's reproductive health, but continued accountability for delivery nationally and locally will be crucial to success. The AGC's focus is now therefore on supporting implementation, while advocating for the needs of those women who are easy to ignore – including younger women – and for those services that remain underprioritised. Abortion, for example, is a vital tool in empowering women to fulfil their reproductive rights, yet access is hampered by underfunding, geographic variation in provision, and outdated legislation. Translating the vision of the Women's Health Strategy into reality must now look across the whole reproductive health pathway, bringing together currently fragmented services to maximise the benefits for women and enabling collaboration between parts of the system.

5.3.2.3 THE ENGLISH HIV AND SEXUAL HEALTH COMMISSIONERS GROUP[7]: CHAMPIONING INNOVATION BUT CHALLENGING LACK OF INVESTMENT

The English HIV and Sexual Health Commissioners Group (EHSHCG) provides a strategic forum for commissioners of SRH services to meet, network and work together to improve the commissioning and delivery of local integrated services and strategies.

There is compelling evidence that easy access to contraception to control fertility is not only a fundamental human right but brings very large returns on investment, with every £1 spent estimated to return £9 of savings (Public Health England, 2018). However, despite the savings benefiting local authorities and the NHS, joining up commissioning of sexual and reproductive health services has always been a challenge. Women who experience a higher burden than men of poor sexual and reproductive health (Parkes et al., 2020) are particularly affected by fragmented services.

This has been raised in inquiries by the All-Party Parliamentary Group on Sexual and Reproductive Health (APPG SRH, 2020) with calls for improved collaboration and integration in relation to contraceptive needs both pre- and post-pandemic. The Royal College of Obstetricians and Gynaecologists' 'Better for Women' report (RCOG, 2019) further advocated for ways to collaborate across systems and centre provision around the needs of women across the lifecourse including the specific needs of young people. The Advisory Group on Contraception echoed this in written evidence to DHSC Integration and Innovation White Paper (Advisory Group on Contraception, 2021).

Frustratingly, although investment in contraceptive services saves money, one of the biggest obstacles is insufficient funding to meet increasing demand. Over the past ten years there has been a 36 per cent increase in consultations and service activity against a £114 million reduction in funding over the same period. A workforce shortage of SRH trained practitioners has further contributed to the problem (Local Government Association, 2022a).

These capacity and monetary challenges have led to some areas struggling to maintain some of the excellent outreach and education and targeted prevention that contributed to the very significant reductions in the under-16 and under-18 conception rates. With the downward trend slowing and a recent uptick in rates, it is vital that we address this now, particularly in relation to marginalised young people experiencing risks of early pregnancy.

Many local authority leads and commissioners have continued to be innovative, devising new ways of improving access through a combination of digital and face-to-face contraceptive services, additional clinics and funding increased training for LARC to add to the workforce in General Practice Local Enhanced Service agreements. Furthermore, many leads are now writing and devising system-wide SRH strategies for their area, using the teenage pregnancy 10-key factors approach to help map what is needed for young people in relation to education, support and contraception particularly (See case studies in Chapter 6).

The establishment of Integrated Care Systems (ICS), a Women's Health Strategy and a Women's Health Hub in each ICS, offers an exciting new opportunity to collaborate and bring some of the commissioning structures together to best serve our population. Placing communities and residents at the heart of design and continuing to take a focus on inequalities and reaching under-served groups will ensure that we provide access and support to more young people who need it.

But commitment and innovation, though essential, are not enough. As the Local Government Association briefing to elected councillors makes clear, SRH services are now at breaking point (Local Government Association, 2022a), a point reiterated in the LGA response to the announcement of the 2024–25 Public Health Grant allocations (Department of Health and Social Care, 2024) '. . . while any real terms increase is positive news, this settlement continues to leave local public health teams with limited resources to maintain essential services such as sexual health services and specialist community public health nursing for the next year' (Local Government Association, 2024). Unless greater recognition and funding is given to councils to invest in prevention services, an increase in young people facing unplanned pregnancy and STIs – and the consequent human and economic cost – is now a real risk.

5.3.3.4 BROOK: BLENDING DIGITAL INNOVATION WITH FACE-TO-FACE SERVICES TO INCREASE ACCESS TO CONTRACEPTION AND SEXUAL HEALTH ADVICE

Over the past few years, Brook[8] has been on an ambitious digital transformation journey; evolving its clinical service offer from just bricks and mortar provision to a blended face-to-face and digital offer.

With no national funding available, only private companies had the resources to develop this offer and while many have robust, well-designed digital offers, they are often a subcontracted add-on to existing face-to-face services. This can create a disjointed user experience, with the two services provided by two separate providers. Brook's vision was to develop an integrated offer of digital and face-to-face provision, informed by the organisation's long experience of providing youth friendly accessible SRH services.

This was driven by insights from clinical colleagues who reported the frustration of young people in the clinic waiting rooms. The majority were judged to be low risk, which lengthened waiting times as younger, higher risk people were prioritised. Those at low risk also often had simpler needs – a repeat pill prescription or an STI test when asymptomatic. By meeting their needs digitally, these users would receive a more convenient and improved experience while freeing up face-to-face time for young people with vulnerabilities needing more intensive support. This insight, together with research and focus groups with Brook's services users and staff, supported conversations with charitable trusts and foundations about bigger ambitions to provide a range of services digitally through what Brook now calls its Digital Front Door (DFD).

Brook's DFD and its integration with face-to-face services now commissioned by two local areas have been developed with some important principles at its heart:

A commitment to safeguarding: The DFD has been developed in partnership with Brook's safeguarding team and is designed to catch and flag young people who need more support. Brook is committed to ensuring that every client receives the level of support they need – whatever their situation or risk profile – so that they can move back and forth between on and offline services. For example, under-16s wanting to engage with the DFD can create an account and request support, but messaging makes it clear that they will need to speak to a member of their local Brook team. Safeguarding flags will alert staff and ensure under-16s are prioritised and promptly contacted.

Taking accessibility seriously: This means not only meeting core standards like WCAG (Web Content Accessibility Guidelines) but taking additional steps to create content and messaging at a level that can be easily understood by all clients. By twinning Brook's digital offer with Brook's clinical and outreach services, more entry points are created for users, ensuring that those with additional access needs have equitable access to care.

Prioritising health literacy: Supported, informed decision-making is one of the biggest barriers to care that Brook has identified. Brook constantly creates and evolves messaging and resources that are clinically accurate, age and stage appropriate and responsive to anticipated need. For example, Brook's *Risk of Pregnancy* tool was created to guide a user through whether they need emergency contraception or not, educating them about fertility and the menstrual cycle in the process. Another example is the *Best Contraception for Me tool* which explains each method as well as acknowledging preferences such as the desire to use methods that improve skin or alleviate heavy, painful periods.

Effective and meaningful user involvement: Brook works with service users to inform priorities for development, develop digital tools collaboratively and refine tools through an approach of continuous improvement. Brook also works hard to engage specific young people, including boys and young men, minoritised and LGBT+ communities, to help create more inclusive, holistic tools and journeys.

Breaking barriers to access: Brook has been laser-focussed on improving the experience of users and prospective users by doing extensive research into barriers to accessing physical services, alongside looking at preference and drivers to engage. For example, in research conducted in 2023, Brook learned that many young people found registering for the Condom Distribution Scheme invasive and wanted the convenience and anonymity of online ordering. In other research conducted with neurodivergent people, Brook learned that they wanted a clear outline of what to expect in advance of a clinic visit. Brook works hard to translate these insights into improvements and innovation that address and break barriers.

Collaboration with frontline colleagues: Digital transformation is only truly successful when people are placed at its heart. Service users are crucial but so too are the staff who will be using and supporting the systems implemented. The Digital Team at Brook have worked closely with their colleagues throughout the DFD project to map and understand existing process, design new ones and test and refine the systems implemented. By doing this, colleagues begin to see themselves in what's created and feel a shared sense of ownership and investment in its success which in turn, leads to better outcomes for service users.

5.3.4 Youth policy: the case for joined-up policy, a focus on inequalities and greater investment

5.3.4.1 THE ASSOCIATION FOR YOUNG PEOPLE'S HEALTH[9]

What has happened in broader youth health policy?

In relation to public health and young people the period since 2018 has seen significant upheaval, owing to the COVID-19 pandemic and subsequent lockdowns. The lack of sufficient policy focus and attention to the particular needs of children and young people during the pandemic has been widely documented (Save the Children, 2023). In addition, post pandemic changes to the public health system, for example the move from Public Health England to the Office for Health Improvement and Disparities (OHID) together with service budget cuts (*BMJ*, 2022) and real-terms cuts to the public health grant, highlight the significant barriers to prioritising public health prevention for young people.

A lack of policy focus on children and young people could be said to be continuing with the publication of a Major Conditions Strategy, replacing the previously promised Health Disparities White Paper. Within the strategy there is no specific section on children and young people's health which many have highlighted, calling for a greater focus on the critical role of prevention (Academy of Medical Royal Colleges, 2023). Despite recommendations from the World Health Organisation, the UK has no co-ordinated youth health policy and no central lead for this function. Childhood and adolescence include a broad range of different policy domains (education, health, social care, welfare support, etc.), which often leads to confusion and inconsistency in the approach to promoting their health. An ongoing frustration is the disconnect between high-level statements about the importance of prevention and early intervention and what actually transpires in policy, funding and practice.

NHS England has maintained and expanded its children and young people's health focus and statutory guidance for Integrated Care Boards requires them to have a Children and Young People's Board member. This is a positive step. However, how the Integrated Care System works for young people is variable and as with other parts of the system requires leadership and resources to ensure effective youth engagement, staff training and service provision. Core to future successful prevention work will be the functionality of the partnership at a local level between the NHS, Local Authorities, schools and the youth and voluntary sectors. The Core20Plus5 for Children and Young People (NHS England, 2022) sets out the approach NHS England is taking to focus attention on tackling inequalities for children and young people in the health system. While this is a positive step it focuses on the areas where the NHS can take action and so does not fully encompass prevention and the multi-agency contribution necessary for effective teenage pregnancy programmes. In 2023 OHID published the revised and updated *You're Welcome* quality criteria for youth friendly health services with a self-assessment form (OHID, 2023) The criteria maintain a specific focus on sexual and reproductive health services and include a new criterion on standards relating to the digital health offer and more emphasis on the involvement of young people in their care and in service design. While the long-awaited update is welcome progress, the challenge will be whether hard pressed and understaffed services are able to effectively complete the self-assessment exercise and address identified gaps.

The wider determinants of teenage pregnancy

While the past two decades have seen significant falls in teenage pregnancy rates there remains considerable variation across regions and between different groups of young people. While targeted outreach plays a key part in providing equitable support for groups of young people more like to experience marginalisation, understanding and addressing the wider determinants of early pregnancy is critical for prevention. Data highlights that young mothers are more likely to live in the highest areas of deprivation, that particular subgroups of young people face additional challenges and how struggles to access support have a greater impact on young people living in more deprived areas.

Deprivation

Increasing numbers of young people are being affected by poverty (Stone, 2023). A large proportion of mothers giving birth in their teens and early 20s live in areas of higher deprivation. Among mothers aged 20–24, for example, approximately a quarter live in the areas of highest deprivation, compared with only 11 per cent of mothers ten years older (Association for Young People's Health, 2020). Furthermore, while overall rates of child poverty may look similar to those in 2015 these mask significant regional inequalities with large metropolitan areas faring badly. The North East, the region with the highest under-18 conception rate, has seen a marked increase. Children and young people with disabilities and from ethnic minority groups are disproportionally affected by poverty across the UK (Stone, 2023).

A particular impact for care leavers

Attention should also be paid to specific subgroups of young people more likely to experience inequality. Young women who are care experienced are three times more likely to be a parent at the age of 18, compared with their non-care experienced peers (PHE & LGA, 2018). Of particular concern is the increase in adolescents going into the care of the Local Authority, an increase of 95 per cent between 2011/12 and 2019/20, with the sharpest rise in 15- and 16-year-olds (Nuffield Family Justice Observatory, 2021). Not all subgroups of young people will experience the same additional risks or barriers but certainly those from health inclusion groups including young refugees and Gypsy, Roma and Traveller young people require particular attention.

Access to prevention services

The policy of austerity, the COVID-19 pandemic and the cost-of-living crisis have all impacted young people's access to prevention services. Young people seek help from a broad range of services within their local communities far beyond traditional healthcare. A combination of support from youth services, schools and colleges and primary care are central to prevention. Each of these settings face distinct challenges but in each young people living in more deprived areas face increased barriers to access.

For example, youth services offer a safe space for young people to access informal support and advice – including relationships and sex education and links to contraception and sexual health advice – but provision has been particularly affected. Participation in youth services is associated with positive health and wellbeing outcomes in the short term for young people with some evidence that these short-term benefits are sustained for many years (SQW for Department for Culture, Media and Sport, 2024). Funding to youth services by local authorities in England and Wales saw a real-terms decline of 70 per cent between 2010 and 2011 and 2018/19, which has resulted in the closure of 750 services since 2010 (YMCA, 2020); and as a result of the pandemic, 17 per cent of youth services face closure and 88 per cent anticipate reducing services (LGA, 2022a). There is also a worrying inequity of access with survey data showing twice as many youth services available in the least deprived areas (National Youth Agency, 2021). This creates more barriers for young people in the most deprived areas getting beneficial support, a situation that has been getting worse over time.

Young people from more deprived areas are also less likely to report an overall positive experience of their general practice and less likely to feel that their needs were met in the last GP appointment they attended (Association for Young People's Health, 2022). The past six years have seen significant and increasing challenges in primary care, creating difficulties getting appointments, a barrier that particularly affects young people. The shift to digital booking systems also seems to have further disadvantaged young people with many systems having age barriers for those under 18. This has highlighted the need for a greater focus on making digital routes into primary care easily accessible for young people (Association for Young People's Health, 2022).

The Children's Commissioner for England has highlighted the issue of persistent school absence which has significantly increased following the COVID-19 pandemic (Children's Commissioner, 2023). While this work focuses on the potential impact of school absence on academic attainment, a lack of school attendance also impacts access to school-based public health interventions and comprehensive relationships, health and sex education. With persistent school absence by the age of 14 a risk factor for early pregnancy (Crawford, 2013), this is particularly concerning.

Alongside services parents and carers should be an important part of prevention strategies. This is a challenging time for many families and lower levels of parental engagement and support is reported by young people from the least affluent families. Parents of adolescents are often the least supported group of parents, and this has not changed in recent years. The development of Family Hubs may help but to date their focus has primarily been on younger children (Department for Education and Department of Health and Social Care, 2023). Moving forward, a greater focus on the 10–19 age range in Family Hubs could be an important part of a prevention approach.

Advocating for young people's health

Within this context of persistent and in some cases widening inequalities, there is a pressing need for advocacy to highlight the particular health and wellbeing issues that affect young people. The Association for Young People's Health (AYPH) works to increase understanding about these issues in policy and practice, ensuring that young people themselves are at the heart of all the work.

For example, AYPH developed a range of resources on understanding how health inequalities affect young people including a conceptual framework (McKeown, 2021) that identifies the levers that can be used to improve support including access to services and young people's experience of care. Importantly, the development of the resources also included consultation with young people on the language (McKeown, 2022) policymakers and practitioners use when talking with young people about inequalities. The work highlighted how language can "other" young people and in some cases – for example in the term 'hard to reach' – seem to place the blame on the young person for not being accessible. While language is complex and dynamic, the solutions can be relatively simple, including being open and honest and asking young people about the language or terminology they prefer.

At a strategic level AYPH advocates for a system that better focuses on the 10–25 age range with joined-up policies on youth health, increased investment in youth services, health services that have the skills to provide youth friendly care and systems to ensure that young people themselves are engaged in policy and practice change in meaningful ways. Partnership working with an integrated approach to young people was a key success factor in the teenage pregnancy strategy. Without a specific focus on this stage of life there is a significant risk of creating further inequalities and missing important opportunities for early intervention and prevention, including early unplanned pregnancy.

5.4 The local experience

5.4.1 What happened after 2010?

The chapter so far has considered the national policy context within which local areas operate. It has discussed the frustrations of wasted opportunities and the optimism of new enablers, up to the present time. We now turn to the experience of those in local areas, working to develop and sustain whole systems approaches to reducing teenage pregnancy and support young parents; seeking to understand the facilitators and barriers to sustaining change as they were felt at the local level. Sustaining momentum of the ten-year strategy throughout its lifetime certainly had its challenges but the work was driven by national government commitment, a cross-departmental national unit, and structures to support implementation. Maintaining the reductions under a different policy regime might have seemed a wholly unrealistic ambition.

However, the majority of local authority areas went on to achieve further reductions – in some cases very impressive declines. As mentioned at the start of the chapter, this is important evidence to challenge the view that the strategy ended in 2010 so could not have contributed to the continuing downward trend.

5.4.2 What happened between 2010 and 2018?

The findings from two studies will be considered in the remainder of this chapter; taking first the study concluded in 2019 (Nichols, 2020) which identified supportive factors in areas with the largest reductions after 2010. Teenage pregnancy leads from each region of England, as well as national policy leads working around related agendas, gave the benefit of their experiences from 2010 until 2018. The findings showed that three basic conditions were supportive to sustaining teenage pregnancy work; visible leadership to maintain teenage pregnancy as a priority (at all levels), systems and governance to ensure the local picture is well understood and progress overseen; and adequate investment for directly related services and more broadly to reduce poverty.

Someone who 'loves' it

Having strong leadership and advocacy of the issue at senior levels was seen to be one of the most protective factors. This was true at the national level as much as locally. The national governance mechanisms which had been in place to oversee and support the original 2000–2010 Teenage Pregnancy Strategy were still highly valued, and their absence felt by many. Notably the cross-departmental Teenage Pregnancy Unit, supported by performance management through the then regional government structures, was seen to be a very effective structure. However, with the success of the original prevention strategy there was a danger that the issue of reducing teenage conceptions was seen to be 'fixed' and therefore the policy focus moved elsewhere. The consequent lack of a strong policy steer was noted as a significant barrier, potentially reducing the levers that those acting locally could use.

To fill this vacuum at least partially, areas with the greatest success had maintained a named responsibility for teenage pregnancy. This was usually integrated into a role around related issues such as sexual and reproductive health services, or children and young people's strategies. This enabled advocacy of teenage pregnancy as an important issue which impacts, and is impacted by, a number of potentially more visible concerns, for example young people's mental health.

Many of those leading co-ordination of local teenage pregnancy strategies had worked in their local area for some time and so had well developed contacts and networks. Maintaining these networks was important to help reinforce the continuing significance of the issue. Having champions within professions was also a feature of areas with greater reductions. Headteachers, GPs, midwives, sexual health consultants and a range of other professionals had provided credibility for the issue among their peers in a way that others could not.

As well as local relationships, maintaining contact with issue-based networks, for example regional PHE sexual health networks, was also important. This helped to maintain a community of practice around the issue, providing mutual support and helping to keep teenage pregnancy on the agenda. Networks helped to share learning across areas and to lobby more effectively for specific issues, for example the need to improve the quality of statutory RSE.

Someone who understands it

Visible leadership also extended across local area systems of governance and planning. Having joint targets, reporting mechanisms and performance management administered through multi-agency boards greatly supported the better performing areas. Unlikely to have remained as single focus Teenage Pregnancy Partnership Boards, these were more frequently subgroups of statutory boards (themselves often a legacy of prior Every Child Matters Children's Trust arrangements). Successful local areas continued to be guided by the original Teenage Pregnancy Strategy evidence-based approach, using the ten key factors and accompanying implementation and planning tools such as the PHE Teenage Pregnancy Prevention Framework (Public Health England and Local Government Association, 2018).

The requirement to report through strong governance mechanisms also meant that local data and intelligence were a priority. Although the national under-18 conception rate was the overarching target, and national data was still provided for this, the most successful areas often had related targets and gathered detailed and timely locally derived data.

A wealth of quantitative information was also gathered, including conceptions and abortions, attendance at sexual and reproductive health services and choices of specific contraceptive methods such as LARC, numbers booking in for maternity services, etc. Successful areas also worked hard to find out directly the challenges and aspirations of young people. Many teenage pregnancy lead responsibilities had been merged into wider commissioning roles. The richness of local information enabled commissioning and service planning with real insight, tailoring approaches to best fit neighbourhood level complexities.

As well as guiding resource allocation, this information enabled an authentic and often stark picture of young peoples' circumstances to be demonstrated to those with the power to maintain the focus at a strategic level. Councillors – notably lead members for children and young people – were often motivated by this.

Someone to pay for it

The newly elected Coalition Government's chosen policy of austerity from 2010 onwards severely reduced many of the services that were most connected to prevention work around teenage pregnancy. The reduction in local authority budgets particularly affected youth services, sexual health services, and school nursing and some of the previous administration's joined-up youth programmes such as Connexions were stopped. School budgets were also under pressure, as was NHS delivered provision such as midwifery. As well as the reduction in absolute financial terms, the removal of the ringfence around public health budgets also contributed to the much diminished financial resource specifically to support teenage pregnancy strategies.

Alongside the reduction in the capacity of services, the policy choice of austerity meant that more families and young people found themselves struggling to cope. This increased the level of demand for what reduced provision was available. Against this background, some areas managed to retain a very much reduced dedicated teenage pregnancy budget, but local leads showed remarkable adaptability and a keen sense of where financial alliances could be made. Many previously standalone roles, such as teenage pregnancy midwives, were mainstreamed. Although this carried the risk that young peoples' needs would be subsumed within a wider service, it did provide some sustainability and, in many cases, helped to educate professionals who previously had little awareness of their role in relation to teenage pregnancy.

The three overarching conditions which supported reduction work beyond 2010 (visible leadership, effective use of data and intelligence, and investment) incorporated a range of complexities. The ongoing relevance of the ten key factors was clear, though many participants recommended that the evidence base be updated to incorporate emerging features impacting on young people's lives through digital contacts (for example the influence of online pornography). The impact of austerity – and the need to address underlying determinants of poverty and low aspiration – was also evident throughout the discussions.

At the conclusion of the study an infographic was produced to illustrate the key findings of 'what works' in local areas (reproduced in this chapter at section 5.8).

5.4.3 What has happened since 2018?

The social, economic and policy context for teenage pregnancy work beyond 2018 has been subject to changing national and global conditions, not least the emergence of the COVID-19 virus. To consider the effects of the changing environment, further research was carried out during 2023. Interviews were conducted with some of the participants from the original doctoral research, who were still working in local areas, as well as participants who had previously provided case study examples to PHE on how they had used the Teenage Pregnancy Prevention Framework. The following presents the key themes from those discussions, in relation to a number of question areas.

Have there been any major challenges or hindrances – either national or local – in delivering teenage pregnancy prevention work in your area?

Three dominant themes featured in the responses. The consequences of the Government's chosen policy of austerity and the recent increased cost of living, losing the priority of teenage pregnancy work, and the COVID-19 pandemic, which as well as having its own specific impact also had an influence on the other two themes.

Austerity policy and cost of living

Financial pressures from reduced local authority (LA) and public health budgets were cited as a major challenge by all respondents who reported a multi-pronged impact on staff, services, and children, young people and families.

The depletion of LA teams previously involved in teenage pregnancy work and an overload on remaining staff made it very difficult to sustain multi-agency engagement in the Partnership Boards and to move agreed actions forward. This was exacerbated by staff exhaustion and frequent role changes with a consequent loss of knowledge.

Reduced investment had led to cuts in upstream prevention work. This followed earlier losses of the Connexions and youth services, both of which had contributed informal RSE and linked young people into services. The further cuts particularly affected three of the 'ten key factors' which are focused on maximising access for young people and reducing inequalities: targeted prevention, taking SRH advice out to education and community settings, and workforce training on RSE and sexual health. There was also a significant reduction in the capacity of the Voluntary and Community Sector (VCS) organisations who had played a crucial role in reaching marginalised young people and filling the gaps left by statutory services. Although early intervention was a policy aspiration, the reality reported by many areas was that upstream prevention had been replaced with downstream crisis management.

The consequence of the chosen policy of austerity on children, young people and families and the impact on the wider determinants of early pregnancy and inequalities was also reported by all areas. The critical challenge cited was how to meet a growing need with less resource. The cost-of-living crisis has added further pressures both on individual families and on LA and NHS budgets which had to absorb staff pay increases with no additional investment.

Losing the priority

Although the degree of challenge varied, a loss or lowering of priority was a consistent theme with complacency, lack of leadership and a shift of focus all mentioned.

A general sentiment that 'the rates are down, so the job is done' was reported by several areas. This was sometimes combined with 'teenage pregnancy fatigue' which was compounded by many staff's excessive workloads resulting from funding cuts.

Although the Teenage Pregnancy Prevention Framework was noted as helpful, having no visible policy leadership or monitoring from national government made it hard to argue for local prioritisation. The lack of focus of teenage pregnancy in regional, professional and peer networks also contributed to a sense of diminishing priority. Some respondents reported that in the 'move on' from teenage pregnancy to other important issues, for example mental health and emotional wellbeing and child sexual exploitation, the critical links to teenage pregnancy prevention – the protective benefits of RSE and referrals to SRH services – had been lost. This was exacerbated by cuts in workforce training which previously would have raised practitioners' awareness, developed basic skills and embedded knowledge about local services.

The COVID-19 pandemic

Unsurprisingly, all areas cited the pandemic as a major challenge which exacerbated many of the pre-existing problems. Leadership and resources were immediately diverted, and non-essential work put on hold. Many staff were pulled into COVID-19 response teams, and some moved into other areas of public health and didn't return to their previous roles. Stress, health issues, long-term sick and retirement decisions further depleted numbers and capacity of staff. This weakened the already fragile teenage pregnancy multi-agency partnerships.

The impact on young people was also a key concern, particularly those with pre-existing disadvantage and those whose insecure home environment posed risks. Despite best efforts to deliver RSE during lockdown, the provision and benefits were limited, and although SRH services swiftly moved online and many tried to keep some face-to-face contact, access to effective contraception was inevitably reduced. Some national conception and abortion data publications were also delayed and depleted data teams struggled to prioritise collation of local maternity and abortion data to monitor what was happening to the local conception rate.

Have there been any changes – either national or local – that have helped or supported the delivery of teenage pregnancy prevention work in your area?

National factors

The national themes reported by respondents included factors specific to teenage pregnancy work, and developments in commissioning and policy that areas felt had the potential to be supportive.

Teenage pregnancy specific factors

The most cited national factor was the **introduction of statutory RSE,** which signalled government's belief in the protective benefits of RSE and provided a mandate for all schools to implement the statutory guidance. However, the universal welcome was strongly caveated by several concerns. Most notable was the lack of government investment in teacher training. Equipping teachers with the evidence, skills and confidence to deliver RSE was considered essential for ensuring an equitable offer of high-quality RSE to all children and young people. While it was accepted that the pandemic had inevitably delayed implementation, the lack of attention to RSE 'catch up' was an additional concern.

Although the extent of the impact varied, the minority but vocal opposition to RSE was also cited as a hindrance to effective implementation with an undermining of teacher confidence. Some areas took mitigating action with briefings from senior leaders and elected councillors. But it was noted that the lack of explicit government backing for schools left many feeling isolated and unsupported.

Some respondents were concerned that important elements of RSE – understanding reproductive health, pregnancy prevention and pregnancy options, were being eclipsed by an understandable focus on healthy relationships and consent. This was partly attributed to very limited curriculum time, but also to a general sense that contraception, pregnancy and STIs was 'old school' RSE rather than essential for young people to understand their bodies and exercise their reproductive choices. Some noted that the problem was exacerbated by teachers' lack of confidence in sexual and reproductive health issues and variable knowledge about young people's rights to confidential SRH services.

Many respondents mentioned having the **Teenage Pregnancy Prevention Framework national guidance** as a helpful factor. Although the lack of visible government leadership was cited as a challenge to maintaining the priority, the Framework clearly stated the evidence and what should be in place and was recognised as official government guidance. The Self-Assessment was seen as a useful tool for engaging or re-engaging partner agencies, reviewing progress and informing action plans.

In the absence of national government leadership, respondents reported that **relevant policy updates** from other organisations were helpful in keeping busy staff informed. These included the Teenage Pregnancy Knowledge Exchange, the British Association of Sexual Health and HIV, the Sexual and Reproductive Health e-newsletter and the Sex Education Forum. The Local Government Association briefings reminding councillors of the continued importance of teenage pregnancy were also mentioned. Although some respondents noted that depleted budgets had curtailed networking in face-to-face events, others reported the **digital environment** had facilitated easier access to national and regional conferences and professional networks, by eliminating travel time and costs. This was particularly beneficial for respondents in rural areas and smaller towns who were able to influence policy discussions, and in some cases lead regional and national working groups around relevant issues.

Broader policy and commissioning developments

On the broader policy and commissioning developments, there was a range of responses on what was already or could potentially be supportive to teenage pregnancy work. In relation to RSE, Ofsted's inclusion of RSE in the Personal Development judgment of school inspections was limited in scope, but helpful in underlining the mandate for RSE delivery in all schools (Ofsted, 2023) Ofsted's report on Sexual Abuse in Schools (2021) was also noted as helpful for shining the light on a widespread problem and highlighting the safeguarding benefits of effective RSE.

Several respondents referenced the Women's Health Strategy (Department of Health and Social Care, 2022) as a potentially helpful initiative with its visible focus and national leadership on reproductive health, improving access to contraception and addressing inequalities, although some expressed concern about the minimal reference to abortion. The potential of meeting young women's reproductive health needs through the commissioning of Women's Health Hubs was also mentioned by some respondents. Similarly, the potential for including teenage pregnancy work in the planning of Integrated Care Systems was also referenced, but by a minority of areas. Some respondents noted that the supportive impact of these wider policy initiatives would only be realised if there was sufficient focus on the specific needs of adolescents and marginalised young people.

Local factors

In the local supportive factors reported, two themes were dominant: the importance of strong leadership and effective multi-agency joint working. There were also mentions of increased efforts to garner more local data and intelligence about young people's needs, and helpful innovations following the pandemic.

Strong leadership

Strong leadership was characterised by passionate, committed and enthusiastic senior leaders and staff, who understood why teenage pregnancy matters and advocated for improved support for young people. Senior leaders mentioned included Directors of Public Health, Directors of Children Services, and Public Health Children and Young People leads. Local councillors were mentioned as particularly helpful in keeping teenage pregnancy on the Council's policy and financial agenda. Respondents also described how the longevity and depth of knowledge of staff leading teenage pregnancy work was critical in the commissioning and delivery of effective programmes. A caveat noted by some was the over-reliance on individuals and the risk of 'knowledge lost' if they moved on.

An understanding that a multi-agency 'whole system approach' is the essence of effective teenage pregnancy work, was reported as a positive legacy of the strategy. Notwithstanding the challenges to partnership work from depleted budgets and being blown off course by the pandemic, respondents reported positive developments and an increased understanding of the benefits of joint working. In many areas new partnerships or structures had not been formalised, but several examples of joint approaches were mentioned. A senior level awareness that the Healthy Schools Programme was a ready-made integrated vehicle to implement statutory RSHE, had resulted in strengthened support and in two areas, re-establishment of the programme. A growing recognition of increasing inequalities and the need to identify the young people and families that services have in common, had prompted developments of multi-agency support. Safeguarding Partnerships were also cited as opportunities to make the links with teenage pregnancy and to focus on preventive actions, although some noted that safeguarding leads sometimes lacked understanding of young people's rights to confidential SRH services.

Several respondents noted how the increasing familiarity with the digital environment, greatly accelerated in response to the emergence of COVID-19, had facilitated multi-agency work, including better attendance at partnership meetings. Some areas reporting a significant increase in the uptake of online training. This provided a practical solution for over stretched 'time poor' practitioners. Some had seen a significant increase in uptake of training by some clinicians when they started to be delivered online, for example, emergency hormonal contraception training for pharmacists. Again, this was felt to be due to the convenience of taking only an hour or so from their day, without the extra travel times.

Increased use of local data and new innovations

The final positive development was an increased interest in gathering local data and intelligence, and some service innovations prompted by the pandemic. Many areas reported scarce resource in their data teams, but some had taken the opportunity to review their plans and investigated the pattern and trend of conceptions across the LA to better target resources. Others were investing in school surveys of pupils and teachers to assess RSE delivery, and consultations with young people to understand wider aspects of their lived experience. Respondents reported using the additional local intelligence to address gaps and improve support – and sometimes to 'wake people up' to the ongoing need. The pandemic prompted innovations that were welcomed focused largely on digital developments to make SRH advice and services more accessible although, as noted below, this was caveated by some respondents.

Since 2018 have there been any specific challenges for young people in your area which may have affected the under-18 or under-16 conception rate?

Three challenges were most often reported by respondents. The impact on young people's lives from austerity policy and the cost of living, the COVID-19 pandemic, and social media. A fourth challenge, mentioned by some, was the dominance of online services and lack of face-to-face support.

There was much concern about the **effects of austerity** and the cost of living crisis. This was both on individual young people's wellbeing and on increasing the risk factors for early pregnancy, notably family poverty and school absence. Some reported the impact was evident in the stark vulnerability of many young parents in their area.

Respondents felt these effects had been exacerbated by the **COVID-19 pandemic.** There was particular concern about the increased numbers of pupils absent from education in Years 9–11 (14–16 years old). These young people are at a crucial point in their academic journey towards qualifications that enable progression to further and higher education. They are also missing the protective benefits of RSE at a time many will be entering sexual relationships. Some respondents noted that these young people should be urgently prioritised in local targeted prevention work.

The negative influence of **social media** was a consistent theme with worries over toxic masculinity and pornography normalising a peer culture of unhealthy and sometime violent relationships. The lack of impactful RSE and conversations to support young people critique and deal with the pressures of social media had been compounded by the minimal RSE during lockdown. Several respondents also noted the influence of social media on negative views of hormonal contraception, which they felt left young women making choices based on the personal opinions of 'influencers' rather than accurate information about benefits and risks of effective contraception.

All areas welcomed the innovation of **digital services** to simplify and increase access to SRH advice. However, worries were expressed that a dominance of online and fewer face-to-face services could jeopardise some young people's access to contraception and sexual health advice as well as losing the benefits of a trusted adult who could assess their wider needs. This was a particular concern where services had been recommissioned and changed immediately after the pandemic or when digital services were viewed as a cheaper option without considering the needs of marginalised young people and those with digital poverty. Some respondents were also apprehensive that the move to centralised integrated all age services risked neglecting the specific needs of young people, particularly those most wary of seeking advice. There was however a welcome increase in engaging young people directly in the commissioning and reviewing of services, including co-developing new C-card schemes.

What do you think the future holds for the teenage pregnancy prevention work in your area?

All respondent expressed a mixture of optimism and concerns about the future of teenage pregnancy work. However, it was striking that even those areas which reported a heavier burden of challenges shared the same elements of hope, albeit to a lesser degree.

Optimism

Despite the concerns expressed, there was a clear thread of optimism from the respondents. Most notable was a widely expressed view that the post-pandemic period offered a window of opportunity for pausing, renewing the focus and resetting their local plans. A view illustrated by one respondent's comment: 'There is no better time to step back, review our teenage pregnancy programme and re-engage partners'.

Some areas were optimistic that the long awaited statutory RSE offered new potential to strengthen engagement with schools – notwithstanding the concerns about lack of national investment in training and the minority but vocal opposition to RSE.

This appetite for seizing the opportunity was underpinned by confidence that the strategy had left a strong legacy of knowledge with people understanding what they should do, and many committed staff still in place. The Teenage Pregnancy Prevention Framework's self-assessment was seen as a ready-made tool for reviewing and renewing plans and working with partner agencies to develop an integrated approach to supporting vulnerable young people. Some areas were optimistic that involvement of new staff in the self-assessment process would grow the knowledge capacity and reach of teenage pregnancy work in the local area. A general level of optimism was perhaps best expressed in the reference to the 'green shoots' of renewed teenage pregnancy work, mentioned spontaneously by several participants.

Concerns

The concerns reflected the dominant themes in the challenges: loss of priority, shortage of investment and capacity, and the impact on young people of the policy of austerity and cost of living pressures.

Many areas felt the 'job done' sentiment was still a risk to maintaining a focus and were concerned that the priority would remain low until the impact of no action was evidenced by a rise in conceptions. Indeed, some noted that recent increases in their local rates (2018–21), although disappointing, had helped to regain attention and prompt action.

The continued shortage of investment to fund staff and services was consistently cited as a key concern. This applied to general Local Authority budgets, the Public Health Grant, and to RSE implementation. There was a specific worry about lack of investment in an RSE trained workforce, which would limit the contribution of RSE to primary prevention of early pregnancy.

With reduced investment and depleted teams, some areas raised concerns about the reliance on individual teenage pregnancy champions leading the work, and the significant risk of lost knowledge if the individual leaves. Formal handovers and succession planning were proposed as essential mitigations.

Many respondents repeated their concerns about the consequences of long-term austerity on children, young people and families and a worsening in the wider determinants of early pregnancy which they feared would lead to a rise in conceptions and poorer outcomes for young parents – a worry that was compounded by services being unable to meet the growing need and lack of resources for upstream prevention.

5.5 Summary of key issues: 2010–2023

Although the context between the 2018 and the 2023 research could hardly have changed more drastically, particularly with the emergence of COVID-19, several enduring themes are clear right across the years from 2010 to 2023.

Leadership

Perhaps the most obvious theme is that of the need for effective leadership, and the highlighting of teenage pregnancy as a visible policy priority. The idea that reducing teenage pregnancy has been accomplished and no longer needs to be addressed, highlighted in the early research, is unfortunately still hampering the work at a local level.

The later qualitative research with local areas again shows a clear understanding of why a focus on teenage pregnancy needs to continue, and that strong leadership is necessary for that to happen. Sustained preventive work is necessary to support every new cohort of young people. This will always be the case but there is a particular concern about persistent inequalities, with fears that these are widening for young people affected by the double impact of austerity policy and the pandemic.

Understanding what works, multi-agency ownership and strong governance

Always a key element of the original ten key factors model, visible leadership at all levels provides for strong governance and performance management: elements which are still seen to be lacking from national government. However, the foundation of strong multi-agency joint working, built throughout the original strategy and beyond, is still helping to maintain local understanding of the relevance of teenage pregnancy as an important issue. Advocates for young people are still in place and continue to link teenage pregnancy with other outcomes of concern, for example mental health. The move to a more digitally connected workforce is perhaps one of the few positive consequences of the emergence of pandemic lock-down measures and may help to spread the ownership of teenage pregnancy as an issue.

It was also evident that local areas know what needs to be done. There were frequent references to the 'ten key factors', the Teenage Pregnancy Prevention Framework and a recognition that a multi-agency approach is key to success. Despite limited capacity, there was an appetite for reviewing programmes and re-establishing partnership groups. Participants were also keen to have the existing body of knowledge augmented to incorporate the increasing impact of the digital world on young peoples' lived experience, for example the impact of social influencers, online pornography, and digital poverty affecting access to services.

Changes to essential services

Almost overnight, COVID-19 changed the landscape for provision of services to address the ten key factors. Regarding sexual health and contraception services, many developments were of necessity put in place almost immediately in the spring of 2020, changes which would have been welcomed by participants in 2018 (e.g. greater online access to services and information). The speed of this transition was rapidly accelerated – developing digital access may have taken many years to introduce in normal circumstances. However, these innovations brought risks as well as benefits. Sexual health services undoubtedly expanded their reach via digital developments but there are concerns that this also 'locked out' many young people, unable to access digitally or in need of face-to-face support. These now need to be evaluated as part of the development of hybrid service models, not simply maintained as the new normal, potentially cheaper, delivery approach.

The impact of the long-awaited change to statutory status of RSE has also unfortunately suffered as a result of the pandemic, coupled with the lack of investment in training to support high-quality implementation. Statutory RSE was called for from the very start of the original strategy and in every one of the Teenage Pregnancy Independent Advisory Groups' reports to Ministers throughout the ten years of the strategy's activity. The lack of high-quality RSE has been a frustration for participants across the research years and to say they were happy about the changed status is an understatement. However, a clear focus is now needed on levelling up the delivery of quality RSE in all schools and ensuring it meets the needs of children and young people living in an increasingly complex world.

Investment

Although the pandemic seems at first glance to be the most significant element impacting on teenage pregnancy work, perhaps the most pernicious element is one the participants of 2018 warned was a fundamental and growing threat – that of the continued chosen policy of austerity. The concern has not changed over the research years and has further deepened. Increasing levels of poverty are now being experienced in the UK; according to the (Joseph Rowntree Foundation, 2023), some 3.8 million people experienced destitution in 2022, including around one million children. This is almost two and a half times the number of those destitute in 2017. Given the link between poverty and teenage pregnancy the worry is well founded that this will impact negatively on families and young people, contributing to increased conception rates and poorer outcomes for young parents and their babies.

The 2018 participants feared that services had already been reduced to breaking point. Unfortunately, in 2023 local areas reiterated this, as did the contributions from national organisations. However, perhaps characteristically of those involved in teenage pregnancy work, in 2023 local areas seemed resolved to find a way to address the worsening financial and social context, often treating the situation as a motivator for refreshing teenage pregnancy strategies and a springboard for strengthening multi-agency working. This resolve and determination to improve RSE, access to contraception and SRH services, and address wider youth inequalities is also evident in the earlier contributions from VCS organisations and stakeholder groups.

Although significant investment challenges remain there have been successes in continuing to commission work to implement local programmes. These are illustrated by the many local case studies described in the next chapter.

5.6 Actions to support sustainability of gains made

The infographic produced for guidance as a result of the first study suggested approaches that would support sustainability of the gains made through delivery of the Teenage Pregnancy Strategy. The subsequent study carried out in 2023 confirmed that the same approaches were still supportive in the post-2019 context and so the infographic is reproduced here:

Teenage Pregnancy Strategies – local authorities
How do we improve support for our young people?
Visibility
Keep visibly caring about it! Teenage pregnancy is still important as it links across a range of other issues. Having senior leaders across services talking about it will help to show IT MATTERS!
Joint governance
Make sure that you have joint governance arrangements through ICS structures as well as within individual organisations.
Planning with insight
What gets measured gets done. Make sure you have detailed local data. As well as conception rates and service data, young people and young parents will give you great insight into what's REALLY happening.
Don't mainstream posts too early - or too late!
Assess the strength of widespread understanding and responsibility for teenage pregnancy before mainstreaming specialist posts. Don't just be tempted to save money! Be cautious if it is still seen as a 'specialist' area but if the wider ownership is there - go for it!
Don't lose sight of the individual
Young people becoming pregnant in the last decade appear to be more vulnerable than in the past. Targeting work to support vulnerable families is important to prevent unplanned conceptions by helping raise self-esteem and aspirations.
Also, ensure that all your young parents have a named support worker. They may not need them but if they do, they need to know who to call on.
Own it!
Make sure someone is named as responsible for development and oversight of all of this. In areas doing well this is usually a commissioner with other young people's/family intervention/sexual health responsibilities which helps to integrate planning and services.
Connect up
Stay linked in with your local and regional networks around young people, sexual health, relationships and sex education or other practice areas. This is a great way to mentor commissioners or others who are new to teenage pregnancy as an issue.
Pay up!
It goes without saying (almost!) services need to be paid for. Even though times are tough, areas doing well around teenage pregnancy have prioritised spending on relevant services (notably sexual health and contraception). This saves so much money in the long run.
Source: Dr Joanna Nichols, University of Bradford 2021

5.7 Concluding recommendations

Scaling up action to make further progress

The local commitment highlighted in the two studies is an encouraging sign that the legacy of the strategy is strong and while views were gathered from a minority of areas, similar commitment is evident across the country. However, it is clear that local prioritisation is hindered by the lack of visible national leadership. To support the efforts of local areas, the following national actions are suggested to help re-assert the importance of a continued focus and to re-establish the principles of a multi-agency system wide approach.

- Restate at national level the impact of early pregnancy on wider health, education and economic outcomes for young parents and their children, the economic and human cost of persistent and widening inequalities, and the relevance of effective teenage pregnancy programmes for the NHS, local authorities and Integrated Care Boards. Proactively publicise Office for National Statistics quarterly and annual conception rates to maintain a focus.
- In consultation with local areas, review and update the Teenage Pregnancy Prevention Framework, incorporating evidence of young people's lived experience, new ways of working, and relevant policy developments. Review the self-assessment to ensure it is a practicable tool for 'time poor' partnerships to identify and address gaps.
- Promote the updated Framework through established channels reaching NHS, local authorities, Integrated Care Boards and relevant Sexual and Reproductive Health and Children and Young People commissioners and embed the whole system approach in a new national Sexual and Reproductive Health Strategy.
- Promote the Fingertips Teenage Pregnancy Profiles to highlight individual local authority trends in under-18 and under-16 conceptions, teenage mothers, and the relevant influencing indicators such as pupil absence, attainment, young people not in education, employment or training (NEET) and family poverty.
- Add to the Fingertips Profiles, the parental and child outcomes to provide local authorities with a comprehensive overview of all aspects of teenage pregnancy.
- Restate and actively promote the evidence for statutory relationships and sex education and its protective benefits for sexual and reproductive health, consensual relationships and supporting young people to access early advice.
- Identify cross-government policies and guidance focused on addressing risk factors for early pregnancy, for example school absence, NEET, vulnerable families, and care experience. Include reference to the associated risks of early pregnancy, the benefits of RSE and early access to sexual and reproductive health services and the importance of local partnership work.
- Establish a national point of contact on teenage pregnancy policy in Department of Health and Social Care (DHSC) with links to relevant cross-government policy teams. Promote learning and sharing effective practice through relevant established networks – UK Health Security Agency sexual health commissioners, DHSC Children and Young People leads, English HIV and Sexual Health Commissioners Group.

And finally, while strengthening policy and support is essential, significant progress will not be made without financial investment by Government, notably investment in Local Authority and Public Health budgets to sustain implementation of the well evidenced teenage pregnancy programmes; investment in the training of teachers to provide high-quality RSE to all children and young people; and investment across government to address the underlying drivers of disadvantage and inequality.

Notes

1 A ward is a geographical area representing an electoral district within a local authority area.
2 The Health and Social Care Select Committee is appointed by the House of Commons to examine the expenditure, administration, and policy of the Department of Health and Social Care.
3 Sex Education Forum is a national VCS organisation dedicated to ensuring all children and young people have access to high-quality, inclusive, and evidence-based relationships and sex education.
4 All-Party Parliamentary Groups are informal cross-party groups that have no official status within Parliament. They are run by and for Members of the Commons and Lords, although many choose to involve individuals and organisations from outside Parliament in their administration and activities.
5 Support for the AGC is provided by Bayer plc, Organon and Pfizer, who fund AGC meetings, activities and the AGC secretariat, delivered by Incisive Health. Sponsor organisations have no influence or input in the selection or content of AGC projects or communications. Members of the AGC receive no payment from Bayer plc, Organon and Pfizer for their involvement in the group, except to cover appropriate travel costs for attending meetings. For more information, see www.theagc.org.uk.
6 The AGC recognises that access to contraception is essential for everyone who can become pregnant, no matter how they identify, and therefore supports and advocates for the right to access contraception for trans, non-binary and intersex people who need it. It is essential that there is an understanding of intersectionality to help minimise inequalities in care and the provision of essential service. We use the word women for simplicity but also in recognition that the majority of those requiring access to contraception identify as women.
7 The EHSHCG is supported by funding from Local Authorities and secretarial support from the Association of Directors of Public Health. Previous funding from Public Health England was stopped in 2021.
8 Brook is a national VCS organisation supporting people with their sexual health and wellbeing through clinical services, education, outreach in community settings and counselling.
9 The Association for Young People's Health is a national VCS organisation working to understand and meet the particular health and wellbeing needs of 10–25-year-olds.

References

Academy of Medical Royal Colleges (2023). Securing our healthy future. Prevention is better than cure.
Association for Young People's Health (2020). Youth Health Data Hub. NHS Digital.
Association for Young People's Health (2022). Young people's views on digital access to primary care. Results from engagement with a youth panel.
Association for Young People's Health (2022b). Youth Health Data Hub.

BMJ (2022). Government pulls £100m funding for weight management services after just one year.
Cabinet Office and Department of Health and Social Care (2019). Advancing our health: prevention in the 2020s – consultation document.
Children's Commissioner (2023). Attendance is everyone's business. Children's Commissioner submission to the persistent absence inquiry.
Children's Commissioner (2023b). Evidence on pornography's influence on harmful sexual behaviour among children.
Convention on the Rights of the Child (2022). Combined sixth and seventh periodic reports submitted by the United Kingdom of Great Britain and Northern Ireland under Article 44 of the convention.
Department for Education (2016). Participation of young people in education, employment or training. Statutory guidance for local authorities.
Department for Education (2023a). Education Secretary's letter to parents: You have the right to see RSHE lesson materials.
Department for Education (2023b). Press release: Review of relationships, sex and health education to protect children to conclude by end of year.
Department for Education and Department for Health and Social Care (2023). Family Hubs and Start for Life programme guide.
Department of Health (2013). A Framework for Sexual Health Improvement in England.
Department for Health and Social Care and Office for Health Improvement and Disparities (2021). News story: New body to tackle health disparities will launch 1 October, co-headed by new Deputy Chief Medical Officer.
Department for Health and Social Care (2021). Integration and innovation: working together to improve health and social care for all. Policy paper.
Department for Health and Social Care (2022). Health and Care Bill: Integrated Care Boards and local health and care systems. Policy paper.
Department of Health and Social Care (2022b). Women's Health Strategy for England.
Department for Health and Social Care (2023a). Major conditions strategy: case for change and our strategic framework.
Department of Health and Social Care (2023b) Women's health hubs: core specification.
Department for Health and Social Care (2024). Public health ring fenced grant financial year 2024 to 2025: local authority circular. Published 5 February 2024.
Eurostat (2017). Teenage and older mothers in the EU.
Faculty of Sexual and Reproductive Health (2022). Hatfield Vision. A Framework to Improve Women and Girls' Reproductive Health Outcomes.
Government Response to the House of Commons Health and Social Care Committee report on Sexual health (14th Report of Session 2017–19).
Hansard. (2022). Relationships and Sex Education Materials in Schools. Volume 717.
House of Commons Health and Social Care Committee (2019). Sexual health. Fourteenth report of Session 2017–19.
House of Commons Women and Equalities Committee (2024). Oral evidence: prevalence of STIs among young people, HC 463.
Joseph Rowntree Foundation (2023). Destitution in the UK, 2023.
Local Government Association (2022a). Breaking Point. Securing the future of sexual health services.
Local Government Association (2022b). Health inequalities: Children.
Local Government Association (2024). Public health grant allocations to local authorities 2024/25. On the day briefing, 5 February 2024.
Ministry of Housing, Communities and Local Government (2023). Local authority revenue expenditure and financing. Outturn data from 2015 to 2016 and 2019 to 2020.
National Youth Agency (2021). Initial Summary of Findings from the National Youth Sector Census.

NHS England (2022). Executive lead roles within integrated care boards.
NHS England (2023). Core20PLUS5. An approach to reducing health inequalities for children and young people.
NHS Digital (2020). Association for Young People's Health: Youth Health Data Hub.
NHS Digital (2023). Sexual and Reproductive Health Ser vices, England (Contraception) 2022/23.
Nichols, J. (2020) *Reducing Teenage Pregnancy in England, 2010 to 2015: A case study.* PhD thesis. University of Bradford.
Nightingale, G. and Merrifield, K. (2023). The health disparities white paper disappearing shows a dangerous pattern for action on health. Health Foundation.
NSPCC and NASUWT (2022). Joint survey.
Nuffield Family Justice Observatory (2021). Older children and young people in care proceedings in England and Wales.
Office for Health Improvement and Disparities (2023). 'You're Welcome'. Establishing youth friendly health and care services.
Office for National Statistics (2022). Conception statistics, England and Wales, 2020.
Office for National Statistics (2023). Conception statistics, England and Wales, 2021.
Office for National Statistics (2024). Quarterly conceptions to women aged under 18 years, England and Wales, 2022.
Ofsted (2021). Review of sexual abuse in schools and colleges.
Ofsted (2023). Education Inspection Framework.
Parkes, A., Waltenberger, M., Mercer, C. et al. (2020). Latent class analysis of sexual health markers among men and women participating in a British probability sample survey. *BMC Public Health*, 20(14).
Public Health England (2018). Contraception: Economic Analysis Estimation of the Return on Investment (ROI) for publicly funded contraception in England.
Public Health England (2021). Women's reproductive health programme: progress, products and next steps.
Public Health England and Local Government Association. (2018). A Framework to Support Young People to Prevent Unplanned Pregnancy and Develop Healthy Relationships. London.
Save the Children (2023). What about the children? How the UK decision-makers considered children and young people during the Covid-19 pandemic.
Sex Education Forum (2017). The 12 principles of good RSE.
Sex Education Forum (2022). Young People's RSE Poll 2021.
Sex Education Forum. (2023). Young People's RSE Poll 2024.
SQW for Department for Culture, Media and Sport (2024). Youth provision and life outcomes. A study of longitudinal research. A Youth Evidence Base report for the Department for Culture, Media and Sport.
Stone, J. (2023). Local indicators of child poverty after housing costs, 2021/22 Summary of estimates of child poverty after housing costs in local authorities and parliamentary constituencies, 2014/15–2021/22. Centre for Research in Social Policy. Loughborough University.
The Advisory Group on Contraception (2018). At tipping point. An audit of cuts to contraceptive services and their consequences for women.
The Advisory Group on Contraception (2020). Shining a light on access to contraception in England: an overview of 2019–20 data.
The Advisory Group on Contraception (2021). Written evidence to the inquiry into the Department of Health and Social Care White Paper: Integration and Innovation: working together to improve health and social care.
UK Government: All Party Parliamentary Group on Sexual and Reproductive Health (2020). Women's Lives, Women's Rights.
UK Health Security Agency (2023). Official statistics. Sexually transmitted infections and screening for chlamydia in England: 2022 report.

UK Parliament (2021). Personal, Social, Health and Economic Education: Training. Question for Department for Education. UIN 50037. Tabled on 15 September 2021.

UK Parliament (2022a). Relationships and Sex Education. Question for Department for Education. UIN 27622. Tabled on 22 June 2022.

UK Parliament (2022b). Women's Health Ambassador. Statement by the Parliamentary Under Secretary of State.

UK Parliament (2022c). Backbench Business. Hansard. Vol. 717.

UNESCO (2018). International technical guidance on sexuality education. An evidence informed approach.

United Nations (2015). Department of Economic and Social Affairs. Sustainable development.

Wellings, K., Jones, K.G., Mercer, C.H., Tanton, C., Clifton, S., Datta, J., Copas, A.J., Erens, B., Gibson, L.J., Macdowall, W., Sonnenberg, P., Phelps, A. and Johnson, A.M. The prevalence of unplanned pregnancy and associated factors in Britain: findings from the third National Survey of Sexual Attitudes and Lifestyles (Natsal-3). *Lancet*, 30 November 2013, 382(9907), 1807–16.

YMCA (2020). 'Out of Service'. A report examining local authority expenditure on youth services in England and Wales.

6 Translating evidence into local action

Continuing to embed the ten key factors for an effective strategy in a new and resource poor landscape

6 Overview

In the previous edition, we described how the ten key factors for an effective strategy were translated into local practice to create the essential whole system approach. The contribution of the ten factors was described with reference to the supporting national strategy actions. Each factor was illustrated by local case studies, written in collaboration with the local teenage pregnancy lead.

In this chapter we have collected a fresh set of current case studies from across the country, submitted by local areas in response to a request sent to the networks of the Teenage Pregnancy Knowledge Exchange[1] and the English Sexual Health and HIV Commissioners Group[2]. Despite the challenges and funding constraints reported in the last chapter, they reflect the commitment of senior leaders, commissioners, practitioners and Voluntary and Community Sector organisations to continue implementing effective practice and to integrate teenage pregnancy prevention into mainstream provision. There were other excellent examples left out due to limited space, and there will be many others that were not submitted. However, we hope that bringing these case studies to a wider audience will prompt national and regional initiatives to share practice and learning between local areas.

The ten key factors whole system approach is designed on the principle of proportionate universalism. Providing comprehensive relationships and sex education (RSE) and easy access to services for all young people, with more intensive support for those at greater risk of early pregnancy, combined with programmes to build resilience and aspiration. More detail on the rationale for each factor and the recommended actions for local areas are included in the previous edition and in the Teenage Pregnancy Prevention Framework national guidance (Public Health England and Local Government Association, 2018).

6.1 Senior leadership to make the case for a continued focus, promote joint working and ensure accountability.

Maintaining a dedicated teenage pregnancy team: Walsall Council

Walsall is a market town in the West Midlands with a population of around 68,000. Since the start of the national strategy the council and their health partners have

DOI: 10.4324/9781003410225-7

Figure 6.1 The ten key factors for effective local strategies.

achieved a reduction of 72 per cent in the under-18 conception rate. However, to ensure the focus on teenage pregnancy continues and doesn't get lost in competing priorities, Walsall Council Public Health team commissions a designated team as part of the Healthy Child Programme[3] (HCP) 0–19 service.

A dedicated teenage pregnancy operational lead champions the strategy action plan which aligns with the Teenage Pregnancy Prevention Framework ten key factors, informed by local knowledge of young people's needs and delivered through a multi-agency partnership. The team includes two teenage pregnancy support workers who provide one to one holistic support to pregnant under-18s, whether they choose abortion or to become a young parent, and deliver youth development prevention programmes with vulnerable young people. The team is supported by a part-time administrator.

The teenage pregnancy operational lead promotes the prevention and support agenda working closely with the Strategy partners to deliver actions and identify gaps and areas of concern. Monitoring of progress and strong partnership working is maintained through the Teenage Pregnancy Strategy Group, which meets quarterly and includes representatives from public health, schools, sexual health, abortion services, school nursing, early help children's services, midwifery, health in pregnancy programme, children in care, youth justice, street outreach teams and Women's Aid. The Integrated Care Board is also represented by the commissioners of abortion and pharmacy services. To strengthen integration of the strategy actions with other programmes, the operational lead also contributes to other partnerships such as Children in Care, the Vulnerable Parents Group, Early Help and the sexual health steering group.

The Public Health Senior Programme Manager who chairs the Group ensures strategic governance oversight through the Council's Overview and Scrutiny Board. This involves key Councillors and senior leaders in the Council and NHS Trust and helps secure accountability and maintain momentum.

Harnessing the potential of Council Overview and Scrutiny to refocus on teenage pregnancy and sexual health: Barnsley Council

Barnsley is a market town in South Yorkshire with a population of around 97,000. Since the start of the national strategy the council and their health partners have achieved a 61 per cent reduction in the under-18 conception rate. However, coming out of the pandemic in the summer of 2021, the Children and Young People Public Health Team revisited the Teenage Pregnancy Prevention Framework self-assessment, and relaunched Barnsley's Teenage Pregnancy Prevention and Supporting Teenage Parents Partnership.

The need to maintain progress and reduce rates further prompted additional focus as part of the Council Overview and Scrutiny process. A number of elected members formed a task and finish group and identified sexual and reproductive health as an area to explore during 2022/23. Given the wide-ranging nature and complexity of the topic, the group agreed to prioritise attention on teenage conceptions and Long-Acting Reversible Contraception (LARC) following concerns over equity of access across the borough. Over the course of the investigation, the task and finish group met with BMBC officers from Public Health; the Cabinet Support Member for Public Health & Communities; clinical staff from Integrated Sexual Health Services; and a local GP who is also Medical Secretary of the Barnsley Local Medical Committee.

The Task and Finish Group undertook several 'check and challenge' sessions with officers and partners regarding the work being carried out, and the current and future and challenges associated with the subject. This involved asking questions of their work and the services available locally.

To support their investigations the group also attended the Barnsley Sexual Health Conference in September 2022 and the Integrated Sexual Health Service open evening in October 2022 where members were given a tour of the facilities and asked questions about access to appointments; safeguarding for staff and service users; access to contraception for young people; and communication methods used to raise the profile of the service.

The group made a total of nine carefully considered recommendations based on their findings. These included specific recommendations to increase young people's access to information and support and to raise the profile and accessibility of LARC and c-card schemes; to consider the most appropriate model to deliver a targeted approach enabling parents to give their babies the best start in life, combined with actions to raise aspirations and self-worth in vulnerable young people to address the wider determinants of early pregnancy. An outcome of the review is the reintroduction of the Family Nurse Partnership Programme in Barnsley.

The recommendations have been used to inform the work of the Partnership Group which continues to have representation from education, RSE lead, sexual health, early intervention, early help, public health nursing, Special Educational Needs and Disability (SEND), children in care nursing and maternity. The Integrated Care Board Named Nurse for Safeguarding is also included. The Partnership meets quarterly and reports to the Best Start Partnership which in turn reports to Council's Senior Management Team. A review of progress will be presented to the Council one year after the publication of the Overview and Scrutiny report.

Involving Barnsley's Youth Council

The work of the Partnership has also been informed by young people's views. In 2022 Barnsley Council's Children and Young People's Public Health team visited the Youth Council to set the context of the focus and presented the local data which showed that teenage pregnancy rates in Barnsley are higher than in other areas. The Youth Council were keen to support this piece of work and saw the value of young people's views shaping this area of service.

The group felt that it would be more appealing for other young people to take part if the piece of work was renamed and focused on Relationship, Sexual Health Education (RSHE), and helped create a survey which would resonate with young people. The survey was promoted online through social media where young people could use a QR code or an online link to go to the smart survey.

The Youth Council encouraged young people to take part in the consultation through secondary school or college drop-in sessions, attending Targeted Youth Support Services youth provisions, peer to peer led group sessions and peer led focus groups at alternative provisions.

278 secondary aged young people took part in the consultation with 76 full or part surveys being completed online and 202 young people taking part face to face in focus groups or by individually completing a paper survey.

Public Health have committed to keeping in touch with the Youth Council to share updates on how the information that they provided has been used and what is happening to improve services.

Embedding teenage pregnancy as a priority in the new Integrated Care System: Cheshire and Merseyside

The Cheshire and Merseyside Local Maternity and Neonatal System (LMNS) sits within one of the largest Integrated Care Services (ICS), with seven maternity providers covering a population of 2.7 million people living across a large and diverse geographical footprint. The Women's Health & Maternity (WHaM) partnership and programme is a workstream within the ICS. Our partnership's ambition is to empower women to take control of decisions about their care.

An estimated total of 455,200 women aged 16–45 are currently resident in C&M and approximately 203,395 individuals (8.15 per cent of the population) are from an ethnic minority background. Several local authorities in Cheshire and Merseyside rank very highly with regards to levels of deprivation, as identified in the 2022 Joint Strategic Needs Assessment.

In 2022, as a response to the national Equity and Equality guidance for local maternity systems (NHSE, 2021), Cheshire and Merseyside LMNS developed a local equity and equality plan (WhaM, 2022), which includes a focus on reducing teenage conceptions. This was driven by local data showing a prevalence in identified areas of social deprivation areas across C&M. Four of the local authorities are in the top twenty highest rates of under-18 conceptions in England – Knowsley, Halton, Liverpool and St Helens – and eight of the nine LAs have rates higher than the national average. In seven of the areas the proportion of conceptions ending in abortion is also higher than the 53 per cent England average, indicating a high level of unplanned and unwanted pregnancies (ONS, 2023)

In response to the local data, in June 2023 the WhaM programme team launched a Cheshire and Merseyside Teenage Pregnancy Forum, and invited commissioners, public health leads, voluntary sector and service providers from each LA. The purpose of the Forum is to explore how to work together to reduce rates across C&M, identify areas of good practice to share within the forum and identify barriers that are impacting on young people's sexual and reproductive health choices. The Forum asked each of the nine LAs to complete the self-assessment in the Teenage Pregnancy Prevention Framework (PHE, 2018). The findings will form a gap analysis and action plan, identify areas for improvement and explore how all nine areas can work collaboratively to improve outcomes, adopting a system wide approach.

Driven by the emerging themes from the inaugural Forum, a second workshop, attended by all nine LAs, focused on RSE and accessing advice and contraception in education and community settings, with examples shared by a local provider's education team. The workshop provided a further valuable opportunity to share practice, policies and contacts and to identify further areas of learning, including hearing from the voice of service users to better understand the lived experience of young people.

The Teenage Pregnancy Forum reports into the Women's Health and Maternity Board, chaired by a non-Executive Director and to Cheshire and Merseyside's Integrated Care Board.

6.2 Strong use of data and local intelligence for assessing need, planning, commissioning and monitoring progress

6.2.1 Using local data to inform priorities: South Tees Partnership

Middlesbrough and Redcar & Cleveland local authorities make up the area known as South Tees, in the North-East of England, with populations of 144,000 and 137,000 respectively. Since the start of the national strategy the two LAs, together with their health partners, had achieved reductions of 53 per cent in the under-18 conception rate. However, Middlesbrough has the highest rate in England and Redcar and Cleveland the fifth highest.

With consistently high rates, South Tees has always had a focus on helping young people to prevent early pregnancy and supporting young parents, with a programme of work led by a multi-agency Teenage Pregnancy Partnership. Nevertheless, the area has struggled to reduce rates in line with comparable LAs in the North-East. In late 2022, following a pause in the Partnership's work due to COVID-19 pandemic, the Partnership was re-established, and a decision taken to review the workstreams by taking a public health approach to understand the local population. The first step was to identify and explore the most recent local conception data.

Due to the time lag for under-18 conception data published by ONS, a local conception measure was created by combining abortion data and birth records. Abortion data was provided by British Pregnancy Advisory Service (BPAS), who are commissioned by the North-East and North Cumbria Integrated Care Board, although 100 per cent accuracy was not possible, as some residents may attend services out of area or be treated within NHS services due to medical conditions. Confidentiality of the data was assured by sending at LSOA[4] level rather than by postcode. A best fit lookup was then used to convert the LSOA to ward level to enable match with the birth data.

The birth records for under-18s are downloaded from Hospital Episode Statistics with demographic and geographical breakdown included. As with the ONS national data, age of conception is calculated by working back from the birth date. Although the calculation is an estimate, comparison between historical ONS birth data and locally sourced data found an accurate match. Sharing of data is enabled by the Office for Health Improvement and Disparities agreement with NHS Digital to provide access to HES data via the Data Access Environment, a secure system that allows local authorities to run queries without the need for data to leave NHS Digital. Both Middlesbrough Council and Redcar & Cleveland Council have data sharing agreements with NHS Digital to access HES data and the maternity datasets are just one dataset as part of the access.

Analysis of the most recent data for South Tees identified three key issues. First, that the rise in conceptions is due to increasing abortions, not births, which are decreasing. Second, the conceptions are heavily weighted towards the most deprived decile; 43 of all conceptions over a five-year period (2017/18–2021/22) were to young women living in eight wards across South Tees, out of a total of 44. Third, in one of the highest rate wards, in contrast to rising abortions across the wider area, there was a high number of births, with a majority to young women identifying as the ethnicity category 'white-other' suggesting a change in the local population.

The data analysis has been a very helpful catalyst for starting conversations in the Partnership, raising awareness of the increase in abortions, highlighting the need for more targeted work in the poorest neighbourhoods and exploring the needs of young people from newer communities. The next essential step is talking to young people across South Tees, particularly those in higher rate areas, to understand their perception of the support currently available and learn what more the Partnership can do to support them to make well informed and healthy choices. The most recent data will continue to be collected and reviewed by the Partnership every six months.

6.2.2 Gathering local data from teachers and young people to inform improvements to RSE. Richmond and Wandsworth.

The London boroughs of Richmond and Wandsworth have under-18 conception rates significantly below the national average and have achieved large reductions over the last 20 years. However, they both remain committed to improving the support young people need to make well informed choices about their sexual and reproductive health. The boroughs have been considered as one case study as they are served by one shared public health team following the launch of a unique shared workforce agreement in 2016.

In 2022 they conducted a sexual health training needs assessment for professionals and commissioned a health-related behaviour questionnaire (HRBQ) from the School Health Education Unit[5] to gain a greater understanding of young people's baseline levels of knowledge and inform the direction of support required for improving RSE. The surveys revealed that while front-line staff held a basic understanding of relationships and sexual health, they often lacked confidence in delivery and wanted further support when dealing with more complex and sensitive topic areas.

The HRBQ survey, conducted with over 4,800 pupils, showed that while 74 per cent of secondary pupils were most likely to say their school covered healthy relationships quite or very well, specific areas for development were identified. For example, only 39 per cent of Wandsworth primary school pupils said they felt they knew enough about puberty and growing up. Further demographic disparities were also noted; 13 per cent of Year 6 boys in Richmond said 'no-one' talked to them about puberty or growing up compared with two percent of girls. Knowledge was also found to be poor in relation to sexually transmitted infections, access to condoms and specialist sexual health services (knowledge-based questions falling below 25 per cent) among secondary pupils. Results were lower in comparison with the same surveys conducted in Richmond before the pandemic, suggesting a further dip in knowledge due to school closures. This reflects the finding of the Sex Education Forum poll that 50 per cent of pupils received no RSE at school during 2020–21 (Sex Education Forum, 2022a).

The data from the surveys are being used to inform the commissioning of RSE related training programmes for professionals working in schools and non-school settings. Going forward the training offer will include RSE sessions for school governors, for professionals working with people with special educational needs and disabilities and for those working with parents. There will be a bespoke webinar developed that explores the impact of traditional notions of masculinity on men's physical and mental health and communication with boys and young men.

Additional training will also be offered that looks at dealing with sensitive issues in the delivery of RSE.

The survey results have also informed a range of related local strategies and operational delivery of outreach sexual health provision for young people, youth service delivery interventions and the Healthy Schools programme at both school and borough level.

6.3 Improving relationships and education (RSE) in schools and colleges to embed primary prevention for all children and young people

6.3.1 Supporting RSE improvements through a whole school approach.

A 'one system' ambition. Surrey County Council

Surrey is a large county in the South of England with a population of around 1.2 million. Since the start of the national strategy the council and its health partners have achieved a reduction of 71 per cent in the under-18 conception rate.

Surrey Healthy Schools champions the holistic links between health, and improved outcomes for children and young people. Developed in 2019, and informed by research, it is an opportunity for collaboration between Surrey County Council, its services, partners and schools to support and promote a strengths-based and trauma-informed approach to the wellbeing, health, inclusion and achievement of children and young people. With clear evidence on the benefits to young people's relationships and sexual health outcomes, Surrey Healthy Schools is a key part of the Council's continuing work to reduce unplanned pregnancies.

The programme is led by an experienced Education Service Manager, with a background in school improvement and education leadership, working directly with an Assistant Director for Inclusion & Additional Needs. Close links between Education, Public Health, and a range of services including domestic abuse, sexual and reproductive health, drug services, physical activity, Surrey Police and Surrey Fire and Rescue, enable effective communication and joined up actions across directorates. Surrey Healthy Schools strategic, operational and governance structures aid additional integration. Findings from biannual use of the Schools Health Education Unit Health Related Behaviours Questionnaire in schools help to identify local need, strengths, and areas for development. Governance is supported by both the Director of Education and the Director of Public Health and membership spans across Surrey County Council.

A progressive and developmental training programme offers courses to all primary, secondary and specialist schools. All training is delivered by subject experts from across services and partnerships, including support for secondary schools from the sexual and reproductive health team. Learning and development is fostered through Surrey Healthy Schools cluster support meetings.

Building on a shared way of working, an interactive online Surrey Healthy Schools Self-Evaluation Tool has been developed. This provides a comprehensive framework of standards to assist schools in the co-ordination, development, action planning and improvement of provision, supporting leadership and management, personal development, behaviour, and teaching and learning. The Tool includes signposting to local services, such as confidential sexual and reproductive health, school nursing (including one-to-one advice for pupils), the support, training and guidance available from Surrey services and partners, and a wide range of more specialist information available from key national bodies.

Maintaining the development of a whole system approach across a large local authority poses many challenges, but building a rigorous methodology and culture on the foundations of strong evidence has enabled many successes and has led to increasingly effective partnership working. With clear structures in place and an alignment of strategy and policy aimed at improving the health and wellbeing of children and young people, benefits of collaboration and a positive vision has helped Surrey County Council progress towards achieving its 'one system' ambition.

Integrating RSE into Healthy Schools: Richmond and Wandsworth Borough Councils

While there is no longer a formally separated teenage pregnancy strategy, support for professionals delivering RSE continues to be a fundamental part of the respective sexual health strategies for Richmond and Wandsworth borough councils, within which the reduction of teenage pregnancy remains a top priority.

A variety of support programmes are on offer, from access to input from external agencies in classroom-based activities and one to one provision in schools, to an ongoing and developing training package for professionals. This is based on identified staff and pupil need collated through local surveys.

RSE training programmes for schools and non-school settings are provided on an annual basis and have included a year's free membership with the PSHE Association in the run up to statutory RSE, training, governor RSE training, RSE policy writing, delivering LGBTQ+ inclusive RSE, developing an age and stage appropriate curriculum, consulting with parents on RSE content and dealing with sensitive subjects (such as pornography and sexual harassment). A full training package for adapting RSE to pupils with SEND has also been delivered. On average, RSE related training reaches over 200 professionals each year.

Support to RSE delivery in schools is delivered within the context of the Healthy Schools London programme, supported by external agencies and offered as part of the public health whole school approach. Alongside school nursing one to one support and school-based health drop-ins for advice and signposting to local services, delivered as part of the Healthy Child Programme, outreach sexual health services have been commissioned to deliver classroom- and assembly-based RSE to promote access to local sexual and reproductive health (SRH) services. Service information and health related topics including sexual health is also promoted through a South-East London young people's health website www.gettingiton.org.uk.

The programme of support from external agencies now also includes targeted 'theatre in education' programmes from Loudmouth Theatre. The evidence-based, actor led, 90-minute performances explore a range of sensitive topics including child exploitation and abuse, County Lines, knife crime, online safety, sexual harassment and domestic abuse. Performances are followed by smaller group discussion workshops and a comprehensive package of supporting resources which include awareness raising information for parents/carers and lesson plans on related PSHE topics. Evaluations conducted a few months on from the workshops demonstrate increased knowledge and positive changes in pupil attitudes. Teaching staff value the interactive engagement of young people and welcome the additional support to their RSE delivery.

> "Children were exposed to a variety of scenarios which they may or may not have discussed before that are presented in a very different way to the discussions we have in the classroom, which will have helped them to retain knowledge. After the workshop, children could talk about the scenarios and how they should be safe online. This knowledge is recapped by us in online safety lessons".

6.3.2 Supporting RSE improvements through a Multi-Academy Trust.

Unity Schools Trust is a family of secondary, primary and special schools located mainly in Suffolk, Norfolk, on the Essex and Cambridgeshire borders and Romford in East London. The Trust is committed to evidence-informed practice, supported by its own research school (Unity Research School) and its partners, the Research Schools Network and Education Endowment Foundation. The delivery of high-quality RSHE is central to the Trust's values of Integrity, Kindness and Inclusion which govern the work in all the schools. The Trust wide RSHE policy ensures consistency in approach and sets high expectations where RSHE is a central component in weekly curriculum delivery. Each school adapts the central policy to reflect their own context.

The Trust places high importance on the leadership of RSHE with leaders invited to termly network meetings to discuss current themes and topics, with each session focusing on an aspect of the curriculum such as consent or online safety. The regular forum also provides updates on policy and practice to ensure the Trust is keeping up with the national picture and continually developing the knowledge and expertise of those championing and delivering RSHE. The importance Unity Trust places in RSHE leadership is underlined by the Trust Executive Team including the Trust RSHE leader who also quality assures provision.

To continually improve quality, each school completes a self-evaluation tool that is updated termly and informs the training provided by the Trust RSHE lead. As part of the regular review, schools discuss openly when RSHE is not meeting need and pupil voice and engagement are highly valued to ensure the curriculum is relevant and helpful. To facilitate involvement, the student trust council members are brought together to allow them to create podcasts, drama and messages which enable the schools to reflect and remodel their approach to delivering RSHE.

Last year the student council entitled their podcast, 'what professionals don't know about keeping young people safe.'

With home-school collaboration beneficial for children and young people, engagement with parents is also highly valued. At each network meeting, leaders share good practice, including the strategies they are using to educate and engage families in curriculum content. For example, through work with the Sex Education Forum, leaders were trained to respond to RSHE 'myths' to equip them to address challenges about a range of issues from LGBTQ+ content, to age restrictions and the fear parents have of their children learning 'too much too soon'. RSHE open evenings are held for parents where curriculum outcomes are shared, forthcoming topics introduced, and live Q&A sessions facilitated.

As well as using data, research and pupil voice to keep RSHE up to date, the Trust connects with partners in the local authority and public health team who provide an RSHE portal resource and connect pupils to local services. While the Trust is continually looking to strengthen the competencies and confidence of teachers, pupil feedback confirms that RSE is improving, responding to their needs and being braver in addressing real life issues. The impact has also been noted by Ofsted in their inspection of RSHE as part of the Personal Development judgement with seven of the Trust primary schools, two secondary schools and one special school all receiving judgements of Outstanding for Personal Development. 'Pupils celebrate diversity and enjoy finding out about people who are different to themselves. This helps them understand evermore about the world around them' (Ofsted Inspection, 2023).

6.3.3 A collaborative approach to faith-inclusive RSE in schools: Nottingham City Council

Nottingham, a city in the East Midlands region of England has a diverse population of 323,700. At the start of the national strategy, the Council had the sixth highest under-18 conception rate in England, but together with their health partners, a sustained focus on teenage pregnancy reduction and specialist support to schools on RSE, the rate has reduced by 74 per cent.

In 2019, the City Council became aware of some concerns from community members around the content of RSE in light of the new Department for Education statutory guidance to schools (Department for Education, 2019). These concerns were fuelled by protests around LGBTQ+-inclusive RSE in the city of Birmingham and information being shared via social media about the content of RSE lessons.

A proactive approach was taken with the leader of the City Council holding an initial meeting with faith leaders to explore the issues. The RSE lead worked with officers from the Communications team to produce briefings and social media messaging to accurately inform citizens about RSE. A briefing session on the statutory guidance was delivered to the community cohesion team by the RSE lead so they could have meaningful conversations with citizens. In addition, the portfolio holder for Education convened sessions with local women's groups to hear concerns. As a result of these conversations, the Council formed an RSE working group with members of the local SACRE (Standing Advisory Council on Religious Education) to explore opportunities for faith inclusion within RSE. Learning from the various focus groups was relayed to teachers through training.

One of the main outcomes of the working group was a guidance document for schools on how to deliver faith-inclusive RSE. The group were keen to develop the confidence of teachers to represent diverse faith perspectives in a safe and supportive way during RSE, allowing children to feel pride in their faith as well as recognising the rights and beliefs of all people. The guidance outlines key perspectives from different faiths and world views on a range of RSE related topics, for example marriage. The development of the guidance was also supported by the City Council's LGBT network.

The support of faith leaders on the SACRE meant the City Council were able to act quickly to address community concerns. Schools use the guidance to increase teacher confidence in addressing faith perspectives in RSE and to reassure parents that their approach to RSE is faith-inclusive.

6.3.4 Supporting RSE for young people with special education needs and learning disabilities (SEND). Sex Education Forum

To help ensure the benefits of statutory RSHE reach children and young people with special education needs or disabilities (SEND), the Sex Education Forum has developed a suite of training courses shaped to context of RSE provision in special schools.

RSE has particular significance for learners who receive personal care, or who may display sexualised behaviour, or for whom therapeutic touch forms part of their learning experience. More independent students with moderate learning disabilities are likely to be more socially active and may need support to develop their confidence in social situations, in navigating their relationships and in looking after their reproductive and sexual health.

Importantly, RSE in special schools does not just take place in RSE lessons. For many special schools, PSHE and developing interpersonal skills is the foundation of the curriculum and forms the basis of their work in and out of the classroom. Special schools also typically have a very large staff of teachers, teaching assistants and personal care assistants. For a holistic whole school approach, all staff need some training, but it can be challenging to give everyone enough training to feel confident to deliver a consistent message.

The Sex Education Forum SEND specialist training offer provides a tiered approach in terms of content, interactivity and depth. Schools can book an 'INSET' (In-service training) training programme comprising of a whole-school session which every member of staff (often 100+) can attend, which gives the rationale for the subject, and core content around consent and touch, public and private, and sexualised behaviour, followed by sessions just for teachers which focus on planning and delivery. Like mainstream schools, special schools tend to have a RSHE or PSHE education lead teacher. A choice of short courses focuses on different age groups. Whole-day courses offer a more interactive and immersive training experience, and include a course focused exclusively on learners with Profound and Multiple Learning Disabilities. The longest course available, *Developing RSE Specialism in SEND Schools,* which is an in-depth five-part programme covering all aspects of developing and delivering RSE, aimed at teachers in SEND Schools who wish to develop their specialism and lead the subject.

By offering this range of courses staff working in special schools can access relevant and cost-effective training, ensuring that learners in SEND schools receive quality and timely RSE, delivered by teachers and staff who feel confident and capable, so that learners can have autonomy over their body, their sexual health and wellbeing, and enjoy their sexuality without harm.

6.4 Youth friendly contraception and sexual health services and condom schemes to provide easy access to trusted and confidential advice

6.4.1 Involving young people to ensure services meet local need

Engaging young people in the commissioning process. Essex County Council
Essex County in the East of England has a population of around 1.8 million. Since the start of the national strategy Essex Council, together with their health partners, have achieved a 71 per cent reduction in the under-18 conception rate.

In 2021 the Council began the procurement for a new Integrated Sexual Health Service. Essex is a large county combining densely populated localities with rural areas which poses challenges in providing equitable access for all young people. The design of a new sexual health service provided an opportunity to include clinical services, support with RSE, training for practitioners, one-to-one support for young people and support for parents/carers in a dedicated young people's offer. The dedicated service specification was informed by local conception data, a sexual health needs assessment, and feedback from health and education stakeholders. Critically, young people, recruited via Essex County Council's youth service, were involved throughout the commissioning process.

The findings of an RSE survey of 16–25-year-olds provided insight on where they would prefer to access information, which topics they would like to learn more about, their awareness of the existing sexual health services and how they prefer to access contraception. Early findings from a further co-designed RSE survey of 11–25-year-olds added the views of younger teenagers.

A separate session with the young people focussed on what they want from a sexual health service, what experience they and their peers have had of accessing sexual health information, examples of effective communications and what a service should consider to be trusted and easily accessible to young people. The young people shared their thoughts and ideas via group discussion and written activities.

Key advice included: disguising sexual health messages 'we won't follow social media pages on sexual health because it's embarrassing', using instead trending apps that could include sexual health messages; and the importance of using safe spaces outside of school for sharing information, 'young people will take more notice of information being given out via groups and clubs rather than school'. They highlighted the importance of reminders of information or appointments with clear instructions telling them what to do and suggested QR codes on posters as 'young people are curious'. They reported the limited impact of themed drop-down days in school: 'we have an amazing day, but the next day it's gone".

The feedback was used to shape a question asking how bidders would ensure young people in Essex were aware of and able to access services. A high-level youth engagement plan was requested addressing two key areas of STIs and a county wide condom scheme. Bidders also had to evidence how young people were involved in their response. A one-page limit was set, and bidders informed that the responses would be evaluated by young people. A panel of 3 young people were supported to evaluate and score responses, and to reach a consensus on the final score for each question.

The appointed provider launched the new service on 1 April 2023 and continues to involve young people via engagement events and surveys. To check the service is meeting young people's needs, the council is exploring options to recruit mystery shoppers aged 16–25 and will continue to run RSE surveys to help shape improvements.

Key lessons learned from the process include: identify local connections who already have the trust of young people; allow sufficient time to involve them and have a back-up plan; being realistic about the time it may take young people to evaluate the bid, and set a realistic page limit of the bidders; send a thank you letter from a senior leader to the young people, recognising the skills they have used in the process; have a communications plan to feedback to young people on the surveys and the commissioning outcome; and co-design as much as possible to ensure the process is young people led and to ensure a common understanding of what is being asked of them.

Youth voice and engagement in the Condom Distribution Scheme. London Borough of Barking and Dagenham

Barking and Dagenham is an outer London borough with a population of around 187,000. Having been one of the capital's highest rate areas, the council and their health partners have now achieved a 77 per cent reduction in the under-18 conception rate with significant progress since 2018.

The council views service user voice and engagement as integral to the successful delivery of any service, with the Condom Distribution Scheme employing co-design processes through the Young Inspectors Programme. The programme is hosted by the Barking & Dagenham Youth Forum, a space which facilitates young people to have a say in issues affecting their lives and communities.

The role of the Young Inspectors Programme within the Condom Distribution Scheme is to 'mystery shop' different pharmacies which offer the scheme within the borough. They are provided with robust training and to ensure equity, every inspector is paid for each inspection they complete.

Although running since 2009, there was a renewal of the programme in 2015 to include the Condom Distribution Scheme, which was brought back into the Council. The feedback from each inspection enables the Youth Health Programmes Co-ordinator to have an open dialogue with pharmacies about their performance. This includes providing constructive feedback and areas for improvement, as well as sharing learning across all providers where necessary. The feedback is also directly fed into formal training which is provided annually.

An example of feedback received from different inspections includes:

- "They were excellent, they were so accommodating, and I felt as though my needs were validated, they were constantly smiling and gave me all the information I needed to know".
- "Although they were lovely this all happened over the counter so I felt like other people in the shop might judge me but other than that they themselves did not judge me and they were so friendly, and I felt safe".
- "I came during the staff break, there was staff available, but they were unwilling to come during their break. I fully understand the need for a break but how I was told I felt dehumanised, and the staff member almost made me cry, with her extremely rude tone, rolling of eyes and dismissive body language. The issue is not the staff unwillingness to come and help me during their break but rather the principle of the matter, I am still human with the same rights and deserve to be treated as an equal".

One of the important pieces of feedback received is how the Young Inspectors are treated. Feeling respected makes a big difference while a judgemental look is an instant barrier. Young Inspectors often noted a friendly and welcoming atmosphere, sharing this as a reason they would return to a pharmacy. However, a challenge often identified is being signposted to other pharmacies if not enough staff are available.

The inclusion of Young Inspectors in the Condom Distribution Scheme has allowed for a number of improvements to the scheme, informed by the intended beneficiaries and most important stakeholders, young people.

6.4.2 Opening the door to young people in primary care: a young person's health hub. Lambeth

The Well Centre is a young person's health hub in Lambeth, South London, open since October 2011. It was created with the ambition to improve access to both physical and mental health support for young people aged 11–20, particularly those who may find it challenging to access support due to concerns about confidentiality or lack of knowledge about how to access primary care. The Well Centre team comprises GPs, a senior mental health practitioner from CAMHS and Health and Wellbeing Practitioners (HWPs) who provide counselling, social prescribing, advocacy and mentoring.

Each young person visiting the Well Centre for the first time gets a holistic biopsychosocial assessment ("The Teen Health Chat") – which means that the practitioner is proactive in asking about preferred gender, sexuality, sexual activity and any contraceptive or sexually transmitted infection screening needs. The young person has an opportunity to discuss any concerns they may have, even if they had come in about something completely different. The HWPs are all trained in condom distribution, STI screening and pregnancy testing and the GPs can offer contraceptive counselling and prescribe both oral contraception and provide Depo-Provera contraception and implants. There are plans to have the local Sexual and Reproductive Health Service provide a service for IUS/IUD fittings once a week within the Well Centre.

The service was initially set up with grants from Guys and St Thomas' and the South London and Maudsley charitable foundations but due to its success has been commissioned by Lambeth CCG since 2015. The service has been used by more than 5,500 young people since 2011 with around 750 new young attendees each year. Young people can self-refer but can also be referred by parents, schools, social services, the police and medical professionals. While the majority since the pandemic have presented with mental health concerns, the proactive nature of the initial assessment has helped meet the SRH needs of a vulnerable population who may not have otherwise accessed care. Of the young people visiting the Well Centre, around 66 per cent are female and 34 per cent male, with the commonest age being age 15–19. There is a widespread in ethnicity reflecting the local population with the majority being from BAME background. The deprivation data (IDACI and IMD) indicates that the Centre has achieved its ambition of providing care for those less likely to access support, with 50 per cent of all young people attending in the lowest most deprived 30 per cent of deciles. One notable success in reaching young men often missed by traditional services has been embedding one of the Health and Wellbeing practitioners in the Lambeth Youth Justice Service where they offer STI screening and a trusted source of advice on safer sex and relationships.

The Well Centre is designed with young people to provide the dedicated safe and confidential space needed to support their sexual and reproductive health. However, Dr Steph Lamb, GP and Clinical Director who created the Well Centre, believes there are opportunities in general practice to provide a similar ethos. "Being clear with young people about their right to confidentiality, being proactive about asking them about sex and sexuality and having an interested and non-judgmental approach can work wonders!"

6.4.3 Confidentiality and safeguarding

Skilling up practitioners

A fear that services won't be confidential has long been, and continues to be, young people's primary concern about asking for contraception or sexual health advice, particularly for teenagers under the age of consent.

Balancing young people's right to confidentiality with keeping them safe has always been an important skill for sexual health practitioners. Reassurance about confidentiality is essential to encourage young people into services so they can get contraception and sexual health advice, establish relationships with practitioners and discuss issues affecting their lives. In the small minority of cases where young people are experiencing or at serious risk of significant harm, practitioners may have to consider involving other agencies to help to keep the young person safe.

To help build the skills and confidence of practitioners to make well informed judgements Brook has reviewed and updated the Sexual Behaviours Traffic Light Tool (TLT). Taking into account the changes in young people's lives, particularly the significantly increased internet exposure to sexual content, including pornography, the Tool has a new three-pronged approach: *identifying* the behaviour and establishing if the sexual behaviour is typical or developmentally appropriate, problematic or harmful; *understanding* what the behaviour is communicating and why the child or young person may be exhibiting it; and *responding* in a way that relates to the motivation of the behaviour. Extending the approach beyond solely identification of harm, helps practitioners better understand the individual needs of young people and provide tailored support. By recommending responses to healthy behaviours as well, the Tool builds the confidence of practitioners to initiate positive conversations about relationships and sexual health and make the important link to RSE (Brook, 2022).

Previously used by senior leaders, the TLT training is now focused on practitioners working directly with young people. An increasing number of Local Authorities are commissioning the training across sexual health services, community settings and schools – to build capacity of the workforce and help ensure a consistent whole system approach.

The *Spotting the Signs* resource, originally developed by Brook with the British Association of Sexual Health and HIV to focus on sexual exploitation, has also been updated to include criminal exploitation and to encompass other risks young people may face, particularly in their online world. Informed by expertise from an advisory group and young people, the resource provides questions for sexual health and other practitioners to integrate into a consultation to explore any concerns (Brook, 2023).

Reassuring young people

Brook has been in the forefront of developing with young people a confidentiality statement which is honest about the limit of confidentiality but doesn't frighten them away from asking for help.

Confidentiality at Brook

At Brook we offer a confidential service. This means that we do not talk about your visit to anyone outside Brook without your permission unless you or another young person is in serious danger. If you have any worries or questions about confidentiality, don't hesitate to ask us.

The statement is provided to young people when they access a Brook clinic and is prominent on the Brook website to reassure young people before they visit a service. The website also links and refers to the statement across its advice and guidance pages, so when young people visit the site seeking information on contraception and condoms, or visiting a sexual health clinic, they learn how Brook's confidentiality policy applies in real life scenarios.

In 2023 Brook held a consultation with the 16–19-year-olds that sit on their Participation Forum on how to make their services more accessible. Among the recommendations was a request for more social media content aimed to help further explain what confidentiality means and how it works in practice. As a result, a new video was created for the Brook Instagram account featuring one of the organisation's education specialists explaining how confidentiality works at Brook clinics. The script for the video was co-produced by Brook's communication and safeguarding teams with the 16–19-year-old members of the Participation Forum.

6.5 Advice and contraception in non-clinical education and youth settings to increase points of access to trusted and confidential support

6.5.1 Reaching older teenagers in FE colleges and other youth settings: South Tees

When sexual health services were recommissioned in 2021 South Tees Directors of Public Health and sexual health commissioning leads agreed to split funding into clinical and prevention provision. One lot for the statutory clinical sexual health service provision, which has six commissioners, including the Integrated Care Board and NHS, and one for the prevention elements of sexual and reproductive health, involving four local authorities. This allowed the clinical service to focus on delivering specialist areas of sexual and reproductive health while allowing involvement from the voluntary sector to bid for the prevention elements, a contract awarded to Brook.

Brook is commissioned to support universal RSE delivery in schools in Years 9–13, covering all aspects of the statutory guidance, with assemblies used to signpost to accurate information on the Brook website and to promote access to local services. Targeted small group RSE is offered in a range of community settings to reach more marginalised young people. To address some of the wider issues that impact on sexual health and pregnancy choices, such as poor emotional health and low aspirations, Brook offers the 1–1 My Life programme. Taking a goal-based approach, the programme builds young people's understanding of healthy relationships, consent, online safety, gender and sexuality, contraception choices and pregnancy options, to equip them to make positive behaviour change around their wellbeing and sexual health.

As 16–18 is the age when sexual activity increases and 84 per cent of under-18 conceptions occur, an important strand of Brook's prevention work is in Middlesbrough College, the largest FE college on Teesside. Building on the RSE students receive in secondary school, the team support young people to proactively manage their sexual and reproductive health, provide information and answer questions, and ensure they know about, and are confident to access the clinical services where they can choose from a full range of contraceptive methods. Pregnancy and STI testing are also provided on site.

Students are supported to sign up to the C-card scheme, a comprehensive service which includes face to face support for younger teenagers aged 13–15, the option of digital C-card for 16+, QR codes for easy in-person registration and a large range of access points, which young people can easily search for in an outlet map on the Brook website. Using an online monitoring platform enables C-card practitioners to access the electronic records of registered users, a joined approach which ensures vulnerable young people, including those at risk of exploitation, can be monitored and safeguarded across different outlets.

To support the South Tees Teenage Pregnancy Partnership build a whole system approach, Brook provides workforce development training to build the knowledge, skills and confidence of the wider workforce to support young people in managing their sexual and reproductive health; facilitates quarterly network meetings with schools and relevant practitioners; disseminates Brook's Digital Toolkit of social media resources for all South Tees children and young people practitioners; and distributes quarterly RSE and sexual health update bulletins to keep practitioners engaged and well informed about local services.

6.5.2 Taking services to where young people are: Croydon Council Sexual Health Mobile Service

The London Borough of Croydon is the largest London borough, with a population of around 391,000. At the start of the national strategy, the Council had one of the highest under-18 conception rate in London, but together with their health partners have achieved a reduction of over 80 per cent.

Croydon Sexual Health Mobile service was launched in October 2020 during the COVID-19 pandemic when access to sexual and reproductive health services was significantly limited. Since then, it has proved to be a very effective way to provide accessible and confidential advice, taking the service directly to young people in various locations including colleges, sixth-form colleges, housing estates, town centre, young people's events and festivals.

The primary aim of the mobile service is to reach individuals who may face barriers to accessing traditional healthcare facilities, such as young people in underserved areas or those who may be uncomfortable seeking sexual health services in a traditional setting. The bus is designed with enough space for confidential consultations and a separate clinical section.

Young people are offered education awareness sessions by well-equipped Education and Training Specialists with many years of experience working in the field of teenage pregnancy, sexual health and teaching Relationships and Sex Education. The staff team build on young people's knowledge and confidence about sexual and reproductive health to promote healthy behaviours, reduce spread of STIs and contribute to the reduction of unplanned teenage conceptions. The bus provides condoms and sign up to the C-card scheme, pregnancy testing and testing for gonorrhoea, chlamydia and HIV, with supported referrals for other forms of contraception. This includes a pathway into the clinic, with a direct line service for young people aged 16 and under. If a clinician is on the bus, services can be provided promptly but if not, a Sexual Health Nurse Co-ordinator is on call.

The mobile service maximises the 'Making Every Contact Count' (MECC) approach with young people, assessing any wider needs they may have and working with other partners across the borough to ensure swift referral to relevant services for any additional support.

Since 2020 the bus has been visited by over 2,200 young people all of whom have benefitted from an open door to confidential sexual health and pregnancy advice in a convenient setting they feel comfortable to use. The service has been well used by young men who welcome the easy access to condoms and STI testing.

6.5.3 Destigmatising discussion about sexual and reproductive health and introducing young people to local services: Dudley Council

Dudley is a market town in the West Midlands with a population in the Metropolitan Borough of around 312,000. Since the start of the national strategy, Dudley Council, together with their health partners, has achieved a reduction of 68 per cent in the under-18 conception rate.

Brook Dudley provides non-medical outreach services to young people in Dudley as part of the young person's level 2 clinical sexual health contract. This is funded by Dudley Council's Children and Young Peoples Public Health as part of the Council's teenage pregnancy and sexual health programmes.

The aim of the outreach is to proactively engage with young people to increase their understanding of how to look after their sexual and reproductive health and give them the knowledge and confidence to access early advice. Reassuring information about local SRH services is key: explaining what they offer, how to access them (online through Brook's Digital Front Door or face to face – see Chapter 5), confidentiality and the welcoming non-judgmental approach of the staff.

The service is currently provided in all Dudley Further Education colleges, with regular drop-in sessions on site, one-to-one advice and group sessions. The team offer sign up to the C-card scheme, chlamydia and gonorrhea testing, HIV and syphilis point-of-care testing, and rapid access to a nurse for emergency hormonal contraception and further support with choosing a contraceptive method. There is additional outreach to some alternative education provision settings and supported housing venues to support young people who may be more at risk but wary of accessing services. All the services are advertised on Brook's website, internally by the Further Education Colleges, at Freshers' Fairs at the start of every academic year and promoted through the networks of professionals who are in touch with young people.

The outreach sessions are staffed by Wellbeing Support Workers (WSW) from the Brook Dudley Clinical team who have undertaken Brook's accredited non-medical competency training. The training, over a period of six months, comprises completion of the SRH elements of Health Education England's e-learning for health, eight theory sessions (run virtually), and completion of a competency programme, with observation in practice from an experience Health Care Assistant or nurse manager. All WSWs are also trained to Level 3 safeguarding and are supported by Brook's nursing staff and safeguarding team, including regular case discussion and safeguarding supervision.

6.6 Targeted prevention to support young people experiencing risk factors for early pregnancy

6.6.1 Targeted youth development programme to build knowledge, confidence and aspiration. Walsall Council

Walsall Council and NHS 0–19s service delivers a rolling 16-week evidence-based targeted youth development programmes to vulnerable young people aged 13–16 years as part of their early intervention teenage pregnancy prevention work. The programme is funded by the Public Health Grant, ring fenced within the 0–19 budget, and delivered by the dedicated teenage pregnancy team, in collaboration with school nursing, health visiting and early help workers.

Young people are invited to join the programme via target schools, social care, early help and looked after children's teams, with groups of 8–10 meeting in a range of settings. The programme focuses on improving young people's understanding of healthy positive relationships, negotiating healthy and unhealthy risks while linking them to sexual health services, with the overall aim of building confidence, assertiveness and responsibility. As part of the programme (Teens and Toddlers) young people spend time in a local nursery, taking responsibility for mentoring a child in need of extra support. This fosters awareness of the reality of parenting while raising self-esteem and giving young people a positive experience of learning, achievement, and aspiration for their future. They can also achieve NCFE[6] level one qualification in interpersonal skills on completion of the programme.

To assess suitability for the programme and to monitor its effectiveness, young people complete a vulnerabilities risk assessment before and after participation, using the Warwick Edinburgh mental wellbeing scale. Pregnancy before 18 is also recorded.

Currently 80 young people participate each year. Over 800 young people have completed the programme with very positive results:

- 73 per cent of young people who participated in our programme said they felt like a person of worth at the end of it.
- 73 per cent of young people with low self-confidence reported improvements.
- 74 per cent of young people who had been at risk of exclusion are no longer at risk.
- 74 per cent of children and young people with shy and withdrawn behaviour improved by the end of the programme.
- 88 per cent of teachers agreed that the teenagers contact with the toddler had a positive effect on the child they mentored.
- Only 1.3 per cent of the cohort became pregnant before 18.

"I was struggling in School as I was misbehaving. Teens and Toddlers helped me a lot, because I've become more assertive, learnt many new things and got a qualification. I am confident and happy, doing well at school and home. I've learnt how to control my emotions".

(Skye, Grace Academy)

Fantastic initiative that improves self-esteem and aspirations of young people and the children they mentor, improves attendance at school and life chances.

(Wendi Blews Mirus Academy)

6.6.2 Taking RSE and SRH support to inclusion health groups: Camden and Islington

Brook works with Central and Northwest London NHS Foundation Trust to deliver a holistic, fully integrated service that prioritises easy access, prevention, early intervention and inclusivity. The service spans clinical provision, RSE in mainstream and special schools and pupil referral units, and targeted prevention through outreach and one-to-one support.

Clinical services are provided through two hubs and outreach-based clinics, in collaboration with partners working with vulnerable and underrepresented groups, and in areas of deprivation. These partners include the Youth Offending Service, Looked After Children and Youth Hubs and wider partners which include the police and leaving care services.

Targeted early help support is provided through 'My Life', a Brook programme co-designed with young people which provides one-to-one support for at-risk young people. 'My Life' typically involves young people attending six sessions delivered by Brook education specialists to increase emotional resilience and self-efficacy in young people to manage their own sexual and reproductive health and wellbeing and linking them to local services, if and when required.

Brook's Education and Wellbeing Specialists also run the Hive Womxn's Youth Group providing a safe haven and RSE for young women who may have missed out on school RSE and be apprehensive about accessing services. The Group is designed to foster honest conversations, empower young women to think critically about their sexual health, understand their right to access confidential services and know where to access information and support. Through interactive and organic discussions, young women are encouraged to explore different types of contraception available, have discussions about consent, healthy relationships and STIs. The goal is not only to provide accurate information but also to develop young people's health literacy and sense of agency, enabling them to make informed decisions about their sexual and reproductive health.

To reach young men and widen awareness of and access to the Condom Distribution Scheme, Brook delivers bespoke training to support The Barbers Round Chair Project. This innovative project trains barbers in Islington to have conversations about mental health – as well as condom use – with Brook's support.

Natalie Clark, Commissioning Manager for Sexual Health, stresses the need to regularly review the offer to young people:

> "Camden and Islington's teenage pregnancy data has seen a downward trend but with a slight upturn in 2021. This is why bespoke group work with young womxn and the barbers round chair programme are so important. Providers and Commissioners need to continually innovate and find new ways to promote safer sexual health and wellbeing to reach all young people".

6.7 Workforce training on relationships and sexual health for non-health practitioners to move prevention upstream and maximise the use of local assets

6.7.1 Building workforce competence through public health funding: Croydon Council

Workforce training has always played a crucial role in Croydon's successful teenage pregnancy programme. Equipping health and non-health practitioners with the knowledge and skills around RSE and SRH gives them the confidence to offer early advice, promote healthy behaviours and link young people into services.

A wide range of SRH training options has been commissioned by Croydon Council Public Health, funded through the Public Health Grant and provided by Croydon Health Services NHS Sexual Health Service. It is aimed at all practitioners working with young people including social workers, youth workers, teachers, early intervention staff, school nurses, Youth Offending Services and local voluntary sector organisations. The training offer is regularly reviewed to include new research evidence and any specific local issues to ensure practitioners are equipped to meet the changing needs of Croydon's population.

During the COVID-19 pandemic the Council identified a continuing need for multidisciplinary training. It was clear that young people were still having sex but were unsure whether and where they could access contraception and sexual health advice. Through innovative thinking and excellent partnership working the team were able to quickly offer online training sessions to larger numbers of practitioners in one session – during team meetings, locality-based meetings and teacher training sessions. Using the principles of the MECC approach, the training equipped practitioners with information about local services which they could share with young people and encourage early uptake of advice.

Although face to face training is still offered, the online provision has increased the reach to larger numbers than were attending before the pandemic. Lack of time and over stretched capacity made it very difficult for practitioners to take time out from a heavy workload, whereas providing training during already established team meetings and network events enables many more to attend. In 2022 over 500 practitioners received the training, helping to build the confidence of the wider workforce to proactively promote sexual and reproductive health to young people.

> "The training has helped me gain in confidence to discuss topics of a sensitive nature with young people who are engaging in risk-taking behaviours. I have then used this newfound confidence to have conservations with young people on a wider scale".

6.7.2 Skilling up practitioners to support vulnerable young people: Salford Council

Salford is a metropolitan borough in Greater Manchester with a population of around 270,000. From the start of the national strategy to 2020 Salford Council together with their health partners achieved a 72 per cent reduction in the under-18 conception rate. However, a significant increase in the 2021 data prompted the council to consider how to improve young people's early uptake of contraceptive advice.

Providing easy routes into youth friendly contraception services is an essential component in reducing teenage pregnancy, but access is often challenging for vulnerable young people, with additional factors compounding the problem. Sexual and reproductive health services are struggling to recruit trained nurses, the emergency of Monkeypox has had an impact on service capacity and since the COVID-19 pandemic young people and practitioners working with them have struggled to access the council's main sexual health services: SHINE.

To address the barriers, the Council in partnership with the Integrated Care Board locality Designated Nurse developed a proposal to build the resilience of the sexual health services system, by training and equipping nurses and other professionals working with young people to provide contraception and advice and, where possible, services. Brook has been commissioned to train staff and build a 'train the trainers' resource to equip practitioners with contraception kits, to inform them of where they can access condoms, what local General Practice and Pharmacies offer and what the 0–19 service (Salford's school health and health visiting provider) and nurses working with vulnerable young people can deliver. Twelve staff will be trained as trainers initially with the aim of cascading the training to 600 practitioners across Salford. The programme is joint funded from the Salford's Integrated Care Partnership Innovation and Improvement Fund with match funding from Salford Public Health Grant.

The proposal includes maximising Brook's useful digital resource – *Contraception: What works for you?* – to promote awareness of the range of methods available and support young people to make their own informed choice of a method which fits their needs. Over the next 12 months an interim pathway will be developed for practitioners working with vulnerable young people to use when they are addressing sexual health and relationships and sex education in the community settings, to enable swift referral into services if additional support is needed.

The training programme is particularly focused on supporting the growing number of vulnerable young people who already face a higher risk of pregnancy but are now experiencing additional challenges of poor mental health and the rising cost of living. Salford has a range of health and non-clinical practitioners engaging with them daily and establishing trusted relationships. By improving their skills, knowledge and understanding of the post-pandemic sexual health system, and its limitations, the training aims to ensure these practitioners are clear what they can offer and how they can support young people into clinical services. Aligning to the principle of the Making Every Contact Count approach, they will also be able to identify any wider needs of the young people and refer them to relevant services.

To evaluate the effectiveness of the programme, practitioners will complete a simple monitoring form on how they have used the training with young people and provide data on protected characteristics to help assess reach to the priority group. Longer term impact will be measured by Salford's under-18 conception and STI rates.

6.8 Supporting parents and carers to discuss relationships and sexual health with their children and work in partnership with schools in the delivery of RSE

6.8.1 Supporting parents through RSE engagement: Islington Council

In Islington, the Council's Public Health funded Health and Wellbeing Team (HWT), responded to growing requests from headteachers for assistance with parental consultation and building teachers' confidence in discussing RSE with parents. Discussions had at times been heated due to some parents' fears of RSE content, often fuelled by misinformation in mainstream and social media.

Initial consultations led by the Council highlighted a shared aim between parents and schools that children needed to develop skills to be healthy and be able to take care of themselves and others.

Keen to build on this consensus, the HWT's PSHE Advisor worked with The Big Think[7] (TBT) to create and pilot a Community Values Dialogue Project.

The first stage of the project involved meetings with the headteachers of the pilot primary schools, training for teachers to model the inquiry and discussions with parents, and a consultation with the school community involving online surveys for parents, pupils and staff.

This was followed by 90-minute RSHE values-led workshops facilitated by the Council and TBT for 30 participants: pupils, parents, teachers, faith/community leaders and school governors. These addressed issues parents felt strongly about: the content of the curriculum, the teaching methods and any fears they had; for example, age appropriateness, learning about different families and naming body parts, including genitalia, using correct anatomical words.

Discussions were facilitated about shared human values, the values of the schools, the respectful relationships and life skills parents were themselves taught in school (or wished they had been) and the results of the survey, including sharing children's worries.

The project concluded with a plan for the schools' communities to work together with the aim of RSE developing children's life skills so they can thrive.

The learning and positive outcomes from the project included:

- There was increased engagement of parents from different ethnicities and the wider community.
- Parents wanted their children to learn about safe, respectful relationships, with particular concerns about online safety, and realised that skills taught in RSE were the ones they wanted for their children.
- There was less parental anxiety, parents felt included in the schools' choices for their children and were more open to working together; this was particularly helped by positive engagement with influential parents in the local community.
- Teachers' confidence grew as positive discussions developed and more parents got involved.

To sustain the work, the Council will be supporting the pilot schools with more workshops, running a second phase with more schools, including secondary, conducting further focus groups with parents and developing an RSE Policy Template and FAQs. The learning from the project will feed into RSHE training for every school.

6.8.2 Supporting Parents and Carers with RSE and sexual exploitation: Wandsworth and Richmond

Schools in Richmond and Wandsworth offer consultation to parents on relationships and sex education content and the use of resources in school-based RSE delivery but engagement of all parents in these discussions remains an ongoing challenge. A number of additional approaches to this have been offered in the boroughs. Parents and carers are made aware, for example, when schools host external agencies such as RSE-related theatre in education programmes through direct messages and/or letters home.

Where parents raise concern about RSE, public health and children's services have supported the development of a joint statement of support for RSE in Richmond for teachers to reference and to assist in conversations where parents request the 'right to withdraw' their child from sex education (Royal Boroughs of Kingston and Richmond, 2021). A similar local RSE guide for schools was developed in Wandsworth.

Additional targeted professional development programmes have also been offered to professionals working directly with parents and carers. One programme, developed locally in partnership with the Sex Education Forum (SEF), enabled participants to consider the barriers and enablers to support parents to take a more active role in relationships and sex education provision, explored techniques for approaching RSE topics and improved confidence in professionals to raise and respond to RSE with parents and carers. The delivery and evaluation of this programme will be used to inform future SEF-targeted parents and carers RSE programmes including piloting the 'Start Talking' training programme for foster carers (see case study below).

Collaboration between the four boroughs of Merton, Kingston, Richmond and Wandsworth led to the publication of a Child Exploitation Parents and Carers Support Pack, led by public health in partnership with the respective local safeguarding children's partnerships and the police Borough Command Unit. The pack, promoted alongside national resources, is primarily for parents whose children have experienced exploitation (or where they are concerned that they may be at risk) either by their peers or adults. It is designed to help parents and carers reduce the risk of further exploitation, help understand what is happening if it does, and provides tips, helpful information, and guidance to protect and support their child going forwards. It includes information on:

- What exploitation is and how it can happen
- Strategies for talking to children about exploitation
- Useful tips for preventing exploitation online
- What to do if a child goes missing
- Living and coping with exploitation

While the pack is a useful tool for parents and carers to access as needed, it is also used as a helpful reference guide for professionals and support workers who provide support for parents and carers.

6.8.3 Supporting foster carers on RSE

Children and young people in care are more likely to miss out on the benefits of RSE. Often experiencing frequent school moves, they are also less likely to receive meaningful RSE from their parents or carers than children living with their family of origin (Mezey et al., 2015).

Sadly, 63 per cent of children and young people in foster care have previously suffered abuse or neglect and 38 per cent show concerning emotional and behavioural needs (Department for Education, 2023). Longer-term health outcomes and risks put the needs of this vulnerable group into sharp focus. Young people in care are in general sexually active at a younger age more likely than their non-looked after peers (Mezey et al., 2015) and are around three times more likely to be mothers by the age of 18 (Public Health England, 2015).

In 2021 the Sex Education Forum identified this gap in provision and formed a partnership with The Fostering Network, securing funding from the Department of Health and Social Care National Reproductive Health, Sexual Health and HIV Innovation Fund to produce a RSE guide for foster carers. Producing a resource for foster carers made sense because nearly 70 per cent of care experienced children and young people live with over 55,000 foster families across the UK (The Fostering Network, 2022).

The 'Start Talking' RSE guide was informed by a series of focus groups with foster carers and care experienced young people. Conversations with those involved in the project showed the strength of support for open and honest discussion about relationships and sex and how this would result in young people being more informed and confident, resulting in better health and wellbeing.

Many of the care experienced young people involved in the project described how they had received little or no RSE and had often relied on educating themselves or asking siblings to fill in the gaps.

The free 'Start Talking' guide resulting from the project covers a range of practical issues, from puberty, periods and body hair, to relationships, sex, pornography, young people with learning disabilities and LGBTQ+ and gender identities (Sex Education Forum, 2022b).

The need for foster carers to access RSE training was identified by all participants (both foster carers and care experienced young people). The Sex Education Forum has now secured grant funding to pilot the development, delivery and independent evaluation of a training programme to groups of foster carers in three local areas in England.

Longer term, it is hoped that the pilot project will help make the case to Government and non-statutory agencies for a more consistent and strategic approach to meeting the RSE needs of all children and young people in care.

6.9 Good communications to deliver accurate information, consistent messages and service publicity to young people

6.9.1 Maximising digital and outreach opportunities to reach young people: Brook

As the only national sexual and reproductive health charity with long experience of young people's needs, Brook is committed to providing information, advice and guidance to anyone that needs it, through its digital and social channels. This is done in collaboration with service users who not only help set the agenda but write content and test every digital tool or service Brook creates.

Brook.org.uk has over 200 pages of engaging and evidence-based content, that is designed to be inclusive and accessible and is always tested with users. Topics range from contraception and STIs to gender, sexuality and mental health. There are real stories, blogs, videos and animations as well as a range of tools to support users with everything from gauging their risk of pregnancy, to helping them decide which method of contraception is right for them.

Brook's commitment to supporting everyone with their sexual and reproductive health extends to building and maintaining a Find a Service tool, designed to help people find exactly what they need, wherever they live and regardless of provider. This ranges from emergency contraception or condoms from a pharmacy to LARC methods from a GP or HIV testing from a sexual health service. Brook also maintains the only national database of home STI testing services.

In response to rising STI rates and a downturn in the use of hormonal contraception, Brook also launched its Best Contraception for Me tool in 2023. Endorsed by the Faculty of Sexual and Reproductive Health, this tool guides users of any gender through a journey to explore their needs and preferences, supporting and educating along the way.

Every Brook education session and resource in schools, colleges and community settings will include links to the Brook website, encouraging young people to access high-quality, evidence-based information in their own time.

Support via the website is only part of the picture, with Brook devoting considerable resource to maintaining a presence across Instagram, Facebook, YouTube, Twitter and TikTok. This enables Brook to inhabit digital spaces where young people congregate and is helpful in providing accurate information at a time when decisions about reproductive and sexual health are shaped by influencers sharing their personal experiences (sometimes as part of advertising paid-for products). Brook is also exploring the use of AI via its social platforms to further strengthen its approach and to provide personalised support for young people.

In order to inform and tailor the information and support it provides, Brook conducts research in the form of surveys and focus groups conducted at local and national level. In 2023 this focused on the downturn in use of condoms and hormonal contraception. Brook ran a survey of young people in England and Wales modelled on the University of Glasgow's CONUNDRUM[8] study, followed by focus groups with young people. Key findings included the important role of social media and online influencers in contraceptive decision making, concerns over side effects of hormonal methods, and an often negative experience with professionals when discussing a change of method. A lack of information, time and sense of autonomy in decision making were cited as key problems (Winters, 2024).

The findings are informing and shaping Brook's work in a number of ways. The charity plans to use the insights to strengthen staff training so that the support front-line staff provide young people reflects what they shared via the survey. In addition to tackling misinformation via AI-powered tools deployed via Brook's website and social media platforms, Brook also plans to use the survey insights to enhance and strengthen the development of its new digital contraception provision pathways in the areas where Brook provides services.

6.9.2 Promotion and Marketing of the Condom Distribution Scheme: London Borough of Barking and Dagenham

In 2015 the London Borough of Barking and Dagenham brought the borough's Condom Distribution Scheme back in house and increased promotion of the scheme to create a buzz around it.

Facilitated by the Youth Health Programmes Co-ordinator, a variety of promotion methods were utilised including social media channels (Facebook, Twitter, and Instagram) and face-to-face engagement with young people in education institutions and youth provisions. The aim was to motivate young people to sign up for the C-Card, making the process as inclusive as possible.

A new condom provider was commissioned, who had a lot of promotional products within their range. This included condoms that glow in the dark, condoms that delay climatic moments, and ones branded for key social causes, such as Pride. Pharmacies were also encouraged to introduce a 'pick 'n' mix' option so that young people could create their own bespoke condom bags. All condoms are Vegan Society certified.

It was also important to promote the website of the London wide condom scheme *Come Correct*, so that young people knew they could access condoms in other London boroughs. Different merchandise was produced with the website but also a message that encouraged young people to sign up online if they were over the age of sixteen. This included pens, wristbands, and sperm keyrings, which were made available through all providers of the scheme.

Recognising that swift and easy access to information is key to increasing awareness and uptake, the website is designed to be mobile friendly and links to the full range of support and guidance. Young people are told where to access this information at educational institutions, youth provisions, pharmacies, and through social media channels.

The introduction of QR codes has made a significant difference as the young person is in charge of creating their own record. Access barriers have also been removed through the introduction of a video condom demonstration for use in pharmacies and during online sign- ups. This took away the embarrassment factor for young people and pharmacy staff, although staff are still taught how to complete the demonstration so that they are able to answer any questions a young person might have following the video.

6.9.3 Making Every Contact Count: Keeping practitioners informed

The following communication for partner agencies in touch with young people is adapted from a template developed by the Sexual Health, Reproductive Health and HIV team in Public Health England during the COVID-19 pandemic.

Adopting the principle of MECC, it is designed for local authority services where frontline practitioners are in regular contact with young people most at risk of unplanned pregnancy and poor sexual health. For example, Drug and Alcohol teams, Looked after Children and Care Leavers, Children and Young People/0–19s/School Nursing, Early Help, Youth Services, School Inclusion, NEET, Mental Health, Youth Offending Teams, Housing and Supporting People, homelessness organisations, organisations that work with migrants and asylum seekers, learning disability services and voluntary sector organisations supporting young people.

The aim is two-fold: to ensure practitioners know where and when SRH services are in their local area so they can make swift referrals, and to encourage them to proactively ask young people whether they have any contraception, pregnancy or sexual health needs.

Helping young people access contraception, pregnancy and sexual health services

As your service supports young people who may be at greater risk of unplanned pregnancy and poor sexual health, we wanted to let you know the details of **our local services where they can get contraception, pregnancy and STI advice.**

Details of our local service offer are here: Add link to local website information, including young people specific services or advice.

To help ensure young people's contraception, pregnancy or sexual health needs are identified, we recommend practitioners in your service proactively offer support to young people following the **MECC** approach of **Ask, Assist, Act.**

Ask: Do you need any help with contraception, emergency contraception, pregnancy support or sexually transmitted infections?

Assist: You can find reliable information on (insert local or national website, e.g. Brook). These are the local services where you can get confidential advice and help.

Act: Find the nearest relevant service or the young person's GP and help them make an appointment.

Optional: If you have any questions or concerns about a young person's contraception, pregnancy or sexual health needs, please contact . . . [insert local contact]

6.10 Support for pregnant teenagers: early pregnancy testing and unbiased options advice, swift referral to abortion or maternity services, and support with post pregnancy contraception

6.10.1 Pregnancy testing, pregnancy options advice and referral pathways for maternity and abortion: Walsall Council

Walsall's dedicated Teenage Pregnancy Team is well established and has strong partnerships with schools and partner agencies across the local authority. Schools, colleges and other agencies notify the team for early support to ensure any pregnant young person receives unbiased advice and support, including from a trained pregnancy counsellor, so they can make their own well-informed choice. Confidential sources of pregnancy testing and pregnancy options advice are publicised as part of wider sexual health promotion to young people in education and community settings.

For those who choose to continue the pregnancy there is a 'parents to be' pathway for 16–19-year-olds with holistic care from support workers within the Health in Pregnancy (HIP) Programme. The Teenage Pregnancy Team receives notification from the midwifery service of all registered pregnancies under 20 years, and to ensure any vulnerability is identified early, works together with the HIP programme to triage cases monthly and arrange additional support. Those of school or college age also have a dedicated teenage parent worker, a specialist midwife and a named Education Welfare Officer. A dedicated fathers' worker supports young fathers through the HIP programme. At 32 weeks of pregnancy, all under-20s see a sexual health adviser to discuss post-pregnancy contraception options, with their chosen method provided post-delivery at the hospital.

For young women who decide not to continue the pregnancy, Walsall Teenage Pregnancy Team have a strong partnership with BPAS, the abortion provider. An abortion referral pathway for schools, colleges and other agencies provides access to a named contact within BPAS which supports professionals when advocating for young people to secure timely local appointments. BPAS also has a representative on the Strategy group who can be contacted if there are specific access difficulties such as an appointment being offered too far from the young person's home or helping to accelerate an early appointment to enable medical abortion. This has proved invaluable in providing bespoke support for young women in Walsall.

Post-abortion contraception is offered as part of the BPAS contract, either provided at the end of the abortion process or through referral to WISH, the sexual health provider. Post-abortion support is also available through BPAS, via phone or face to face, and from a counsellor in the Teenage Pregnancy Team.

The strong partnership between the Teenage Pregnancy Team, the maternity service and the abortion provider not only ensures smooth referral pathways, but also provides the Team with real time conception data which helps inform targeted prevention work.

6.10.2 Reducing second and subsequent pregnancy in teenagers in Bristol

The Teenage Pregnancy Outreach Nurse service was commissioned in 2008 due to a high repeat pregnancy rate (22 per cent) for teenagers in Bristol. They work with two distinct groups of young people: those having abortions, miscarriage or ectopic pregnancy under the age of 18 and those continuing with their pregnancies who are under the age of 19 at delivery.

The service sees all Bristol and South Gloucestershire teenagers who come to the Pregnancy Advisory (Abortion) Service at Unity Sexual Health Services to formulate a contraception plan, fit a LARC at the time of abortion if appropriate and then individually support teenagers in contraceptive use for six months, or longer if needed. The nurses also work with those who continue with their pregnancies by taking direct referrals from midwives and the Family Nurse Partnership (FNP) and contacting young women at 36–40 weeks gestation to discuss their contraception plan. They can fit or arrange for teenagers choosing an implant to have it fitted on the postnatal ward or to have a bridging method such as Depo Provera. They encourage and facilitate starting a method of contraception by day 21 post-delivery if the mother is not breastfeeding on demand and again offer support for six months or longer. All young mothers have direct access to members of the nursing team via text or phone. Overall, uptake of LARC methods is high.

In the NHS Bristol, North Somerset and South Gloucestershire Integrated Care Board, during the first six months of 2022 the proportion of under-19-year-old women having an abortion who had had one or more previously, was 3 per cent against the England average of 9 per cent.

As well as working closely with the FNP team, the service also offers sexual health screening and outreach and networks with a variety of agencies including supported housing projects, the Youth Offending Team, and the Barnardos' Project against Sexual Exploitation. This reflects the increasingly complex and often safeguarding needs of the young women the service is supporting.

Notes

1 The Teenage Pregnancy Knowledge Exchange was established in 2013 at the University of Bedfordshire as the first national source of expert knowledge and advice on all aspects of teenage pregnancy.

2 The English HIV and Sexual Health Commissioners Group provides a strategic forum for commissioners of sexual and reproductive health services to meet, network and work together to improve the commissioning and delivery of local integrated services and strategies.
3 The Health and Social Care Act 2012 sets out a local authority's statutory responsibility for commissioning public health services for children and young people aged 0 to 19 years. The Healthy Child Programme aims to bring together health, education and other main partners to deliver an effective programme for prevention and support.
4 Lower Layer Super Output Areas are geographic areas designed to improve the reporting of small area statistics in England and Wales.
5 SHEU is an independent research unit based in Exeter, which conducts health and wellbeing surveys on behalf of schools and local authorities.
6 NCFE is the UK's longest-standing awards body.
7 The Big Think is a Human Values Foundation education charity programme that creates opportunities and spaces for genuine conversations with children and caregivers, with shared values inspiring and uniting communities.
8 **CONUNDRUM (Con**dom & **Con**traception **UND**erstandings: Researching Uptake & Motivations) is an ongoing collaboration between sexual health stakeholders, including young people, policymakers, practitioners and researchers, who are committed to improving sexual health among young people in Scotland.

References

Brook (2022). Sexual Behaviours Traffic Light Tool. A guide to identify, understand and respond to sexual behaviours in children and young people.
Brook (2023). The Spotting the Signs Tool.
London Boroughs of Wandsworth and Merton and the Royal Boroughs of Kingston upon Thames and Richmond upon Thames (2021). Child Exploitation. Parents and Carers Support Pack.
Mezey, G., Meyer, D., Robinson, F., Bonell, C., Campbell, R., Gillard, S. *et al.* (2015). Developing and piloting a peer mentoring intervention to reduce teenage pregnancy in looked-after children and care leavers: an exploratory randomised controlled trial. *Health Technol Assess*, 19 (85).
Public Health England and Local Government Association (2018). A Framework to Support Young People to Prevent Unplanned Pregnancy and Develop Healthy Relationships. London.
Royal Borough of Kingston on Thames and Royal Borough of Richmond upon Thames (2021). Safeguarding the health and wellbeing of children and young people in Kingston and Richmond – joint statement to support the new Relationships Education, Relationships & Sex Education, and Health Education statutory guidance and curriculum content.
Sex Education Forum (2022a). Young People's RSE Poll 2021.
Sex Education Forum (2022b). Start Talking. A guide for foster care.
The Fostering Network (2022). Fostering statistics.
Winters J. (2024). Education, access, stigma and young people: attitudes to contraception, condoms and sexual health. (EASY). Brook.

7 Improving the lives of young parents

Developments and challenges since 2018

7.0 Overview

The Teenage Pregnancy Strategy was the first government initiative to include a focus on improving support for young parents alongside the prevention programme (Social Exclusion Unit, 1999). While the primary goal was to halve the under-18 conception rate by equipping young people to delay early pregnancy, the strategy recognised that those who chose to become young parents should have high-quality support to enable them to fulfil their ambitions, to promote independent living and to decrease the risk of longer-term social exclusion. In the previous edition we described the detail of the strategy's support programme, how it was implemented through the national, regional and local structures, and what we learned. We reported the positive finding of a doubling in the proportion of teenage mothers in education, training or employment (Wellings et al., 2016), but that many outcomes remained poor, and a continued focus was needed. We noted that the combination of no longer having a specific strategy, the dismantling of the national and regional support structures and the new commissioning landscape following the Health and Social Care Act, posed significant challenges for local areas in maintaining a co-ordinated support offer for young parents. These challenges were exacerbated by significant funding cuts resulting from the coalition government's chosen policy on austerity.

In this chapter we take stock of developments and challenges since 2018. We cover the most recent outcomes for young parents and their children; the findings and recommendations of reports investigating their needs; a summary of the evidence for effective approaches, with new developments and learning from the Family Nurse Partnership[1]; an update on aspects of support initiated by the strategy: education of young parents, Care to Learn childcare funding and supported housing; new evidence on the lived experience of young fathers and initiatives to meet their needs; the national guidance – *A Framework for supporting teenage mothers and young fathers* (PHE and Local Government Association, 2016) – and current local case studies illustrating NHS, Local Authority and Voluntary and Community Service (VCS) organisations examples of specialist support. We conclude by summarising the key themes and suggest actions for further progress.

DOI: 10.4324/9781003410225-8

7.1 Outcomes and influencing factors for young parents and their children

With the 72 per cent reduction in under-18 conceptions over the past 23 years, and an increased proportion of young women who do conceive choosing to have an abortion, there has been a very large reduction in the numbers of young parents. In 1998 about 23,800 young women who conceived under 18 continued their pregnancies. This dropped to 9,300 in 2015 and to 5,800 in 2021. Numbers of young mothers under 20 have also declined from 63,000 in 1998, to 33,000 in 2015 and 21,000 in 2021 (Office for National Statistics, 2023d). This large reduction in maternities confounded earlier speculation from some critics of the strategy, that improving support would incentivise teenage parenthood.

However, it appears from the Family Nurse Partnership (FNP) Adapt study (pp. 162) and from reports from local services that this diminishing cohort of young parents have increasing and complex needs. While every young parent has their own individual story, the geographical area and individual risk factors for early pregnancy highlight the vulnerabilities with which some young people enter parenthood: family poverty, persistent school absence by age 14, slower than expected educational attainment between ages 11 and 14 (Crawford et al., 2013) and having care experience, where a combination of negative experiences can compound vulnerability. Young women and men who have experienced four or more Adverse Childhood Experiences are between three and seven times more likely to experience an accidental teenage pregnancy, become a teenage parent and have a lifetime diagnosis of a sexually transmitted infection (Wood et al., 2022). As discussed later in the chapter, it is a concern that the trends in these underlying risk factors have been rising since 2015 and have been exacerbated by the COVID-19 pandemic. Notably, family poverty (Joseph Rowntree Foundation, 2023; Policy Press, 2022) school absence and educational attainment (Committee of Public Accounts, 2023), young people's mental health (NSPCC, 2022) and a sharp rise in the numbers of 15- and 16-year-olds going into local authority care (Nuffield Family Justice Observatory, 2022). Reports have also noted social and developmental delays in babies and children born and growing up during the pandemic (Parent Infant Foundation, 2022).

It has always been difficult to quantify the extent to which pre-existing disadvantage, or the challenges of parenting at a young age, contribute to the inequalities experienced by young parents and their children. Most likely it is a complex interplay of both. What is clear is that routine and research data continue to show disproportionately poor outcomes, with some worsening over recent years.

Babies and children born to mothers under 20:

- Have a 25 per cent higher risk than the overall average of **infant mortality** – dying in the first year of life (Office for National Statistics, 2023b).
- Have a 21 per cent higher rate of **stillbirth** compared with babies of mothers of all ages (Office for National Statistics, 2023a).

- Are 3.5 times as likely to die from a **sudden unexpected death in infancy** compared with the overall population and almost 7 times as likely compared with mothers aged 35–39. The overall risk has risen from a 3.1 times as high risk in 2016 (Office for National Statistics, 2023c).
- Are at significantly increased risk of being born **extremely preterm and with extremely low birth weight** (Marvin-Dowle et al., 2018).
- At age 5, children born to mothers under 19 have an almost nine-month **developmental delay behind the average on verbal ability** (Morinis et al., 2013).
- Are at higher risk of **living in poverty**. Over half (55 per cent) of children in households in Scotland with a mother aged under 25 were in relative poverty in 2015–18, compared with 24 per cent of children overall (Scottish Government, 2022).
- Have a higher than expected risk of being taken into care; 42 per cent of mothers in **recurrent care proceedings** are estimated to have been aged 14–19 when they had their first child (Nuffield Family Justice Observatory, 2022).

Of the influencing factors on infant health, breastfeeding, smoking and maternal nutrition:

- Babies born to mothers under 20 are about as third as likely to be **breastfed** as the overall average, whether considering exclusive breastfeeding or any breastfeeding (NHS England. 2023).
- More than 3 in 10 mothers under 20 are **smoking** at the start of pregnancy, more than double the average for all ages. Of those who smoke at booking, 61 per cent continue to smoke at the end of the pregnancy. However, this is the lowest proportion of all age groups and suggests that although young women are less likely to stop in advance of, or when they realise they are pregnant, they are more likely to quit during the pregnancy (Public Health England, 2021).
- Younger women are more likely to be **underweight** at the start of pregnancy with 1 in 8 (12 per cent) under 18s underweight at the booking appointment, compared with 4.5 per cent of all women. 31 per cent were classified as **overweight or obese** compared with 49 per cent of all women (Public Health England, 2021).

Young parents

Young mothers under 20 are at higher risk of experiencing **pre-natal** and **postpartum depression** compared with mothers of all ages (Reid and Meadows-Oliver, 2007; Lanzi et al., 2009) and are two to three times more likely to experience **depression, anxiety** and **PTSD** during pregnancy and postnatally (Estrin, 2019; Tabet, 2016). Parental depression is the most prevalent risk factor for negative impact on poor child development outcomes (Sabates and Dex, 2012).

Older adolescent mothers and fathers aged up to 24 are also more likely to experience **poor mental health** compared with their non-parent peers (Action for Children, 2017).

In 2020 young mothers under 20 had a **death by suicide** rate of 27/100,000 compared with 3.8/100,000 for all-age maternal death by suicide. The figures refer to deaths during pregnancy and in the first year after birth. This is an increase from a rate of 2.5/100,000 in 2014–16 with the rise pre-dating the COVID-19 pandemic (National Perinatal Epidemiology Unit, 2021)

Set against some of the articles in the United Nations Rights of the Child[2] (UNCRC), these outcomes are a stark reminder of the inequalities young parent families face and of how much more needs to be done.

Article 6: Every child has the right to life: *25% higher risk of infant mortality and 3.5 times more likely to suffer a sudden unexpected death in infancy.*

Article 24. Every child has the right to the best possible health. *A significantly increased risk of being born extremely prematurely and having an extremely low birthweight.*

Article 27. Every child has the right to a standard of living that is good enough to meet their physical and social needs and support their development. *Over twice as likely to be living in relative poverty compared to children overall. More likely to have one or both parents with poor mental health. Higher risk of being subject to recurrent care proceedings.*

Article 29. Education must develop every child's personality, talents and abilities to the full. *Nine-month delay in development of verbal ability.*

While national data make a compelling case for action, data from local services provides a microcosm of need, conveying the burden of stress and disadvantage experienced by some individual young parents, which contribute to the poor outcomes for them and their children.

This is vividly illustrated by the data gathered by WILD Young Parents in Cornwall from referral information, other professionals and from trusted conversations with the young mothers and fathers as they join the service. Of the 352 young parents assessed: 76 per cent had experience childhood trauma; 63 per cent self-harm and suicidal ideation; 39 per cent substance abuse; 27 per cent domestic abuse; and 26 per cent sexual abuse (WILD Annual Report, 2022).

The impact of this complex web of disadvantage is explored in a synthesis of qualitative studies focused on young women's perceptions of their mental health and wellbeing experiences during and after pregnancy (Lucas et al., 2019). The study highlights the importance of understanding how young women's mental health is closely linked to physical and structural factors rather than individual capacities alone. As well as contributory factors of childhood experiences and challenges in family and social relationships, mental health problems are also influenced by the external conditions of young mothers' lives. Housing instability and financial and food insecurity figured highly as increasing stress, which young mothers understood was profoundly impactful on them and their children, but couldn't avoid. These stresses are likely to be greater since the COVID-19 pandemic (Joseph Rowntree Foundation, 2023; Policy Press, 2022) and the rising cost of living. When WILD young parents were asked what they were finding harder since 2020, 29 per cent said having a secure home, 48 per cent keeping their home warm, 55 per cent paying for electricity and 53 per cent having enough food.

For some young parents the interplay of different aspects of these vulnerabilities can compromise their capacity to safeguard themselves and their babies. In WILD's assessment of 292 children's safeguarding needs: 38 per cent had a social work assessment; 30 per cent were at risk of neglect; 20 per cent had a child protection plan; 17 per cent were at risk of physical harm; 16 per cent had a child in need plan; 13 per cent had care proceedings; and 5 per cent were at risk of sexual harm (WILD Annual Report, 2022).

This is sadly further illustrated in the NSPCC analysis of case reviews published since 2018, which involved parents who were teenagers when their baby was conceived or born (NSPCC, 2021). Previous experience of trauma, domestic abuse, sexual exploitation, drug and alcohol use, unstable living situations and poor mental health were all identified as contributory factors. A similar combination of vulnerabilities and challenges was evident in the study of Recurrent Care Proceedings, which found 42 per cent of the mothers involved had their first child as a teenager (Nuffield Family Justice Observatory, 2022).

With such clear evidence of inter-generational inequality, it is not surprising that there has been a continued call to recognise and address the needs of young parents from NICE (Antenatal Care guideline, 2021), Nuffield (Mothers in Recurrent Care Proceedings, 2022), the Royal College of Paediatrics and Child Health (State of Child Health, 2020), MBRRACE UK (Saving Lives, Improving Maternity Care, 2022) and NSPCC (Learning from case reviews, 2021). All recommend specialist and co-ordinated support starting early in pregnancy with specialist maternity care to secure the protective benefits of antenatal care, and continuing into parenthood.

A consistent theme is the importance of practitioners building a trusted relationship with young parents so they feel able to share their concerns and challenges without fearing a judgement that they can't cope. Notably a key learning point from the NSPCC review and the MBRRACE report was the need for practitioners to understand better how factors such as experience of trauma or domestic abuse can impact young parents' capacity to care for themselves and their child, and to be more enquiring into the underlying causes of poor mental health. In the MBRRACE report, all the teenage mothers who died by suicide had complex problems of mental health, domestic abuse and substance misuse abuse. Echoing the recommendation from the earlier Ofsted report on Serious Case Reviews (Ofsted, 2011), NSPCC highlighted that practitioners need to be aware that in a young parent family there may be three children in need – mother, father and infant – with each requiring a trusted relationship and careful attention.

7.2 Providing effective support: what we know from the Strategy and what more we have learned

7.2.1 Sure Start Plus

As part of the Teenage Pregnancy Strategy, Sure Start Plus was piloted in 35 local authorities to provide intensive support for pregnant teenagers and young parents with the aims of improving their social and emotional wellbeing, health and learning, and strengthening their families and communities. Each pregnant teenager in Sure Start Plus had a personal adviser who gave one to one support, drew in specialist support tailored to their needs, and was a key point of contact and co-ordination for other agencies.

The programme was evaluated using a mixed method approach, including comparison with 35 non-Sure Start Plus sites, matched for deprivation scores and teenage pregnancy rates. The findings were intended to inform future policy on young parent support, including reshaping existing services to make them more responsive to the needs of young parents.

As the intention of the programme was to be innovative and explore different ways of delivering services, Sure Start Plus was characterised by diversity, with a range of models developed in the pilot areas. This posed some challenges for the national evaluation to distil the learning, as did the difficulty of differentiating the impact of the programme from other support initiatives in both the pilot and the matched areas. However, compared with matched local authorities without Sure Start Plus, positive impact was demonstrated in a number of areas.

The evaluation (Wiggins et al., 2005) found the projects were successful in addressing the young person's expressed and immediate needs and averting crises: increasing support for emotional issues; improving the young women's relationships, including reducing the incidence of domestic violence; and improving the housing situations of young parents. Some of this work may have been at the expense of reaching the programme health objectives, for example reducing smoking or increasing breastfeeding where there was no significant impact. Sure Start Plus advisers reported these objectives were difficult to achieve with such a vulnerable and disadvantaged group at a time of transition and upheaval in their lives. However, the evaluation found that for some of these vulnerable young women, once crises had been averted, they had begun to lay foundations for their future by learning parenting skills to give their children positive experiences, building up their social support networks and returning to education.

Choosing unrealistic primary outcomes in research studies of young parent support programmes was also an issue for the Randomised Controlled Trial (RCT) study of the Family Nurse Partnership. Recognising the limitations of short-term outcomes, the evaluation recommended that a sample of Sure Start Plus users be followed up five years after using the programme to try to determine longer-term consequences of taking part in the programme. This was not acted on, but a longer view of impact has been taken by the Family Nurse Partnership (section 7.2.3).

The evaluation also found no significant impact on young fathers, possibly because during the first two years of the programme, few areas did any specific work with young fathers. Although by the third year, two thirds of the programmes had a specific strategy, work with young fathers in most areas remained a secondary priority. Limited funding was a factor in preventing the appointment of dedicated fathers' advisers. However, the failure to recognise the importance of supporting young fathers to improve their and their family's outcomes is a recurrent theme which is discussed later in this chapter (pp. x).

7.2.2 The essential role of a trusted adviser

The essential ingredient of the programme appeared to be the role of the adviser who acted as a 'critical friend' to the young parent, building their confidence and aspirations, and providing a specific point of contact and co-ordination for other agencies. The role provided help earlier and for longer, acting as a bridge between crisis support and future development. The evaluation cited this as a unique aspect of the programme, as other services tended to provide either crisis management, or on-going support, but seldom both.

Asked to say what they liked about the one-to-one support, young mothers cited friendliness and having an individual relationship with one worker who never pushed them away, and never gave up on them. Confidential support with personal issues; practical help and advice with, for example, benefits and housing; help in accessing groups and other activities; home visits; accompanying them to appointments; and liaising with agencies on their behalf all contributed to a strong sense of reliable consistent support.

> "The Sure Start Plus adviser) was one of those people you could make friends with straight away. She's a warm lovely person. She can sit there and you can talk to her because she's a friend to you . . . and I just throw it all at her! She does help you with (any problem)".
>
> (Young mother aged 17)

This sentiment is echoed by young parents in other dedicated support programmes, illustrated in the case studies later in the chapter. It underlines the critical importance of all young parents, mothers and fathers, having a trusted adviser, providing continuity of care and co-ordinating tailored support to meet their individual needs.

This was the primary recommendation from the evaluation (Wiggins et al., 2005). Every local area should fund personal advisers whose primary role would be to provide a holistic, one-to-one package of support. The advisers should target services at the most vulnerable and socially excluded pregnant teenagers and young parents and expect to work intensively with them during pregnancy and throughout the child's first year. For young parents with continuing multiple needs there should be an option for further one to one work until the child's fourth birthday. There should be separate advisers for young women and young men to ensure the needs of young fathers are not subsumed by the more obvious support needs of young mothers. Support for young parents with less critical needs should be provided through short term, one to one interventions and group work combined with support to access other services. A caseload of between 25 and 50 was recommended to enable the essential intensive work to be carried out effectively.

The adviser would act as a lead professional delivering a tailored support package in close liaison with a multi-disciplinary team, bringing in specialist support for individual needs – for example counselling, smoking and reintegration to education. The evaluation cited strong links with partner agencies as the other cornerstone of Sure Start Plus; without these, the referral system did not work and the support plan for individual young parents floundered. At the core of the team, it was recommended that an operational level forum should meet at regular intervals to discuss joint initiatives, referral pathways and individual cases. Active forums to share problems and solutions should be supported by formal strategic links with the local accountable body for children and young people. The limited implementation and impact of these recommendations is discussed later in this chapter.

7.2.3 The Family Nurse Partnership: progress and developments

The Family Nurse Partnership (FNP) was not part of the strategy action plan but was introduced in 2007 as part of Government's on-going quest for effective interventions to reduce inequalities experienced by young parents and their children. It was initially piloted in 10 local authority areas, increasing to around 130 areas by 2015. FNP is a licensed programme, developed in the US in the 1970s at the University of Colorado, where it is known as the Nurse Family Partnership. It is a programme providing intensive support for first time young mothers, through structured home visits from a specialist trained family nurse. Initially offered from early pregnancy (before 28 weeks) until the child's second birthday, changes made to the programme in England in 2020 enable family nurses and young mothers to consider an earlier graduation from the programme, after their child's first birthday, when mother and child are ready to transition to universal services. The programme has a maximum of 64 visits: 14 during pregnancy, 28 in infancy during the first 12 months, and 22 during the toddler phase between 13 and 24 months.

FNP has three aims: to improve pregnancy outcomes, child health and development and parents' economic self-sufficiency. The methods are based on theories of human ecology, self-efficacy and attachment, with much of the work focused on building strong relationships between the client and family nurse to facilitate behaviour change, and attempting to tackle the emotional problems that prevent some mothers and fathers caring well for their child.

Implemented in eight countries, evaluation of the Nurse Family Partnership over the past 45 years has shown significant benefits for vulnerable young families in the short, medium and long term, across a wide range of outcomes (Olds et al., 2014). To test the impact of FNP in the England the Department of Health commissioned a three- year formative evaluation (Barnes et al., 2012), followed by a large-scale RCT. The formative evaluation found the programme could be delivered successfully in England and showed encouraging signs of positive impact. Families valued the programme, with young mothers less likely to smoke in pregnancy and more likely to breastfeed. By the end of the programme mothers were very positive about their parenting capability, reporting high levels of warm parenting and low levels of harsh discipline. A significant achievement was a narrowing of inequalities, with young parents reporting levels of parenting stress similar to that in the general population and FNP children also developing in line with the general child population (Barnes et al., 2012).

The Randomised Controlled Trial chose to look at four primary outcomes in mothers receiving FNP: maternal smoking, birth weight, timing of second pregnancy and children's attendance at Accident and Emergency departments. A number of secondary outcomes were also monitored: breastfeeding, child language development, maternal education and employment, care giving quality, maternal mental health, domestic abuse, child immunisations and child injuries (Robling et al., 2015).

The results showed FNP appeared to improve some of the secondary outcomes relating to child development, particularly early language development at 24 months. Better protection for children from serious injury, abuse and neglect was also indicated, with earlier identification of safeguarding risks. This was most likely due to the greater level of family nurse contact and the trusted relationship, which may have enabled the young parent to disclose problems earlier. There was also some small improvement in mothers' social support, relationship quality and self-efficacy, which may provide longer term benefits for the child.

However, the RCT showed no impact across the primary outcomes, even when looked at by sub-group or by variation in programme implementation. Compared with matched sites, young parents' participation in education, employment or training and other secondary outcomes also did not appear to be influenced positively by FNP. The evaluation suggested the lack of impact demonstrated in England may be due to the target group not being as disadvantaged as those in the US cohort. The relatively high levels of universal and specialist support received by young parents in the control group may have also made it more difficult to distil the 'added value' of FNP. As with Sure Start Plus, there were some examples within individual programmes of effective support on smoking and breastfeeding, illustrated by the case study below, but numbers were too small to be picked up in the national evaluation.

In 2021 a follow-up data linkage study tracked outcomes for mothers and children enrolled in the RCT a decade earlier (Robling et al., 2021). This study found a similar rate of child maltreatment referrals and registrations and child protection plans in social care data for FNP children, compared with children of young parents who had not been enrolled in FNP. However, descriptive analysis in the study found FNP children were less likely to be referred on multiple occasions and spent less time in care. Meanwhile, FNP children were 26 per cent more likely to achieve a good level of development in school reception year (age 4–5) and more likely to achieve the expected standard in reading in Year 1 (age 6–7), both relevant to the Public Health Outcomes Framework indicators on school readiness. The study also found that: "Writing scores improved as a result of the Family Nurse Partnership for boys, and for children of younger mothers and of mothers who were not in employment, education or training when first recruited to the study". Although the study did not monitor developmental progress of individual children, the improved reading and writing scores suggests a potential link with the improved language skills at 24 months, identified in the RCT.

CASE STUDY 7.1

Challenging barriers to sustained breastfeeding

N joined her local Family Nurse Partnership at 17. With the help of her Family Nurse and through the use of a range of FNP 'Facilitators' (specifically designed tools) – such as 'Babies First Feed', she successfully began breastfeeding her baby. Having stopped attending college while she was pregnant, N returned to resume her studies soon after giving birth, putting her baby in the attached nursery, with the intention of continuing to breastfeed. Despite initial success, the arrangement became difficult when staff at the college started to criticise N for leaving classes to breastfeed and actively encouraged her to have someone bottle-feed her baby when her workload increased.

N discussed this with her Family Nurse, articulating both how proud she was at being able to breastfeed her baby and her shock at the negative response of the college. Through exploring N's feelings with her, the Family Nurse was able to use the opportunity to reinforce the positive decision N had made and highlight the continued benefits of breastfeeding for both her and her baby. She encouraged and supported N to challenge the college, which she did successfully, leading ultimately to the college developing a new breastfeeding-friendly approach. In addition to helping N to breastfeed, the long-term positive, therapeutic relationship between her and her Family Nurse helped to improved N's self-confidence and self-efficacy which was crucial in her feeling empowered to raise the issue with her college.

The RCT confirmed two important findings similar to the Sure Start Plus evaluation. First, that a large proportion of the young parents was particularly vulnerable and had entered parenthood with significant disadvantages. Notably only 14 per cent reported that they had planned the pregnancy. Second, the programme was very popular with the young parents. The Family Nurses had developed respectful and trusting relationships with their clients and uptake of the visits was good. Importantly, they had succeeded in engaging with a group who, because of their prior experiences, are sometimes reluctant to access services and trust professionals.

> "Having a baby young was really hard, people judged me and questioned me as a mum. It felt like nobody believed in me!"
>
> "When I met my family nurse she didn't judge or question me. She believed in me and helped me believe in myself. She didn't patronise me or 'baby' me. I got treated like an adult and as though what I thought mattered. We had a really rough few months with my little girl and I really don't know what I'd have done without my family nurse. Over time she has become someone I can trust, turn to and rely on".
>
> FNP client, Telford

7.2.4 Family Nurse Partnership next steps

Although the England studies showed mixed results, the Early Intervention Foundation[3] has taken into account the significant impact shown in RCTs in the US and the Netherlands and has maintained a high evidence rating for FNP (Early Intervention Foundation, 2015/2021 Family Nurse Partnership | EIF Guidebook). The results of the trial have informed further development of the programme.

In a programme of change begun in 2016, the FNP National Unit continues to improve and adapt the FNP programme in England by testing a series of innovations and improvements to strengthen outcomes, increase value for money, ensure greater flexibility and share learning with other services.

This included a range of swiftly implemented changes, such as an extension of the eligibility criteria up to age 24 years for mothers with additional vulnerabilities, as well as provision of improved data reporting to explore any impact of the programme locally and nationally on, for example, safeguarding and child development. This has provided local areas with greater flexibility to target FNP according to local population needs.

More complex changes to the programme were put through rapid-cycle testing in 11 and then 20 FNP areas between 2016 and 2019, before being implemented in all areas in 2020. A series of modifications to better 'personalise' the programme were designed, based on a newly introduced collaborative assessment tool, the New Mum Star. Co-designed by Triangle (originators of the Outcomes Star framework), family nurses, FNP clients and the FNP National Unit, the New Mum Star provides a tool to enable young mothers and family nurses to work together to identify strengths and areas of need. This helps to shape and personalise the content of programme. It also informs decisions about early graduation from the programme or variation in the intensity of visits (Family Nurse Partnership National Unit & Dartington Service Design Lab, 2020).

> "The structure of the New Mum Star guides the developing brain of the young person . . . through a process of reflection and planning. It helps set a framework for . . . breaking down goal planning into manageable chunks. By going back to that repeatedly throughout the programme, you are reinforcing that process and developing these skills, which are important skills for parenthood and for life".
>
> Family Nurse Supervisor

> "The way the tool is structured can also help tackle difficult subjects. Nurses will use their clinical judgement and skill to facilitate a conversation, contributing what they think alongside the [mum's] own assessment. Together they can then talk about where she is on her journey and what she needs to change to move forward".
>
> Family Nurse Supervisor

> "Yeah, I think [the New Mum Star] just . . . it makes people, like the mums think properly of, if they're not doing well in it, how can they improve it, or if

> they're doing good, how can they do anything else to improve it even more, and stuff like that. It definitely helps, and obviously it's made me think more about what I wasn't doing good with him".
>
> FNP client

> "You understand yourself a bit more. You can better express yourself more, it gives you the words really, especially when you're speaking with the family nurse".
>
> FNP client

This collaborative and responsive approach to programme development has also led to adaptations in practice to improve responses to intimate partner violence and neglect in FNP in England. Established as a result of feedback from family nurses about a sense of increasing need, in conjunction with emerging evidence from the RCT, the development work drew on insights from the international Nurse Family Partnership community and has been tested and developed in collaboration with FNP teams (Family Nurse Partnership National Unit and Dartington Service Design Lab, 2020). As a result, an enhanced learning package is now in place for all family nurses in England, along with a pathway to guide nurses in identifying and responding to intimate partner violence and neglect, implemented by all FNP teams in 2023.

Lastly, in response to growing demand from commissioners, the FNP National Unit developed a knowledge and skills exchange programme in 2016, built on the evidence-based methods used in FNP. This has led to FNP teams' involvement in workforce development of health visitors and early years practitioners in their local areas, building knowledge and awareness of approaches such as motivational interviewing and how to engage marginalised clients. In this way, FNP skills and knowledge about working with highly vulnerable families can benefit a wider local population beyond those young parents who are eligible for the programme. In some areas, this has also led to significant system developments, including the development of services supported by local FNP teams.

CASE STUDY 7.2

Extending the reach and skills of FNP: Norfolk

Since 2017 the Family Nurse Partnership team in Norfolk have developed and supported a teenage parent pathway. Every young mum-to-be aged 19 and under at conception is eligible for an enhanced service and is offered either Family Nurse Partnership or Teenage Parent Programme. This approach is designed to widen access to evidence-informed practice in the county for young parents and to enhance the developmental progress of their babies.

Teenage parent practitioners provide 16 visits beginning in pregnancy and until the child reaches 2 years of age, including Ages and Stages Questionnaire assessment visits completed every 6 months. Ages and Stages Questionnaires provide a way to measure child development from age 0 to 6. The caseload is held by named health visitors.

The Family Nurse Partnership team supervisor provides clinical triage, assessing the needs of teenage mums-to-be notified by midwives and ensuring the appropriate service is offered according to their needs. Clinical triage is based on their life experiences, including Adverse Childhood Experiences (ACEs), and factors such as: current or previous involvement with children's services or being in care, or having a learning disability, or having a history of mental health services input. The Family Nurse Partnership cohort in Norfolk have an average ACEs score of 6.5, where four ACEs are thought to be detrimental to longer-term health outcomes. Family nurses also provide skills and knowledge training for teenage parent practitioners, as well as group and one-to-one supervision. In addition, the Family Nurse Partnership team provides case discussion supervision sessions for staff across Norfolk who deliver the Healthy Child Programme[4].

This approach expands the impact of Norfolk's Family Nurse Partnership team, from the intensive direct work with 170 teenage parents enrolled in the local FNP programme, to a total of 750 young families who are supported through Norfolk's Teenage Parent Pathway in 2021/22.

Owing to the changes made within Norfolk in 2017, the Family Nurse Partnership Programme is delivered with a focus on urban areas of Norfolk, where there are the highest rates of conception to under-18s. Consistently, these urban areas feature within the relatively most deprived 10 per cent and 20 per cent Lower-layer Super Output Areas nationally.

Despite the increasing vulnerability of the young parents-to-be recruited to FNP within Norfolk, outcomes continue to be positive, with developmental progress of babies and infants evidenced through the use of Ages & States Questionnaires (ASQ: 3 & ASQ: Social & Emotional).

CASE STUDY 7.3

FNP engagement with fathers: Swindon

Leaders in Swindon identified a need to better engage with young fathers to help build their capacity as parents to provide safe, nurturing care for their babies.

The FNP supervisor developed a service model based on theories, practice and implementation underpinning FNP, working alongside a fathers worker and the FNP National Unit.

The father's worker has a therapeutic and early years background. She sits within the FNP team, receiving supervision, psychological and safeguarding support alongside the family nurses. She has a caseload of 16 young fathers whose current or former partners are enrolled in FNP. Most are aged between 16 and 25 years old. Some access a longer programme of one-to-one support, lasting from pregnancy up until their child is aged 12 months; others take part in a shorter programme lasting around six months.

The aim is to enable young fathers to build attachment and parenting skills, while helping them address any poor mental health they may be experiencing or unsafe behaviours, including anger, violence, drug-taking and criminality, often linked to adverse childhood experiences in their own lives. The fathers worker helps young dads understand when their behaviour is unsafe and to take responsibility for being calm and emotionally regulated around their baby. The service provides dedicated help to enable fathers to learn to parent independently, whether or not they remain in a relationship with their child's mother.

The service has also undertaken outreach work with local midwives in response to feedback from young fathers, who said they felt excluded in antenatal and postnatal care which often felt exclusively focused on mothers. Some young fathers talked about not being spoken to in the room during appointments or included in correspondence, or supported to take an active role in the birth when their partner was in labour.

This has helped midwives reflect on how small changes to clinical practice can enable fathers to feel more involved in classes and appointments. This builds opportunities for fathers to develop practical and emotional aspects of their parenting from early on, such as changing a nappy or bathing a baby, as this provides key moments to build attachment through touch, play, singing or talking. Knowledge built during pregnancy through antenatal care can provide fathers with a blueprint for building a bond with their baby after they are born.

A formal qualitative evaluation of the pilot's first 18 months was completed by researchers from Leeds Trinity University. This showed improved short- and medium-term outcomes in aspects such as assessments and identification of a father's needs, professionals' and the fathers' understanding of risk, parental confidence, self-efficacy and parent child relationships, young fathers' behaviours, attitudes, and relationships with others, including receptivity to professionals. Family nurses report lower levels of parental conflict for mothers who are separated from their partner, where the partner is engaged with the father's worker.

There are now around 50 areas in England where FNP is available for young parents in 2023, down from a peak of 132 areas in 2015. FNP is a targeted service for young parents, with evidence of impact, however public health commissioners are under pressure to meet the needs of broad populations at a time of limited resources. The responsiveness to context, led by the FNP National Unit, has led to more personalised programme delivery for young families and a keener focus on FNP teams' integration within local systems, supporting service development and skill-sharing with the wider universal services workforces. For Barnsley Council, which stopped commissioning FNP in 2016, these changes – coupled with FNP's strong evidence base and locally high levels of teenage pregnancy and deprivation – have led to a decision to commission FNP again from 2024 (see the case study in Chapter 6).

7.3 Supporting young parents into education and training

In 1999, as part of the strategy's aim to increase the proportion of young parents in education, employment or training, a new Standards Fund Teenage Pregnancy Grant was introduced for 48 local government areas with high conception rates to help reintegrate and support school age mothers into education, including appointing a dedicated Reintegration Officer. Qualitative research was commissioned in ten areas to understand the facilitators and barriers (Dawson and Hosie, 2005).

The study found that the young women who had a positive experience of education before they became pregnant were more likely to get a supportive response from their school when disclosing their pregnancy and continued to have a good record of attendance and achievement whether attending mainstream school or alternative provision.

However, for many of the young women, pre-existing disengagement from school was a dominant theme in their experience of education. Less than half were attending school regularly at the time they became pregnant. Difficulty with schoolwork, bullying and a sense of failure were all cited as reasons for truancy and increasing levels of non-attendance. The study reported these young women benefitted hugely from attending specialist units and non-school education provision. Attendance was greatly improved during and after pregnancy and they were more likely to continue their education post-16. The role of Reintegration Officers was also key. Whether in mainstream school or specialist provision, young mothers felt better supported in choosing and following the best option for their circumstances. Importantly, Reintegration Officers had a particularly positive impact on young mothers who had previously been missing school – the most vulnerable cohort – suggesting that a dedicated role contributes to narrowing inequalities in education and future life chances.

The study concluded that school age pregnancy in young women, who are already enjoying school and coping well, should not lead to disengagement. Nor is disengagement inevitable for the most vulnerable. With the right provision, and sufficient resources to provide specialist support, pregnancy can provide the opportunity to re-motivate young women to return to learning and build their confidence and aspirations. Recommendations from the study included the provision of specialist education support in all areas, especially for young women with prior negative experiences of education and poor school attendance; the appointment in all areas of Reintegration Officers, or an equivalent dedicated role, to provide the considerable attention needed to support the most vulnerable young women; and for mainstream schools to take on the lessons from specialist units, particularly in relation to developing a non-judgmental and supportive ethos for pupils disclosing pregnancy.

Since 2010 the number of young mothers of statutory school age (16 and under) in England has fallen by 66 per cent (Office for National Statistics, 2023a) from 7,628 to 2,569. However, many of the smaller cohort have similar education experiences to the vulnerable young parents in the study. Of the participants in the FNP trial, 46 per cent had been suspended, expelled or excluded from school. With persistent absence a strong associated risk factor for early pregnancy, the increase in school absence post-COVID-19, is a worrying potential indicator of further education inequality for young parents.

It's a concern therefore that there are no national data on the numbers or locations of specialist school age pregnancy education units or alternative provision. Moat House in Stockport, described below, continues to support young parents to achieve excellent outcomes, but the Meriton Centre featured in the first edition closed in 2017.

CASE STUDY 7.4

Combining nurture with education: Moat House School, Stockport

Moat House in Stockport is a secondary school, with a nursery, founded in 1979 to support 14–19-year-old girls who are pregnant or new mothers. Alongside academic qualifications, Moat House teaches wider life skills, including cookery and parenting. Moat House is supported by Stockport Council with the young mums referred via secondary schools, midwives, Family Nurses or social care.

All the students who attend are studying for English and Maths qualifications, and there is an offer of other GCSEs too, including Science, English Literature, Health and Social Care, Business Studies, Statistics, Art and Religious Studies. The key focus is on education and ambition within an environment described more like a house than a school, with a nurturing family ethos.

Moat House's success can be seen in the examination results students achieve, with most emerging with grades at or above those predicted by baseline assessment, and many students destined for college and/or university.

The school also employs a Mental Health Lead, as many of the students enter parenthood with pre-existing vulnerabilities and need extensive wellbeing support. There is also a Young Parents Educational Lead funded by the council who is based at Moat House and provides bespoke information, advice and guidance to all the students and helps them make the post-16 transition into college.

Moat House provides holistic support for every parent and baby. The school and nursery work closely together, and these links between the two parts are one of the primary reasons for our success. At a very early stage students spend time getting to know the nursery staff and during pregnancy will work with a nursery key worker to complete a "Preparation for Baby" programme – a series of sessions which cover topics such as sterilising bottles and safer sleeping. This is sometimes offered to both parents of the baby if they are a couple and some school age fathers have completed the courses. Baby massage, baby yoga and baby signing classes are also successful at Moat House.

Teenage pregnancy rates dropped during the past decade, and nationally much of the support for young parents elsewhere has been lost. Moat House was also at risk but during a high needs funding review by Stockport Council the potential for its nurturing approach to improve outcomes for other vulnerable young people was recognised. As a result, during the COVID-19 pandemic, Moat House implemented a pilot project to offer its small number of places to those who would benefit, but who were not necessarily young parents.

Today Moat House is thriving, with an offer of 10–15 personalised places for vulnerable young people, who require a bespoke, nurturing approach, alongside the cohort of 12 young parents. Since the start of 2022 Moat House has also experienced a significant increase in referrals from very young parents and has received requests from neighbouring authorities for places for young parents. This reflects an ongoing need for specialist education support for school age parents, particularly those who have previously disengaged from school.

The school and nursery have been consistently rated as Outstanding by Ofsted:

> "The relationships between staff and students are outstanding. There is a culture of mutual respect and care in which students can thrive and make exceptional progress in their learning and wellbeing".
>
> Ofsted Inspection, 2019

There are also no data on young parents continuing in mainstream school. Walsall has an excellent example of wrap around care with a dedicated teenage pregnancy worker and named Education Welfare Officer, with an additional young fathers' worker, (see Chapter 6), but there is no national overview to indicate whether this is the exception or the norm. Neglect of this important issue is underlined somewhat by the Department for Education's failure to review and update the strategy's original *Guidance on the education of school age parents*, published over twenty years ago (Department for Education and Employment, 2001). New guidance for schools and local authorities, *Working Together to Improve School Attendance* (Department for Education, 2022) was published in 2022 but the reference to school age parents was minimal and provided no advice on addressing their sometimes complex needs. Norfolk Council's excellent initiative to develop its own guidance has been very helpful for other local authorities but is filling a gap which arguably should be addressed at national level given the inequalities young parents and their children face.

CASE STUDY 7.5

Pregnant pupils policy for schools: Norfolk

In March 2021 the Medical Needs Service at Norfolk County Council was contacted by the Deputy Clinical Lead for the Norfolk Healthy Child Programme 5–19, to enquire around existing guidance for pupils who are pregnant. Searches quickly revealed that no such guidance existed, at national or local level. Government guidance on school age parents published in 2001 had not been updated and other guidelines referred to pregnant women with no reference to school pupils. The service lead subsequently undertook to develop a Norfolk policy. Links were made with the local Teenage Parent Pathway, with the Healthy Child Programme and the Family Nurse Partnership, to ensure that the policy reflected accurate health guidance as well as education needs.

Research revealed clear links between education and poverty, lower attainment for teenage mothers, persistent absence and an increased likelihood of suspension or exclusion. This highlighted the importance of identifying key strategies to support pregnant pupils, both young mothers and fathers. The draft policy was shared with a wide range of colleagues in both health and education. It includes key links for support for all involved, and guidance on government benefits and access to health services, for example. It was important to provide schools with practical steps to support the young expectant, and then new, mother in school. These range from uniform adaptations, safe spaces, approved absences for medical appointments, seating in assemblies and examination arrangements, to name but a few.

The needs of young fathers and their right to paternity leave are also included. The policy includes a template care plan to be agreed with school, midwife, the pupil(s) and parent carers, so that all parties work together.

The policy was well received and is updated annually in line with statutory guidance such as Keeping Children Safe in Education. It is a measure of the policy's quality that other local authorities have sought to integrate versions of it into their practice (Norfolk County Council, 2022).

7.3.1 Post-16 education

Until 2013 it was compulsory for young people to remain in education until the age of 16, but as a result of the Raising the Participation Age legislation, the law now requires that young people continue in education, employment or training until the age of 18. However, understanding the situation for young parents aged 16 and 17 is similarly impeded by a lack of data.

The Department for Education's statutory guidance for local authorities, *Participation of young people in education employment or training* (Department for Education, 2016) makes minimal reference to young parents. Local authorities are responsible for identifying young parents who are not participating and for ensuring there is appropriate support in place to help them return to education or training as soon as practicable. Young parent is one of the vulnerable 'characteristic' codes which local authorities are asked to record but not all do, and no national data are published to monitor progress. There is also no specific requirement to ask or record whether young men are fathers, even though the responsibilities of parenting are likely to impact on their engagement in education or training (see Connected Young Fatherhood research; section 7.6.4). With the loss of the Connexions Service and diminished local authority resources for the 'NEETs' workforce (Wallace, 2023), it is a concern that young parents – both mothers and fathers – will not receive the additional support needed and risk falling through the gaps.

7.4 Care to Learn childcare funding

Helping young parents with childcare so they could return to education was a specific action of the strategy. Following a pilot of subsidised childcare, the national Care to Learn programme was launched to provide financial support to teenage parents to continue their education or training. To qualify the young person must: be under 20 on the date they start their course or learning programme; be the main carer for their child(ren); be living and studying in England; and meet the residency criteria. The course or learning programme must have some public funding and the childcare must be registered with Ofsted or the Care Quality Commission.

An evaluation in 2009 found Care to Learn played a vital role in increasing the proportion of young parents in education or training, concluding that the success rate for those funded by Care to Learn was comparable to the national average for all learners. "This represents a significant achievement given that young parents are combining learning with childcare responsibilities" (Vaid et al., 2009).

Between 2013/14 and 2022/23 take-up of Care to Learn fell from 5,674 students to 841 (Department for Education, unpublished data). This is explained largely by the significant drop in numbers of young parents, but other factors may also be at play. Some young parents may be in education but using other sources of childcare, including family members, and others may be choosing to delay return to education until their child is older. Lack of publicity about the scheme and fewer dedicated support services to promote it may also be contributory factors.

In 2022 the Department for Education reviewed Care to Learn to test the original hypothesis that providing funding for childcare would help young parents engage in and complete their further education studies. The small study involved meetings and surveys with local service partnerships, education providers and young parents and found unequivocal support for the scheme (Department for Education, unpublished report, 2023). It was concluded that many young parents would be unlikely to engage in education without it, and the Care to Learn funding programme should be retained. Twenty years after the start of the scheme, this was an encouraging sign that the additional needs of young parents are still recognised. The announcement of increased weekly amounts was also welcomed – having stayed at the same level for 20 years – although in some areas of the country it may still be insufficient to cover the rising costs of childcare.

Services, education providers and young parents all called for better publicity of Care to Learn. In the absence of any national promotion, this is left to local areas to ensure all relevant services from maternity to education providers know about and promote the programme. However, publicity alone may not be sufficient to re-engage young parents in education without holistic support to address individual needs and circumstances. Practitioners in the study noted the importance of building rapport, using motivational interviewing and supporting young parents to set achievable goals, while education providers highlighted the importance of flexible timetables, support with home study and access to learning mentors.

CASE STUDY 7.6

Promoting Care to Learn locally: Nottinghamshire

To address the low take-up of Care to Learn in Nottinghamshire, an apprentice working with the Council's Families Information Service developed a publicity leaflet with young parents and the local Family Nurse Partnership.

Over 2,500 leaflets have been distributed to relevant services, with over 100 scans of the QR code featured on the leaflet which directs young parents to the

Government website where they can make their application. The Council will be monitoring the take-up of Care to Learn in the 2023–24 academic year to assess the impact of the publicity.

7.5 Housing for young parents

A specific aim of the strategy was to ensure that all lone young parents who couldn't live at home were given housing with support. This was to address the social isolation, and the challenges young parents can experience from living on their own in independent tenancies. The aim was included in government housing policy led by the Office of the Deputy Prime Minister, later the Department of Communities and Local Government, with resources drawn from relevant funding streams. By 2007 the numbers of single parents living independently without support had dropped by 75 per cent, but around 1,000 remained unsupported. In 2009, as part of the government's child poverty strategy, different models of supported housing for young parents were piloted in seven local areas. The evaluation made six recommendations (Quilgars et al., 2011).

- Young parents need support through a wide variety of housing provision, tailored to their individual need. All types of provision should include courses on developing skills and confidence for independent living, which were highly valued by young parents.
- The support model needs to be delivered flexibly, enabling support workers to provide young parents with help in all areas of their lives, referring on to specialist services when necessary.
- Expectations for returning to education and training needed to be realistic and include long-term goals as well as short term planning.
- The quality of frontline staff was paramount. Young parents greatly valued, and gained substantial confidence from their relationship with support staff if they trusted them and felt able to ask for help without being patronised. The support worker was also critical as a 'hand-holder' along the path to independent living, including accompanying young parents to other services and appointments.
- Further development was needed in the support for young fathers, both in providing one-to-one advice on different aspects of their lives and in commissioning models of housing support which enable couples to live together.
- Improved evidence should be gathered to inform cost benefit analyses of supported housing models.

The case study in Torbay described below (Case study 7.7) is an excellent example of a supported housing model which reflects these recommendations. But there appears to have been no progress on the final recommendation to gather improved evidence, and no data are collected to assess need or provision across the country. However, the importance of secure housing for young parents is evident in reports mentioned earlier, and in a recent longitudinal study of the housing pathways of young parents summarised below. With insecure and unsuitable housing cited as a key contributory factor to poor parental mental health and safeguarding risks for children the apparent lack of policy priority is a concern.

7.5.1 ***Housing Young Parents: the housing experiences and support needs of young mothers and fathers***[5]

Housing Young Parents was a qualitative longitudinal study of the housing pathways, experiences and support needs of young mothers and fathers. The research was conducted in collaboration with a charity that provides housing support to young people. A total of 22 young mothers and fathers participated in interviews and observations and five housing support professionals were also interviewed. Young parents were tracked during a pivotal point in their lives, following their entry into parenthood. Becoming a parent changed their housing needs and aspirations and the study followed their housing pathways as they unfolded.

Family and housing are inextricably linked and connected to the life chances of young parents. A safe, secure and stable home is of essential importance as the foundation of family life. Yet, young parents often have highly precarious housing pathways that are shaped by their relationships and support networks. Living with their own parents can sometimes offer stability if their families have adequate resources to house and support them. However, for those who want, or need, to live independently, their housing choices are highly constrained. In the context of a long-standing and worsening housing crisis, there is limited affordable housing stock, and this means that some young parents are often pushed into accepting housing that is poor quality and/or in an undesirable location (for example, away from their local support networks). While difficult housing experiences can lead to snowballing problems that become overwhelming, having a safe, secure, and quality home provides a base from which young parents can engage in other activities in life, such as education and employment.

Despite a challenging housing landscape for young parents, targeted support can be a critical source of help. Housing support services with a wide reaching and holistic remit, can help bridge the transition to independence, and support young parents to establish and maintain their own family home. However, it is essential that the overall quality and availability of social housing improves to meet the conditions needed for home as a foundation for family life. Young parents would benefit from greater choice and support to make informed decisions around housing, and this could be achieved with an expansion of housing support services to increase their reach and remit.

CASE STUDY 7.7

Accommodation with dedicated support: Torbay

Torbay Council Children's Services commissions Westward Housing to deliver Torbay Young Parents' Service with the aim of providing support and accommodation for young families aged 16–24 to live together successfully in their community. The service provides support in a safe living space for up to 12 months, giving young parents – both single and couples – the opportunity to build skills, knowledge and confidence to move towards living independently. The service offers outreach to young parents waiting to come into the service and resettlement support of up to four weeks for those moving on.

As each parent's situations varies, individual needs are carefully assessed through referral information and trauma informed discussion with the dedicated support workers. Tailored support is provided through a combination of one to one and group support, including developing parenting skills, weaning and cooking, budgeting and tenancy-related support and finding education or voluntary work experience, while a multi-agency approach ensures joined up working with practitioners involved in each family's care. To engage young fathers who are not living as a couple, the service has set up a 'dads group' to provide emotional support and develop practical parenting skills.

Through a partnership with the local authority Family Hub[6], additional onsite input is provided by Action for Children, including a course on babies' brain development, while a local dentist visits to promote understanding and the importance of dental health. Sexual health and contraception are included as part of each parent's support plan with referrals to the local SRH clinic and condoms provided by the c-card trained support worker. Bringing outside agencies into the service which is familiar and comfortable makes it easier for young parents to engage. It also builds their knowledge of and confidence in accessing services when they are living independently.

The cornerstone of the service is the dedicated support workers and the trusted relationship they develop with the young parents. Drawn from a variety of backgrounds, one of the key criteria for recruitment is the passion to work with young parents and their children. To ensure suitability, young parents are involved in the recruitment, showing candidates around and asking them questions and feeding back their views to the interview panel. To date there has been 100 per cent agreement on the best candidates!

The service is monitored through a 'distance travelled' approach, assessing progress across a range of measures, as well as reviewing qualitative feedback from young parents:

> "Since being in my flat I am more independent, and I know I can live by myself and manage my bills".
>
> "I have learnt parenting techniques for the future, and this has made me understand my child more".

7.6 The Importance of Supporting Young Fathers

Since 2018 there has been a welcome increased focus on understanding the lived experience and needs of young fathers. I am grateful to the researchers who have led much of this work for their contributions to this section.

7.6.1 [7]The experience and needs of young fathers

Calls for targeted support for young fathers (commonly defined as young men who enter parenthood up to the age of 25, a quarter of whom are estimated to be under 20) have been growing over the past decade. Evidence gathered through the ESRC-funded *Following Young Fathers* study has provided further impetus for this change (reported fully in Neale and Tarrant, 2024, drawing on and extending earlier evidence: Neale, 2016; Neale and Lau Clayton, 2014; Neale and Davies, 2015, 2016; Neale and Patrick, 2016; Ladlow and Neale, 2016; Tarrant and Neale, 2017a, 2017b). This qualitative longitudinal study explored the lived experiences and support needs of a diverse sample of young fathers over time and sought to consolidate a scattered body of existing evidence to better inform policy and professional practice. The aim was to facilitate a greater congruence between the lived experiences of young fathers and policy and practice responses.

A growing body of research evidence reveals that for much of the 21st century, young fathers have been neglected in British policy and professional practice. During implementation of the Teenage Pregnancy Strategy, attempts were made to understand and address the needs of young fathers (Teenage Pregnancy Independent Advisory Group, 2002; Clark, 2002; Department for Children, Schools and Families and Department of Health, 2007), but no benchmarking mechanisms or national frameworks were put in place to turn principles into practice and embed and sustain the changes needed. Nor were there any developments to collect health or educational data for young fathers, despite them often experiencing poor outcomes.

The marginalisation of young fathers has been reinforced by a *social deficit* model of young fatherhood, a moral condemnation of these young men for supposedly running away from their responsibilities and 'causing' the ills that they suffer (although research evidence suggests that only a small minority of young fathers are likely to fall into this category; Neale and Tarrant, 2024). This stigmatising of young fathers is pervasive, and doubly so for young men who also face the additional stigma of poverty and welfare dependency. This neglect of young fathers in policy and professional practice has created a policy vacuum that has enabled a *social deficit* model to flourish.

Over the past decade the increasing research focus on exploring the lived experiences of young fathers has brought a welcome shift in perspective. The *Following Young Fathers* study, and the *Following Young Fathers Further* and *Connected Young Fatherhood* research summarised below, are part of a wider pool of studies that have sought to understand the dynamics of young fathers' transitions into parenthood and beyond. We know that most enter parenthood in an unplanned way, without access to adequate relationship and sex education or guidance – at school or at home (Sex Education Forum Poll, 2022); that they struggle with the 'unreal' time of the pregnancy and may face ongoing stress and anxiety in their lives as they try to fulfil their new responsibilities. The professional neglect and stigma that they face compounds these difficulties. It creates an emotional burden that impacts on their identities as parents and their capacity to fulfil their responsibilities, and it may have negative consequences on their mental health for years to come (Neale and Tarrant, 2024).

At the same time, this body of literature consistently shows that young fathers develop deep and enduring commitments to their children. They wish to be engaged fathers, to 'be there' for mother and child, to provide for them through a breadwinner role, and to be acknowledged by service providers and in public discourses as young men with an important contribution to make, who are deserving of support and encouragement. This *social engagement framework* for understanding young fathers is evident regardless of the young men's socio-economic and relationship status, and the many challenges that they face as young parents (Neale and Tarrant, 2024). Fatherhood offers a chance to change their lives, to grow up a little faster, to set new goals and improve their life chances. Parenthood becomes an accomplishment, a source of pride and responsibility, and a potential source of giving and receiving love (Arai, 2009; SmithBattle, et al., 2019). Moreover, there is mounting evidence to suggest than when young fathers are engaged in these ways, this can be beneficial to them, the mothers and their children (Wilson and Prior, 2011; Neale and Tarrant, 2024).

This is not to deny the social problems and challenges that many young fathers face. Those who are well resourced, with educational skills, stable homes and supportive family backgrounds have the capacity to manage their fatherhood responsibilities with relative ease and are likely to sustain their parenting commitments over time. However, those who are poorly resourced are more likely to face downward trajectories, shaped not simply in relation to their parenthood status, but prefigured by poverty, difficult childhoods, unstable families, and a lack of educational, employment and housing opportunities. The challenges are compounded for those young men who engage in offending behaviour linked to drug and alcohol abuse, and/or who experience volatile relationships with young mothers and the maternal households. Where an accumulation of these problems occurs over time, they are more likely to lose contact with their children. They may also need sustained professional support to manage the deep suffering that arises from impoverished childhoods and associated relational and mental health problems. Given the depth of these problems, it is striking that a substantial majority of young fathers remain committed to their children and continue to strive to be good fathers.

A *social engagement* framework for understanding the lives and support needs of young fathers needs to sit alongside and tempers the *social problems* evidence, offering a more balanced, holistic and empirically driven framework for shaping policy responses. It also provides an important corrective to existing assumptions and prejudices that lead to a *social deficit* model of young fatherhood. In policy and professional practice there is a clear need to develop new cultures of understanding that enable young fathers to be seen in a different and more compassionate way (Neale, 2016; Neale and Tarrant, 2024).

7.6.2 How services respond to young fathers

The evidence presented suggests that young fathers deserve to be supported not only for what they can contribute to their children's lives, but as young and often vulnerable young men who may have experienced deep suffering in their earlier years. The *Following Young Fathers* study shows just how difficult it is for young fathers to invest in their roles and identities as fathers when their own basic needs as young citizens are not being met. A *social engagement* framework for understanding young fathers has been slow to feed into policy and professional practice and research evidence that is scattered and difficult to access creates a knowledge gap for professional practice. Moreover, there is a lack of demographic evidence upon which to base practice developments or gauge their effectiveness. If young fathers don't seem to count, it is because they are not routinely counted, or even identified. Acknowledging young fathers in policy documents carries little weight without clear directives and funding streams to enable local providers to turn principles into practice, particularly where there are no reliable data around which targets can be built and effectiveness monitored and appraised.

For much of the past two decades, evidence from a range of studies, including *Following Young Fathers,* shows a tendency for practitioners across the statutory sector to treat these young men with uncertainty and suspicion. A culture of discretion for professionals in their treatment of young fathers has perpetuated their invisibility and the tendency for them to remain unrecognised and under-served. Professional support is commonly tempered by cultures of surveillance and sidelining. Surveillance stems from the assumption that young fathers are irresponsible and a potential risk to themselves or to their children. While safeguarding assessments and actions are critically important, surveillance without support can undermine young fathers' confidence and potential for change:

> I feel like I've got to act perfect . . . do what they say and if I don't then summat bad is gonna happen.

Sidelining is a pernicious practice in which young fathers are effectively ignored or shown the door, rather than welcomed as clients (Neale and Davies, 2015; Neale and Tarrant, 2024):

> It was like I wasn't there. They didn't speak to me. They didn't involve me . . . I said (to the midwife), 'how come you never address me? When you've got something to say about my son you never tell me'. . . and she just said it's easier and she's mum after all . . .

Sidelining can also occur at an organisational level, where services fail to publicise support for young fathers, or where schools and colleges refuse fathers time off to attend maternity appointments. More benignly, perhaps, practitioners may view young fathers as 'hard to reach', underpinned by assumptions that they are not interested in a role as a parent or deserving of professional support. This is no less harmful. It places the onus for engaging with services on young men themselves, when the reality can be turned on its head: the services themselves are hard to access (Hadley, 2014; Neale, 2016). The concept of hard to reach can often be a mask for easy to ignore.

Young fathers are fully aware of such stigmatising practices. Sidelining or judgmental attitudes may colour their responses to practitioners, creating a vicious circle of non-engagement and mutual distrust, and cementing the disengagement of young fathers from services (Neale and Davies, 2015; Neale and Tarrant, 2024). The underlying problem is the policy vacuum in which service providers develop their practice. In a context of unclear remits, limited resources, lack of knowledge and few targets and benchmarking tools, practitioners have been working very much in the dark.

Despite this picture, pockets of provision based on a social engagement model of young fatherhood, and driven by an ethos of support, have been under development for some years in selected local authority areas, although provision remains highly patchy and largely confined to specialist services. Evidence from the *Following Young Fathers* study shows that such provision is greatly valued by young fathers:

> [It was] the best support you can have really. . . . I didn't have a clue what I was doing, like, I was skiving school . . . but he got me referred onto college, and that got me back into education, right. . . .Well I'd have been lost [without him].

Where statutory service providers (e.g. maternity units, or children's centres) have used their discretion to seek out and welcome young fathers and to support their efforts, this can also make a huge difference to young men's trust and confidence, with behavioural changes costing nothing:

> [The hospital staff] involved both of us . . .There was a lot of laughing and joking. The staff and scans . . . they was all fantastic . . . They explained what the pregnancy's going to be like and giving birth . . . .It was really good.
>
> (Institute of Health Visiting, 2014)

A separate small study in Lincolnshire further illustrates the impact of simple, no cost initiatives that are father-inclusive. The health visiting team increased the participation of fathers in the Primary Birth Visit from 20 per cent to 70 per cent simply by changing the wording of their 'invitation' letter (from *Dear Parent*, to *Dear new Mum and Dad*), and making clear that they wished to arrange 'an appointment that is convenient for you both'.

Some overarching principles for re-thinking support for young fathers have been sharpened through The *Following Young Fathers* study (Neale and Tarrant, 2024):

- Moving from a presumption that young fathers are a problem, to a starting point in all services that the involvement of young fathers is beneficial to the young mother, their child and the young man himself.
- Ensuring the small minority of serious safeguarding cases are not perceived as the norm.
- Identifying and including young fathers in all early assessments and providing tailored support that can be sustained over time to meet their individual needs.
- Using dedicated practitioners to provide specialist support for vulnerable young fathers but also to model effective working for non-specialist practitioners to develop a supportive ethos in universal as well as targeted services.

More recent policy directives (Public Health England and Local Government Association 2016, 2019) have begun to put these principles into practice, helping to raise awareness of the value of young-father-inclusive practices across a range of mainstream settings. The Royal College of Midwives have published a new Engaging Fathers Pocket Guide and series of resources (2023), developed with the Fatherhood Institute to help midwives and other support staff engage effectively with fathers. Hopefully this will be widely shared and adopted by maternity staff. However, critical to sustained improvements in culture and practice will be building awareness and skills into midwifery training. This applies to the training of all practitioners working with families, such as health visitors and those working in the new Family Hubs.

There are also encouraging developments in the commissioning of services. The Family Nurse Partnership development of a bespoke support service for young fathers has been long awaited but is very welcome (see Case Study 7.3), with the learning being picked up and developed in other FNP sites. WILD young parents (see Case Study 7.11) is an inspiring VCS example of recognising and addressing the needs of young fathers. This is creating a much-needed sea change in cultures of professional support, although a lot remains to be done to roll out and co-ordinate such support across local authority areas and provide the necessary funding to invest in the futures of young men and their children.

A range of creative initiatives (some of which utilise research-practice partnerships) are also under way to put these new principles into practice, as the case studies below show.

7.6.3 Co-creating father-inclusive support pathways with and for young fathers[8]

Funded £1.7 million through the UKRI Future Leaders Fellowship scheme, Following Young Fathers Further (FYFF, 2020–27) is the most extended international and qualitative longitudinal study about young fatherhood globally. FYFF builds from a cumulative set of studies in the UK that have established a dynamic evidence base about young fathers and built collaborative partnerships between young fathers, practitioners, and policy makers over time for the purposes of enriching and enhancing professional practice and policy. Two notable studies include the baseline, *Following Young Fathers* (Neale and Lau Clayton, 2010–15), and an applied fatherhood research study called *Responding to Young Fathers in a Different Way* (Tarrant and Neale, 2017a).

Since January 2020 the FYFF team has followed a cohort of 42 young fathers over time, ten of whom participated in the original FYF study and ten of whom are young fathers in Sweden. The team has captured their evolving parenting journeys and support needs against a backdrop of recent global and socio-economic crises, not least the COVID-19 pandemic and the more recent cost of living crisis. The comparative empirical research with British and Swedish fathers has confirmed that young fathers in both countries express clear intentions to 'be there' for their children, aligning with shifting cultural imperatives towards engaged fatherhood (Andreasson et al., 2020).

The FYFF findings indicate that compared with young fathers in Sweden, British young fathers are heavily undermined in their efforts for father engagement by the conditional nature of austerity driven welfare policies, restrictive parental leave systems, and precarious youth labour markets. During the pandemic, a period of rapid policy and practice change, existing social disadvantages experienced by young fathers were further compounded as they navigated their parenting journeys (Tarrant et al., 2022). Combined with the challenges support services were also experiencing in reducing the spread of the virus and focusing their efforts on shifting their support online, the support needs of young families intensified at the very same time that services were under unique pressures to remain afloat (Tarrant et al., 2022).

The qualitative longitudinal timeframes of the linked FYFF studies have also underscored new innovations that prioritise support for young fathers. In particular, the team has collaborated with young fathers and multi-agency professionals who champion young fathers to co-create new place-based social interventions premised on a model of effective practice called the Young Dads Collective (Coram Family and Child Care, 2017). Two place-based models have been co-created since 2016: the Young Dads Collective North and the Grimsby Dads Collective. Each has provided unique opportunities for young fathers and professionals to challenge the broader exclusion of fathers from services and to address the complex set of barriers that professionals and services face in instigating father-inclusive practice and support offers (Pfitzner et al., 2017; Tarrant, 2023). The co-creation methodoogy, supported by the QL timeframes of the FYFF study, has facilitated new and productive relational ecologies and dialogues between young fathers and multi-agency professionals over time, for the purpose of co-designing and creating bespoke training and parenting education programmes. Based on the view that young fathers are 'experts by experience' these unique support offers have enhanced the social and familial participation of young fathers by supporting them to develop new skills and newfound confidence in themselves. They have also directly informed the training of multi-agency professionals as part of the continuous professional development by advocating on behalf of themselves and others about the broader benefits of father-inclusion.

CASE STUDY 7.8

The Grimsby Dads Collective (GDC): North East Lincolnshire.

The Grimsby Dads Collective is a community-driven support intervention founded in Grimsby, a town in North East Lincolnshire, UK. Unique in the specialist father support space, the GDC has been co-created with and for young fathers. Guided by Professor Anna Tarrant, the co-creation process has brought together both local and national partners including Coram Family and Child Care, NSPCC Together for Childhood, YMCA Humber and the Following Young Fathers Further research team. In collaboration, the GDC is working together to tackle what is a general but complex problem that cannot be addressed by one group alone. In response to evidence that young fathers feel sidelined and/or subject to surveillance in their interactions with professionals (Neale and Davies, 2015; Neale and Tarrant, 2017a), the shared aim is to co-create and embed father-inclusive support pathways and environments, with and for young fathers, in a support context that is 'mother-centric' and excludes fathers, including those 'on the margins' (Bateson et al., 2017; Ferguson, 2016).

The GDC builds on an existing model of effective practice called the Young Dads Collective (Coram Family and Childcare, 2017) and a replicated version in the North of England (May et al., 2017; Tarrant and Neale, 2017a). Identified by practitioners in Grimsby as a potential solution for offering more enhanced support for marginalised fathers, a core aim of co-creating the GDC was to support and empower young fathers, both as engaged fathers and as citizens, in an area of the UK where rates of teenage pregnancy and adolescent parenthood remain relatively high.

The GDC has multiple strands. In a national and regional context where young fathers are under-served, it creates a space for young fathers to benefit from and provide peer support to one another. In collaboration with professionals, the model trains young fathers as 'experts by experience'. They are supported to develop their narratives about their experiences and support needs as fathers and to advocate on behalf of themselves and others to audiences of multi-agency professionals through the co-delivery of bespoke training. In particular, young fathers promote strengths- rather than risk-based views of young fatherhood, as well as the broader benefits of father-inclusive practice for the whole family. Core to the theory of change is the transformation of the existing support and policy ecosystem, on a platform of knowledge exchange that is rooted in lived experience and the existing evidence base.

As the Grimsby Dads Collective continues to develop and make a positive impact on the lives of local fathers and their families, it serves as a replicable model for other communities to create similar support offers that empower young dads in their essential role as caregivers and enhance their opportunities for their more comprehensive social participation in their families and society.

CASE STUDY 7.9

DigiDAD: an e-learning programme for young fathers: North East England.

With the North-East Young Dads and Lads, a specialist support service for young fathers in the North East of England, the FYFF team are also co-creating creative content with and for young fathers for a pioneering and innovative e-learning platform. A key aim of the e-learning platform is to provide young fathers with an online community and comprehensive early years (age 0–2) parenting and relationship skills support, addressing gaps in their informational needs. Currently, the platform hosts over 40 films and animations featuring the voices and/or images of young fathers and professionals. These cover a diverse range of topics from early parenting, court and law proceedings, and perinatal mental health. The content on the platform is used by NEYDL's staff in their one-to-one work with young dads and can also be accessed by young dads independently, whether they are engaged with NEYDL or not.

7.6.4 'Connected Young Fatherhood': young fathers' experience of employment post-pandemic[9]

'Connected Young Fatherhood' was a collaborative research study between Leeds Trinity University, the County Councils Network, DaddiLife, and Leeds City Council, funded by Research England. Building on from the '*New Pathways for Young Fathers'* project (Clayton and Lee, 2020), the study explored young fathers' employment experiences since the pandemic and the resulting implications on employment pathways and professional support. Online and telephone Interviews were conducted with 15 professionals in the family sector, six employers and 25 young fathers.

The study found that all the young fathers were deeply committed to their children and felt that paid employment was beneficial in terms of providing financial stability for their family. Young fathers also felt that paid work offered other benefits, such as enhancing feelings of self-pride, being a good role model for their children and fostering positive mental health. Since the pandemic, there was a heavier emphasis upon the importance of finding or staying in roles which offered job security. This was particularly seen within the accounts of young fathers who lost their jobs during lockdowns and by those who did not benefit from the furlough scheme.

Young fathers who expressed positive employment experiences, in terms of job security, recognition, adequate pay, feeling respected, having an empathetic manager and having flexible working conditions, reported higher levels of job satisfaction and often had better opportunities to develop professionally. For this group of young fathers, the pandemic had initiated agile ways of working, which they were keen to maintain post-lockdown, given the benefits it had for balancing home and work life, alongside a sense of control and well-being.

On the other hand, the negative impacts of the pandemic, coupled with the cost of living crisis, have left some young men feeling vulnerable and 'stuck' within their current occupations, or out of work itself. Regional inequalities in relation to work opportunities, and the evidence of pay gaps, job insecurity, discrimination within the workplace, and poor mental health (because of working conditions), were expressed by many of the young fathers who we spoke to. These difficulties could then lead to negative impacts in other areas of their lives, including reports of poor health and challenging family relationships.

When young fathers experienced difficulties in their work or family life, it was clear that professionals were in a prime position to support them. If young fathers are able to build trusting relationships with professionals, and where support is respectful, this can then make a significant difference to the young fathers in terms of being listened to, developing appropriate coping mechanisms, and improved decision-making. The study found a small number of examples of good practice across the country, but provision on the whole for young fathers (and young parents) has been reduced over the years which can have significant implications.

Employers too can play a vital role in supporting young fathers, particularly through a more understanding approach which recognises that young fathers may feel at risk at the workplace due to discriminatory views and gendered expectations around working parents (e.g. assumptions that mothers rather than fathers will be the ones who attend to childcare issues and appointments). Better training around the needs of young fathers and the creation of more inclusive practices and policies in the workplace would be beneficial here. Employers expressed a desire to better support young fathers but cited the need for appropriate funding and information from Government about available help for employees.

7.7 Promoting effective practice: national guidance – what has happened, what more needs to be done

As we reported in the previous edition, in 2016, responding to requests from local areas for national evidence-based guidance, Public Health England developed a new *Framework for supporting teenage mothers and young fathers.* The Framework enshrined the principle of all areas providing young parents with dedicated support starting early in pregnancy and continued through a co-ordinated care pathway, with close multi-agency collaboration. To help each agency understand their role, an infographics format was used to highlight the relevance of young parents to the priorities of each individual service, with key actions for tailored support designed as a self-assessment checklist. The Framework was updated in 2019 and promoted to local areas with a briefing from the Local Government Association urging councillors to continue a focus on young parents to reduce inequalities, and to commission specialist support in line with the national guidance.

The case studies below, and others described in this chapter, are encouraging examples of locally funded specialist support which reflect the evidence and the guidance recommendations.

7.7.1 Current examples of specialist support provided by the NHS, VCS organisations and Local Authorities

CASE STUDY 7.10

Specialist maternity team for young parents: East Sussex Healthcare Trust.

Following the publication of The Better Birth Maternity review in 2016, East Sussex Healthcare Trust piloted three Continuity of Carer teams in 2018. In July 2019 one of these teams was restructured as The Lighthouse Team, providing continuity of care and an enhanced service for young parents under 20 and those aged 20–22 with additional vulnerabilities.

This decision was prompted by the high under-18 maternity rate in Hastings, which in 2017 was 68 per cent higher than the England average (Office for National Statistics, 2023a-d). Hastings is the 13th-most deprived local area in England which contributes to the vulnerability of young parents and their children with regards to financial difficulties, domestic abuse, substance misuse and smoking, mental health difficulties and safeguarding concerns.

As young parents often find accessing care difficult for a number of social, emotional or financial reasons, the Lighthouse Team provides ante and postnatal support in various settings to suit the family. This is usually in their home which provides a more relaxed setting for the team to offer their holistic care approach. This has resulted in a low rate of missed appointments, more consistent monitoring and better maternal and infant outcomes including lower rates of small for gestational age babies. Depending on individual need the team can offer extra antenatal appointments and additional support with emotional wellbeing and mental health issues, and any safeguarding concerns. Working closely with other services, the team signposts and supports young parents to access antenatal education and specialist advice on benefits and housing and healthy pregnancy support for smoking cessation, substance misuse, nutrition and exercise.

In the postnatal period families are seen for 28 days on an individualised care basis for clinical checks, feeding support, emotional support and parenting advice. Discussion about their preferred method of post-partum contraception starts in the 28th week of pregnancy with the midwifery team able to provide three months of contraceptive pills, the contraceptive injection or implant. Alternatively, they are referred to local sexual and reproductive health outreach services for further contraception needs.

Funded by NHS England the Lighthouse Team is made up of seven full-time equivalent midwives and is led by the specialist midwife for young parents. Each midwife has a caseload of up to 28 per year and they provide 24/7 cover for intrapartum care with the families followed to the obstetric unit or supported for home births. Regular 'meet the team' events occur to invite the caseload to meet each other for support and to meet the team midwives in preparation for labour. Some additional funding from the Local Maternity System has increased midwifery hours and enabled the appointment of a care co-ordinator/administrator to assist the team. Further plans include exploring how best to support young fathers.

CASE STUDY 7.11

WILD Young Parents: Cornwall.

WILD Young Parents is the largest British voluntary sector young parent organisation supporting over 15,000 parents and children over the past 30 years. Based in Cornwall and part funded by Cornwall Council, WILD aims to give young parent families a fair start and to prevent repeated patterns of intergenerational trauma and adversity. Informed by evidence, learning from families and developing a theory of change, WILD has built a model that bridges the practice gap between what babies need from their parents and how young parents can overcome the cumulative barriers to provide this.

WILD delivers over 700 group sessions for young parents and their babies across Cornwall, reaching 600 families and working more intensively with 350 families, including longer term help for families experiencing care-proceedings and individual support for young fathers. As well as providing trauma informed support, creativity is a central component of WILD's approach to build confidence and resilience. Early years music and language projects nurture child development while young parents are involved in WILD allotments, a WILD choir, and art projects – resulting in a young father's national exhibition – and a new theatre project called the Rant Club. Developed with Trifle Gathering Productions, a trauma informed theatre social impact theatre group, the project enables a safe connection with anger and frustration through imagination, bravery and storytelling.

WILD assesses the individual needs of each parent, and tailors the type and intensity of support accordingly. The impact is regularly monitored through surveys with young parents and significant improvements shown on parental and infant mental health, parenting confidence and enjoyment, and health issues. Families facing more complex challenges who have safeguarding plans or who are at risk of their child being taken into care have shown greater improvement when WILD provides more intensive support. The most popular reasons parents gave for being with WILD were the friendship, sense of belonging and shared experience with other parents, and the support they received in feeling welcomed, safe, comforted, included and being able to talk about difficult experiences without judgement.

WILD works in close partnership with local services. The CEO is the VCS representative on Cornwall's Safeguarding Children Partnership and the team is represented in local food, housing and mental wellbeing alliances, MARAC (Multi-agency risk assessment conference), multi-agency suicide prevention and perinatal mental health groups, and the new Start for Life plan. Training is also provided for health visitors, foundation for life team, early years leads and childminders.

WILD has now formed a national Young Parent Network, to connect and share ideas, collaborate and learn and be part of a collective national voice for young parent families.

CASE STUDY 7.12

HomeStart Teenage Pregnancy Project: Manchester

Manchester City Council has a long history of providing support services for young parents. Since 2022 the service has been commissioned by Public Health through Home-Start, an organisation with a successful track record in supporting parents of all ages, with a dedicated Co-ordinator providing a key point of contact and working closely with other services.

With many young parents having a history of Adverse Childhood Experiences, chaotic lifestyles and little or no support from their own families, their needs are often complex. By establishing a strong relationship with the young parents, the Co-ordinator is able to explore their situation to identify their needs and co-ordinate tailored support during pregnancy and in the transition to parenthood. Support can be weekly and may include priority issues, such as housing, finance and safeguarding concerns, but also focuses on building young parents' self-esteem and confidence in parenting and exploring their future aspirations.

Reflecting the evidence from Sure Start Plus, having a trusted adviser is the cornerstone of the project, enabling young parents to share their feelings and needs without fear of judgement.

Most young parents are referred early in pregnancy from Manchester's young people's specialist midwives, facilitated by the Co-ordinator attending their clinic. Other sources of referrals include school safeguarding leads and local sexual and reproductive health services.

Key to delivering effective support for young parents is the Co-ordinator's established relationship with other services. Strong links with education, mental health, family hubs, SureStart and sexual health help with swift referrals. The Co-ordinator also attends Social Care multi-agency meetings to ensure information sharing and safeguarding as appropriate.

The impact of the project is measured by parents self-assessment at the start and end of support and regular intervals in between. Listening to what young parents want and need will be central to further development of the project.

CASE STUDY 7.13

Working together with care experienced young parents to build new and supportive relationships: Hertfordshire.

Ohana is a free support group established in Hertfordshire in direct response to the voices of care experienced young parents. Many new parents feel disconnected from friends and family but those with care experience where traditional family and social networks are more limited, reported an added sense of isolation, which made the already challenging job of parenting even harder. This was particularly exacerbated during and after the pandemic. Ohana has been developed with care experienced young parents to help them and their children build new and supportive relationships, outside of the professional world.

Funded by Hertfordshire County Council, Ohana is staffed by a blend of employed co-ordinators and volunteers, and has a three part offer: drop-ins to a peer support group which meets weekly, face to face or online, organises fun and holiday activities and days out, offers courses such as 'My Baby's Brain, and brings in guest speakers and other services in response to interest or needs of the group; access to an Ohana Champion, a volunteer who offers emotional and practical support on a long term basis; and support from Lifelong Links which helps to find and bring together people who can provide support in the future.

Young parents can access all or part of the Ohana offer as they choose; some seeking regular contact, some more intensive support and some joining the group for holiday activities.

As the key aim of Ohana is to respond effectively to the needs of care experienced young parents, their inclusion has been a cornerstone from the start. They were involved in drawing up the job descriptions of the Ohana Champions, take part in the two-day DBS training of the volunteers and are on the interview panel.

Ohana young parents are also sharing their care experience to influence and improve social work practice more widely. They have contributed to the 'post card' messages for corporate parents developed by the Children's Social Care Research and Development Centre (CASCADE) at Cardiff University and ran a workshop at the East of England Social Work Conference.

The benefits of Ohana are best illustrated in the testimonies of young parents but it has also been praised by Ofsted in the 2023 HCC Children's services outstanding Ofsted judgement.

> "I wanted to say thank you for all your support and Ohana is amazing. I struggle to feel happy, but I always feel genuinely happy when I come to the group, so thank you again".
>
> "I don't know what I would do without Ohana. It has really helped me. I am more of a woman now all thanks to the group".
>
> "Ohana means family and family means nobody gets left behind or forgotten".

7.8 Scaling up action to make further progress

In taking stock of developments on the support for young parents since 2018, two main elements stand out.

First, stark inequalities persist. While the number of young parents is much reduced, many of those entering parenthood appear to be carrying an increased burden of vulnerabilities which contributes to poorer outcomes for them and their children. Of particular concern is the increase in some of the drivers of both pre-existing risk factors and poorer parent and child wellbeing resulting from reduced funding, the COVID-19 pandemic and the cost-of-living crisis; most notably, family poverty, young people's poor mental health, school absence and delays in child development.

Second, despite significant funding challenges, it is clear from the case studies collected that much good practice is in place, more is being learned from the further development of FNP and there is a growing focus on understanding and meeting the needs of young fathers. However, although the FNP National Unit in Department of Health and Social Care provides leadership on the FNP programme, there is no national strategic overview of the arrangements all local areas have in place, nor a specific outcomes framework with relevant indicators to assess national and local progress on outcomes. As a result, it is not possible to know whether there is an equitable offer of support for young parents across the country, or whether inequalities are narrowing or widening. Moreover, reference to the national Framework (Public Health England and Local Government Association, 2016; updated 2019) is missing from some key policy guidance. The following actions are suggested to help re-establish a system wide approach to young parents, scale up effective support and monitor progress.

Improving understanding of need and effective action

- In consultation with local areas, update the national multi-agency Framework for supporting teenage mothers and young fathers; incorporate a trauma informed approach, and develop a self-assessment tool for partnerships to identify and address gaps;
- promote the updated Framework through established channels reaching relevant NHS and local authority and ICB leads involved in the commissioning of maternity, early years, young people and family support services;
- strengthen reference to the additional needs of young parents and include link to the Framework in relevant policy guidance, for example Family Hubs and Supporting Families; and
- strengthen the skills of relevant practitioners in NHS and local authority commissioned services by including awareness of young parents needs and the impact of complex vulnerabilities in initial and post-qualification training.

Improving data collection and information to monitor progress

- Disaggregate and report on routinely collected maternal and infant data by age of mother;
- Develop a specific outcomes framework, building on the Fingertips Teenage Pregnancy Profiles to include data on young mothers and their children to monitor progress at national and local level;
- develop indicators for measuring health, education and wellbeing outcomes for young fathers;
- draw on the learning from well-established support services to develop an evaluation tool to help local services measure their impact;

- draw on research and consultations with young mothers and fathers to inform practice; and
- promote learning and effective practice through relevant networks, for example the National Teenage Pregnancy Midwifery Network, the newly established Young Parents Forum and the Following Young Fathers Further network.

Finally, significant progress will hinge on adequate resourcing as highlighted by the Royal College of Paediatrics and Child Health (State of Child Health, 2022). Not only sufficient funding for local areas to deliver the universal and specialist services required, but also funding to address the underlying drivers of disadvantage and inequality.

Notes

1 Family Nurse Partnership is an intensive home-visiting programme for first-time young mothers and families.
2 With thanks to Jo Davies, CEO Wild Young Parents, for sharing this approach of presenting outcomes in the frame of the UNCRC.
3 The Early Intervention Foundation (EIF) is an NGO established in 2013 and is one of the British Government's 'What Works Centres'. EIF evaluates evidence and provides advice on effective early intervention to improve outcomes for children and young people.
4 The Health and Social Care Act 2012 sets out a local authority's statutory responsibility for commissioning public health services for children and young people aged 0 to 19 years. The Healthy Child Programme aims to bring together health, education and other main partners to deliver an effective programme for prevention and support.
5 Housing Young Parents: a micro-dynamic study of the housing experiences and support needs of young mothers and fathers Linzi Ladlow. PhD 2015–2021 University of Leeds. With thanks to Linzi Ladlow for contributing this section of text.
6 In 2022 a total of 75 local authorities in England received funding to establish Family Hubs. These bring together a range of services to be a 'one stop shop' for families with babies, children and young people from birth until they reach the age of 19 (or up to 25 for young people with special educational needs and disabilities).
7 With thanks to Professor Bren Neale for contributing this section of text.
8 With thanks to Professor Anna Tarrant, University of Lincoln, for contributing this section of text.
9 With thanks to Professor Carmen Clayton, Leeds Trinity University, for contributing this section of text.

References

Alrouh et al. (2022). Mothers in recurrent care proceedings: new evidence for England and Wales. Nuffield Family Justice Observatory.

Andreasson, J., Tarrant, A., Ladlow, L., Johansson, T. and Way, L. (2020). Perceptions of gender equality and engaged fatherhood among young fathers: parenthood and the welfare state in Sweden and the UK, *Families, Relationships and Societies*.

Arai, L. (2009). *Teenage Pregnancy: The Making and Unmaking of a Problem*. Bristol: Policy Press.

Barnes, J. *et al.* (2012). *Nurse Family Partnership Implementation Evaluation*. London: Birkbeck University of London.

Bateson, K., Darwin, Z. Galdas, P. and Rosan, C. (2017). Engaging fathers: Acknowledging the barriers, *Journal of Health Visiting,* 5(3), 126–132.

The Child Safeguarding Practice Review Panel (2021). Fieldwork report: National Review of Non-Accidental Injury in Under-1s.

Clark, E. (2002). *Baby Fathers: New Images of Teenage Fatherhood.* With a foreword by Cathy Hamlyn, Head of the Teenage Pregnancy Unit. London: Teenage Pregnancy Unit.

Coram Family and Child Care (2017). *Left Out: How Young Dads Access Services in North East London. www.familyandchildcaretrust.org/young-dads-collective* (accessed 25 July 2023).

Crawford, C., Cribb, J. and Kelly, E. (2013). Teenage Pregnancy in England. CAYT Impact Study, report number 6. London Centre for Analysis of Youth Transitions, NatCen, IoE, IFS.

Dawson, N. and Hosie, A. (2005). The Education of Pregnant Young Women and Young Mothers in England. University of Newcastle and University of Bristol.

Department for Children, Schools and Families and the Department of Health (2007). *Teenage Parents, Next Steps. Guidance for Local Authorities and Primary Care Trusts.* London: DCSF.

Department for Education (2022). Working together to improve school attendance. Guidance for maintained schools, academies, independent schools and local authorities.

Department for Education (2016). Participation of young people in education, employment or training. Statutory guidance for local authorities.

Department for Education and Skills (2001). 'Education of School Age Parents' Circular DfES/0629/2001.

Early Intervention Foundation (2015/2021). *Early Intervention Foundation Guidebook.* London: EIF.

Family Nurse Partnership National Unit and Dartington Service Design Lab (2020).

Ferguson, H. (2016). Patterns of Engagement and Non-Engagement of Young Fathers in Early Intervention and Safeguarding Work. *Social Policy and Society*, 15, 99–111.

Following Young Fathers. 2015. *Briefing Papers 1–8.* University of Leeds.

Hadley, A. (2014) Teenage pregnancy: huge progress . . . but more to do. Community Practitioner, 87(6), 44–47.

Hogg, S. and Mayes, G., (2022). First 1001 Days Movement and Institute of Health Visiting. Casting Long Shadows: The ongoing impact of the covid-19 pandemic on babies, their families and the services that support them.

Institute of Health Visiting (2014). *Good Practice Points for Health Visitors. Engaging with Fathers.* London: Institute of Health Visiting.

Joseph Rowntree Foundation (2023). The essential guide to understanding poverty in the UK.

Joseph Rowntree Foundation (2023) Destitution in the UK 2023.

Knight, M., Bunch, K., Patel, R., Shakespeare, J., Kotnis, R., Kenyon, S. and Kurinczuk, J.J. (Eds), on behalf of MBRRACE-UK (2022). Saving Lives, Improving Mothers' Care Core Report – Lessons learned to inform maternity care from the UK and Ireland Confidential Enquiries into Maternal Deaths and Morbidity 2018–20. Oxford: National Perinatal Epidemiology Unit, University of Oxford.

Lau Clayton, C. (2017), Young Fathers and their Perspective of Health and Well-Being in Portier, F. (Eds), Population Health Perspective. Routledge.

Ladlow, L. and Neale, B. (2016). Risk, resource, redemption? The parenting and custodial experiences of young offender fathers. *Social Policy & Society*, 15(1), 113–127.

Lanzi, R.G., Bert, S.C. and Jacobs, B.K. (2009) Centers for the Prevention of Child Neglect. Depression among a sample of first-time adolescent and adult mothers. *J Child Adolesc Psychiatr Nurs*, 22(4), 194–202.

Lockwood Estrin, G., Ryan, E.G., Trevillion, K., Demilew, J., Bick, D., Pickles, A. and Howard, L.M. (2019). Young pregnant women and risk for mental disorders: findings from an early pregnancy cohort. *BJPsych Open*, 5(2), e21.

Local Government Association and Public Health England (2019). Supporting young parents to reach their full potential.
Lucas, G., Olander, E.K., Ayers, S. et al. (2019). No straight lines – young women's perceptions of their mental health and wellbeing during and after pregnancy: a systematic review and meta-ethnography. *BMC Women's Health*, 19, 152.
Marvin-Dowle, K., Kilner, K., Burley, V.J. and Soltani, H. (2018). Impact of adolescent age on maternal and neonatal outcomes in the Born in Bradford cohort. *BMJ Open.*
Morinis, J., Carson, C. and Quigley, M.A. (2013). Effect of teenage motherhood on cognitive outcomes in children: A population-based cohort study. *Archives of Disease in Childhood*, 98, 959–964.
Neale, B. and Davies, L. (2016). Becoming a young breadwinner? The education, employment and training trajectories of young fathers. *Social Policy and Society*, 15(1), 85–98.
Neale, B. and Lau Clayton, C. (2014). Young parenthood and cross generational relationships: The perspectives of young fathers. In Holland, J. and Edwards, R. (Eds), *Understanding Families Over Time*. London: Palgrave, pp. 69–87.
Neale B and Davies L. (2015). *Rethinking support for young fathers.* Following Young Fathers Briefing Paper 6. University of Leeds.
Neale, B. (2016). Introduction: Young Fatherhood: Lived experiences and policy challenges. *Social Policy and Society,* 15(1), 75–83.
Neale, B. and Patrick, R. (2016). *Engaged Young Fathers? Gender, Parenthood and the Dynamics of Relationships.* Following Young Fathers, Working Paper Series No. 1.
Neale, B. and Tarrant, A. (2024). *The Dynamics of Young Fatherhood: Understanding the Parenting Journeys and Support Needs of Young Fathers*. Bristol: Policy Press.
NHS England (2023). NHS Maternity Statistics, England, 2022–23: MSDS Breastfeeding CSV Data.
NICE guideline [NG201] (2021). Antenatal care.
Norfolk County Council (2022). *Pregnant pupils policy for schools.*
NSPCC (2021). Learning from case reviews briefings: young parents.
NSPCC (2022). The impact of coronavirus (covid-19): statistics briefing.
Nuffield Family Justice Observatory (2022). Mothers in recurrent care proceedings: New evidence for England and Wales.
Office for National Statistics (2023a). *Births by parents' characteristics: 2021 edition.* London: ONS.
Office for National Statistics (2023b). *Infant mortality (birth cohort) tables in England and Wales: 2020 edition.* London: ONS.
Office for National Statistics (2023c). *Unexplained deaths in infancy, England and Wales: 2021 edition.* London: ONS.
Office for National Statistics (2023d). Conception Statistics, England and Wales, 2021. London: ONS.
Ofsted (2011). *Ages of concern: learning lessons from serious case reviews.* A thematic report of Ofsted's evaluation of serious case reviews from 1 April 2007 to 31 March 2011. Manchester: Ofsted.
Olds, D.L., Kitzman, H., Knudtson, M.D., Anson, E., Smith, J.A. and Cole R. (2014). *Effect of Home Visiting by Nurses on Maternal and Child Mortality Results of a 2-Decade Follow-up of a Randomized Clinical Trial,* JAMA Pediatrics, p. 472.
Pfitzner, N., Humphreys, C. and Hegarty, K. (2017). Engaging men: a multi-level model to support father engagement, *Child & Family Social Work,* 22(1), 537–547.
Public Health England and Local Government Association (2016; updated 2019). *A Framework for Supporting Teenage Mothers and Young Fathers*. London: PHE and LGA.
Public Health England (2019). Health of women before and during pregnancy: health behaviours, risk factors and inequalities. An updated analysis of the maternity services dataset antenatal booking data.
Public Health England (2021). Supporting tables – analysis characteristics of women who stop smoking in pregnancy, MSDS 2018 to 2019.

Quilgars, D., Johnson, S., Pleace, N., Beecham, J. and Bonin, E. (2011). Supporting independence? Evaluation of the teenage parent supported housing pilot – final report. Centre for Housing Policy, University of York.

Reid, V. and Meadows-Oliver, M. (2007). Postpartum depression in adolescent mothers: an integrative review of the literature. *J Pediatr Health Care*, 21(5), 289–98.

Robling, M. *et al.* (2015). Effectiveness of a nurse-led intensive home-visitation programme for first-time teenage mothers (Building Blocks): a pragmatic randomised controlled trial. *Lancet*, 387, 146–55.

Roe, A., Alrouh, B. and Cusworth, L. (2021). Older children and young people in care proceedings in England and Wales. Summary. London: Nuffield Family Justice Observatory.

Royal College of Midwives (2023). Engaging dads pocket guide.

Royal College of Paediatrics and Child Health (2022). *The State of Child Health: 2020.* London: RCPCH.

Sabates, R. and Dex, S. (2012). *Multiple risk factors in young children's development.* CLS Working Paper 2012/1. London: IoE Centre for Longitudinal Studies.

Sex Education Forum (2022). Young People's RSE Poll 2021.

Scottish Government (2022). Tackling child poverty delivery plan: fourth year progress report 2021–2022 – focus report on households with mothers aged 25 or under.

SmithBattle, L., Phengnum, W., Shagavah A.W., and Okawa S. (2019). Fathering on Tenuous Ground: A qualitative meta-synthesis on teen fathering. MCN: *The American Journal of Maternal/Child Nursing,* 44(4), 186–194.

Social Exclusion Unit (1999). *Teenage Pregnancy.* London: SEU, Cmnd 4342.

Tabet, M., Flick, L.H., Cook, C.A.L., Xian, H., Chang, J.J. (2016). Age at First Birth and Psychiatric Disorders in Low-Income Pregnant Women. *Journal of Women's Health,* 25(8), 810–817: a USA study of 744 low-income mothers.

Tarrant, A. and Neale, B. (2017a). *Learning to Support Young Dads, Responding to Young Fathers in a Different Way*. Project Report.

Tarrant, A. and Neale, B. (2017b) *Supporting Young Fathers in Welfare Settings: An Evidence Review of What Matters and What Helps*, Responding to Young Fathers in a Different Way: Evidence Review.

Tarrant, A. Ladlow, L., Johansson, T., Andreasson, J. and Way, L. (2022). The Impacts of the Covid-19 pandemic and lockdown policies on young fathers: Comparative insights from the UK and Sweden, *Social Policy and Society,* 1–11.

Teenage Pregnancy Independent Advisory Group (2002) First Annual Report. London: TPIAG.

Teenage Pregnancy Unit and Department of Health (2004). *Long term consequences of teenage births for parents and their children.* Teenage Pregnancy Unit Research Programme Briefing. London: TPU and Department of Health.

Trivedi, D., Brooks, F., Bunn, F. and Graham, M. (2009). Early fatherhood: A mapping of the evidence base relating to pregnancy prevention and parenting support. *Health Education Research,* 24(6), 999–1028.

Turner, D., Garthwaite, K., Patrick, R., Power, M., Tarrant, A. and Warnock, R. (Eds) (2023). Covid-19 Collaborations: Researching Poverty and Low-Income Family Life during the Pandemic. *The British Journal of Social Work,* 53(4), 2470–2472.

UK Parliament, Committee of Public Accounts (2023). Persistent absence and support for disadvantaged pupils. Seventh report of session 2022–23.

Vaid, L., Mavra, L. and Sims, L. (2009). The Impact of Care to Learn: tracking the destinations of young parents funded in 2006/07 and 2007/08. Centre for Economic and Social Inclusion and Learning and Skills Council.

Wallace, M. (2023). Trends in Adolescent Disadvantage: Policy and Outcomes for Young People under Labour, the Coalition, and the Conservatives (1997 to 2019). London School of Economics and Political Science and Centre for Analysis of Social Exclusion.

Wellings, K., Palmer, M.J, Geary, R.S., Gibson, L.J., Copas, A., Datta, J., Glasier, A., Scott, R.H., Mercer, C.H., Erens, B., Macdowall, W., French, R.S., Jones, K., Johnson, A.M.,

Tanton, C. and Wilkinson, P. (2016). Changes in conceptions in women younger than 18 years and the circumstances of young mothers in England in 2000–2013: An observational study, *Lancet*, 388(10044), 586–595.

Wiggins, M., Rosato, M., Austerberry, H., Sawtell, M. and Oliver, S. (2005). Sure Start Plus. National Evaluation: final report. London: Social Science Research Unit, Institute of Education, University of London.

Wilson, K. and Prior, M. (2011). Father involvement and child wellbeing. *Journal of Paediatrics and Child Health,* 47(7), 405–407.

Wood, S.K., Ford, K., Madden, H.C.E., Sharp, C.A., Hughes, C.E. and Bellis, M.A. (2022). Adverse Childhood Experiences and Their Relationship with Poor Sexual Health Outcomes: Results from Four Cross-Sectional Surveys. Int. J. Environ. Res. Public Health, 19(14), 8869.

8 Adolescent childbearing globally

Tangible progress made, but much more to be done – developments since 2018

8.0 Overview

Drawing from credible global surveys, this chapter begins by pointing to the progress that has been made globally in reducing levels of adolescent childbearing – slow and uneven, but tangible progress, nevertheless. Second, it describes the widely differing contexts in which adolescent childbearing occurs globally. Third, it describes the evolution of global, regional and national responses to adolescent childbearing. It shines a spotlight on successful national government-led programmes in countries in different world regions – Moldova (Central Europe), Ethiopia (sub-Saharan Africa, SSA), England (Western Europe), Argentina (Latin America and Caribbean, LAC) and Thailand (South-East Asia) – which show what can and has been done with the application of wise and courageous leadership, good science and strong management. It ends with data on countries, communities, families and individuals being left behind and calls for tailored efforts to address these inequities, providing an example of a remarkable 40-year initiative from Jamaica.

8.1 Levels and trends in adolescent childbearing globally

Adolescent girls aged 15–19 years in Low- and Middle-Income Countries (LMIC) have an estimated 21 million pregnancies each year, 50 per cent of which are unintended (Sully et al., 2020). In 2021 an estimated 12.1 million girls aged 15−19 years had given birth globally; this figure was 499,000 for 10−14-year-old girls (United Nations Department of Economic and Social Affairs, 2024a, online version).

Globally, the adolescent birth rate (ABR) has decreased from 64.5 births per 1,000 women aged 15−19 in 2000 to 42.5 births per 1,000 women of the same age in 2021. However, rates of change have been uneven across different regions of the world with the sharpest decline occurring in South Asia, and slower declines in the LAC and SSA regions (United Nations Department of Economic and Social Affairs, 2024a, online version). Although declines have occurred in all regions, SSA and LAC continue to have the highest rates globally at 101 and 53.2 births per 1,000, respectively in 2021 (United Nations Department of Economic and Social Affairs, 2024b, online version).

DOI: 10.4324/9781003410225-9

There are also enormous differences in rates between countries within regions. In LAC for example, Nicaragua recorded the highest estimated ABR at 85.6 per 1,000 adolescent girls in 2021, compared with 24.1 per 1,000 adolescent girls in Chile (United Nations Department of Economic and Social Affairs, 2024b, online version). Even within countries there are large variations. For example, in Zambia, the percentage of adolescent girls aged 15–19 who have begun childbearing (women who either have had a birth or are pregnant at the time of interview) ranged from 14.9 per cent in Lusaka to 42.5 per cent in the Southern Province in 2018 (Zambia Statistics Agency, Ministry of Health, Zambia, ICF, 2018). In the Philippines in 2017, the percentage of adolescent girls aged 15–19 who have begun childbearing, derived from the household surveys, ranged from 3.5 per cent in the Cordillera Administrative Region to 17.9 per cent in the Davao Peninsula Region (Philippine Statistics Authority and ICF, 2018).

While the estimated global ABR has declined, the actual number of births to adolescents continues to be high. The largest number of estimated births to 15–19-year-olds in 2021 occurred in SSA (6,114,000), whereas far fewer births occurred in Central Asia (68,000). The corresponding number was 332,000 among adolescents aged 10–14 years in SSA, compared with 22,000 in Central Asia in the same year (United Nations Department of Economic and Social Affairs, 2024b).

8.2 The contexts in which adolescent pregnancies and childbearing occur

Adolescent pregnancies are a global problem occurring in high-, middle- and low-income countries. Studies of risk and protective factors related to adolescent pregnancy in LMICs indicate that levels tend to be higher among those with less education and/or of low economic status (Chung et al., 2018). Progress in reducing adolescent first births has been particularly slow among these vulnerable groups, leading to increasing and continuing inequity (Neal et al., 2020).

Several factors contribute to adolescent pregnancies and births. First, in many societies, girls are under pressure to marry and bear children. Child marriage – marriages before the age of 18 – places girls at increased risk of pregnancy, with girls who are married very early typically having limited autonomy to influence decision-making about contraceptive use and delaying childbearing (Petroni et al., 2017).

As at 2021 the estimated global number of child brides was 650 million (UNICEF, 2021). Second, in many places girls choose to become pregnant because they have limited educational and employment prospects. Often, in such societies, motherhood – within or outside marriage/union – is valued, and marriage or union and childbearing may be the best of the limited options available to adolescent girls (UNICEF, 2021).

Access to accurate and up to date information and education about sexuality, reproduction and sexual and reproductive health is limited. This has important consequences. First, many adolescents are poorly informed about the physical and emotional changes taking place at puberty and are ill-prepared to deal with them.

Second, many adolescents are unaware and ill-equipped to protect themselves from sexually transmitted infections and unwanted pregnancies, and to have sex safely and pleasurably when sexual activity begins – generally during adolescence (Liang et al., 2019). They are also ill-prepared to refuse unwanted sex from peers or from influential adults who use physical or emotional pressure to coerce them to have sex. And third, they do not know where and how to seek help from the family and from health and social services when problems occur (Herat et al., 2018).

In many places, contraceptives are not easily accessible to adolescents. Even when contraception is available, adolescents may face stigma in seeking contraceptives, lack the agency or the resources to pay for them, and the knowledge on where to obtain them and how to use them correctly. Further, they are often at higher risk of discontinuing use due to side effects, and due to changing life circumstances and reproductive intentions (Herat et al., 2018).

Restrictive laws and policies regarding the provision of contraceptives based on age or marital status pose an important barrier to the provision and uptake of contraceptives among adolescents. This is often combined with health worker bias and/or lack of willingness to acknowledge adolescents' sexual health needs (Chandra-Mouli and Akwara, 2020).

Child sexual abuse increases the risk of unintended pregnancies. A recent WHO report estimated that 120 million girls aged under 20 years have experienced some form of forced sexual contact (WHO, 2020). This abuse is deeply rooted in gender inequality; it affects more girls than boys, although many boys are also affected. Estimates suggest that in 2020, at least one in eight of the world's children had been sexually abused before reaching the age of 18, and one in every 20 girls aged 15–19 years had experienced forced sex during their lifetime (WHO, 2020; UNICEF, 2020).

8.3 The global response to adolescent pregnancy and childbearing

There has been awareness of the need to address adolescent pregnancy and childbearing in countries around the world for over 50 years (WHO, 1993). But the issue did not get the attention it deserved until it was placed on the global public health and social development agendas by the International Conference on Population and Development (ICPD) in 1994. That enabled international organisations and indigenous champions to press governments to pay attention to this area (Chandra-Mouli et al., 2019).

In 2000 the Millennium Development Goals (MDG) were announced; Goal 5 on reducing maternal mortality provided a new impetus for the work on preventing early pregnancy and childbearing in adolescents. UN agencies and other international organisations pressed for attention to adolescent pregnancy (and to HIV in adolescents and young people as part of Goal 6) and supported policy and programme development in countries willing to work in this area. Despite concerted efforts, there was little engagement because in the first decade of the MDG era, adolescent health was not really seen a priority (Chandra-Mouli et al., 2019).

In the early 2010s there was growing realisation worldwide that adolescents were being left behind, and that this had implications not only for their health and wellbeing but for efforts to reduce maternal and childhood mortality. International organisations responded with data on the scope of the problem and policy and programme guidance based on research studies and project experiences. They also used the platforms set up by the ICPD and the MDG to pay greater attention to the sexual and reproductive health of adolescents (Chandra-Mouli et al., 2019).

In the past five years of the MDG era (i.e. 2011–14), GirlsNotBrides, a global partnership of NGOs and the newly established Joint UNICEF-UNFPA Programme to Accelerate an End to Child Marriage, injected energy and resources to strengthen ongoing efforts to end child marriage, and Family Planning 2020 initiated efforts to support countries in including adolescent contraception in their national commitments (Chandra-Mouli et al., 2019).

The Sustainable Development Goals and the updated Global Strategy for Women's, Children's and Adolescents' Health which were launched in 2015, placed adolescents at the center of the agenda. Adolescent pregnancy prevention is on the agenda of the Sustainable Development Goals and the International Conference on Population and Development + 25 Agenda (Global Sustainable Development Goals Indicator Platform, online); it is also solidly positioned on the agenda of regional political bodies (The Sexual and Reproductive Health and Rights Scorecard for the Southern African Community, online). Over the years, research evidence and programmatic experience have been built. This has informed policy and programme support tools (WHO, 2011; UNFPA, 2022a). Global partnerships such as FP2030 are encouraging and supporting countries to develop bold and innovative commitments (FP2030, 2021). Global financing institutions such as the Global Financing Facility are providing countries with the funds they need to translate their plans into action (Global Financing Facility, 2022). They and others – such as the Global Fund for AIDS Tuberculosis and Malaria – are pressing for stronger synergies between HIV and early pregnancy prevention programmes (The Global Fund, 2022). Global initiatives such as The Challenge Initiative are supporting countries to translate country aspirations into context-specific programmes, delivered at scale with quality and equity, and to make full use of approaches such as Self Care and the direct-to-consumer movement (Bose et al., 2021). There is much more to be done. There are both enormous opportunities to exploit and challenges to overcome but the prospects for progress are better today than they have ever been.

8.4 National responses to adolescent pregnancy and childbearing

For years, NGOs have led efforts to prevent adolescent pregnancy in countries of both the global North and the South. From their projects and from research studies, there is a solid evidence base of effective approaches to prevent adolescent pregnancy and increase access to and uptake of contraceptives by adolescents. Until recently, these proven approaches were being implemented only in small-scale and time-limited projects. This is beginning to change (Chandra-Mouli et al., 2020).

Despite governments identifying adolescent pregnancy as a priority and including the issue in their policies and strategies, national efforts to address prevention tend to be weak because of one or more of the following reasons. Lukewarm commitment because of other competing priorities, discomfort with addressing the sensitive aspects of adolescent pregnancy including the provision of comprehensive sexuality education and contraception especially to unmarried adolescents, weak capacity within governments leading to weak governance and management, no systematic efforts to engage civil society bodies and groups, reluctance to tap into the expertise of nongovernment organisations with expertise in this area, and lack of any real accountability for the execution or the results of programmes (Chandra-Mouli et al., 2017).

However, a small but growing number of countries have put in place successful government-led national adolescent pregnancy prevention programmes such as those in Argentina, Ethiopia, Moldova and Thailand. There are valuable lessons to draw from these countries. They put adolescent pregnancy on the national political and governmental agendas; they planned scale up methodologically; they raised resources and effectively managed scale up, identifying and addressing challenges as they went along; they built support and anticipated and addressed resistance; and they worked strategically to ensure sustainability. The England Teenage Pregnancy Strategy is another notable example. The lessons are summarised here and described in detail in the previous edition.

They put scale-up on the agenda: Alliances of internal and external change agents worked together to highlight the need and to build consensus for investment and action on adolescent pregnancy prevention, using windows of opportunity as they arose.

They planned scale-up meticulously: They developed evidence-based strategies grounded in supportive national policies. They simplified the package of interventions to only the essential elements and communicated clearly what needed to be done, where, how and by whom.

They raised resources, and effectively managed scale-up: They committed adequate resources – from both internal and external sources – and managed implementation by engaging and retaining different stakeholders. Further, they used findings of assessments and reviews to reshape implementation.

They built support and anticipated and addressed resistance: They built understanding and support for what they were doing. Alongside that, they anticipated resistance and decided whether to avoid it in some way or to address it head on.

They worked strategically to ensure sustainability: They used data creatively to communicate the progress being made. They advocated for – and succeeded in – integrating elements of the scale-up effort into wider national policies, strategies and indicator frameworks.

Their efforts led to impressive results. The adolescent birth rate in Argentina declined from 33.7/1,000 in 2013 to 13.7/1,000, from 53.4/1,000 in 2012 to 21/1,000 in 2022 in Thailand and from 41/1,000 in 2014 to 26/1,000 in 2021 In Moldova. In Ethiopia, the decline was less impressive, i.e. from 16.3 in 2000 to 13.4 in 2019, although there were overall far fewer pregnancies among young adolescents. In England the conception rate among young women under 18 fell by 72 per cent between 1998 and 2021.

The experiences of these five countries – one each in Central Europe, Western Europe, LAC, South Asia and SSA, show what can be achieved with the application of good science combined with good evidence and strong leadership and management. They challenge and inspire other countries to do what is doable and urgently needs to be done – now.

8.5 Case studies: Moldova, Ethiopia, Argentina, England and Thailand

Moldova[1]

How adolescent pregnancy was put on the national agenda

The period following the break-up of the Soviet Union in the 1990s led to significant social and economic disruptions in Moldova. Government service delivery systems including education, health and social welfare faltered with lack of governance and resources. Young people aged 10–24 were among the worst affected, with increased mortality and morbidity from injuries, including self-inflicted ones, and poor mental health. Early unintended pregnancies and STIs rose (Bivol et al., 2013). Recognising that the existing health service delivery system was not geared to effectively prevent or treat young people's health, the Ministry of Health – with the support of international organisations – set about reorienting the health service delivery systems to be more responsive to their needs (Bivol et al., 2013).

Planning scale up

In the early 2000s a situation analysis of the adolescent friendliness of health services was conducted with the results informing the concept of Youth Friendly Health Services (YFHS). A regulation underpinning the concept was issued in 2007, with quality standards published in 2009. In 2008, a costing exercise succeeded in securing funding from the National Health Insurance Company to ensure young people's free access to health facilities across the country. With support from international organisations, NGOs and government, health facilities began operationalising the concept. The YFHS were required to promote, prevent and treat all adolescent health issues, including pregnancy and sexual health; provide health education and counselling for young people and their parents/guardians, in person and through a telephone hotline; and collaborate with the mass media and, more latterly with social media. Finally, to take into account the range of health service providers, a basic and an extended YFHS package was provided to embed a youth friendly approach across the health system (Bivol et al., 2013).

How scale-up was managed

The Ministry of Health's recommendations were disseminated energetically and integrated in different health care delivery systems:

- All children, students, pregnant and post-partum women have their medical insurance covered by the Government. Family doctors offer a free basic package of services even for those who are uninsured.
- A network of 41 free and confidential youth friendly health centres (YFHC) spans the country, as part of the national primary care delivery system. The Centres provide condoms, other contraceptives, pregnancy tests, medical abortion, testing and treatment for STIs, including confidential HIV counselling, testing and treatment.
- Free confidential, HIV counselling, testing and treatment is available across the country.

To complement service improvements, the Ministry of Health supported local activity to ensure young people are aware of and confident to access the services – with outreach education and workshops in schools and recreational facilities and through a multifaceted online effort. Measures were also put in place to build local support for the service provision to adolescents, with YFHC staff reaching out to parents and other community members (Carai et al., 2021).

Finally, Moldova gathered and used data, at different levels of the health system to inform the delivery of services to adolescents and complemented this with learning from studies and evaluations.

Building support and addressing resistance

With the dissolution of the Soviet Union, many systems and structures were radically transformed. Within that context and the availability of data on the health problems faced by young people, there was broad support for the policy and programme changes that were made. Over time, spurred by external influence, resistance has slowly grown, especially to comprehensive sexuality education. Also, given that funds are allocated from the national budget, questions are sometimes asked about whether providing sexual and reproductive health services to young people should be a priority when there are many other things that need attention and investment. Support from government authorities, health professionals, NGOs and international organisations continues to maintain the importance of adolescent health and prevention of early pregnancy and address concerns of communities (Caraiet al., 2021).

How sustainability was addressed

Sustainability was built in three ways. First, norms and standards for youth friendly health services were set out by the Ministry of Health, outlining the services that would be delivered, to which group of young people, who would deliver these services and where. Sexual and reproductive health was included in this package, as part of a holistic adolescent health focus. Second, directives by the Ministry of Health were communicated energetically and their application supported by the different health service delivery systems. The competencies required by different health service providers were also identified, training and re-training curricula updated, and an innovative system of sharing and learning was put in place (4). Finally, agreed funding for the provision of the specified package of health services to young people was included in the National Health Insurance Company. Beyond this, the team led by Neo Vita which led this effort are watchful of both opportunities to consolidate the sustainability and political or administrative developments that might challenge it (Carai et al., 2021; Lesco et al., 2019).

What were the results?

The adolescent fertility rate (15–19 years) declined from approximately 41/1,000 to 26/1,000 between 2014 and 2021. The same is true for abortion rates in this age group (from 7.3/1,000 to 6/1,000). Condom use at last sex has increased from 6 per cent to 13 per cent and the use of contraceptive pills among sexually active adolescents – has increased from 6 per cent in 2014 to 10 per cent in 2018 (Republic of Moldova, National Bureau of Statistics, 2022).

Ethiopia[2]

How teenage pregnancy was put on the national agenda

In 2000 the Ethiopian government recognised and decided to use the transformational power of the Millennium Development Goals (MDG). As called for by the United Nations, it addressed the MDGs as a package and addressed them all. Within this context, the Federal Ministry of Health (FMOH) identified as a priority, a reduction in maternal and childhood mortality in the rural areas where over 80 per cent of the population reside. Recognising that adolescent pregnancy, particularly early childbearing, contributed to a substantial portion of maternal deaths, the government decided to ensure that the reproductive health of adolescents and young women should be addressed in efforts to reduce maternal mortality (Assefa et al. 2017).

Planning scale-up

To achieve this, the FMOH launched an ambitious Health Extension Programme to deliver information and education, provide a basic package of health services in the community, and to strengthen linkages between information, education and health services. The overall aim was to empower rural households to take responsibility for improving and maintaining their own health with reducing maternal and child mortality a key area of focus (Assefa et al., 2017).

The FMOH set out to delay and space childbearing through improving access to, and uptake of contraception, and to reduce pregnancy-related mortality and morbidity by improved access to obstetric care. It also put in place complementary measures to prevent child marriage – defined as a marriage before the age of 18 – such as promoting the enrolment and retention of girls in school, educating them about child marriage and motivating them to resist it, and working to change community and the wider societal norms about child marriage (Assefa et al., 2017; UNICEF, 2018; Akwara et al., 2022).

Managing scale-up

A new cadre of health workers was created. Salaried health extension workers with a clear set of functions were linked to health posts, the most peripheral points of access in the health system. Over a five-year period, nearly 35,000 individuals (almost all females) selected by communities using a structured process were recruited, trained and deployed. Alongside this, a cadre of mid-level health workers were recruited, trained and deployed in health centres to provide midwifery, neonatal and emergency care services, and health centres themselves were constructed/rehabilitated and equipped. Contraception is promoted by the health extension workers and provided in health facilities for both unmarried and married adolescents without or without children (Assefa et al., 2017; Akwara et al., 2022).

A multi-level monitoring system was put in place and supported with data-driven planning and management. Progress was monitored from the local to the national levels, and a core team with technical experts and chaired by the State Minister of Health, reviewed progress, set priorities and developed plans. Problems that arose as the implementation was rolled out, were identified and addressed at the appropriate level (Assefa et al., 2017; Akwara et al., 2022).

Building support and addressing resistance

The FMOH built support for this initiative at the national level through partnerships with a number of medical professional associations, including the Ethiopian Society of Gynaecologists and Obstetricians and Ethiopian Midwifery Association. It built support at the local level by engaging health extension workers from the communities they would serve in. These workers were fully aware of the social and cultural context and were trained and supported to be both sensitive to it, and to engage in dialogue to challenge and change norms such as low utilisation of contraception or maternal health services (Assefa et al., 2017; Akwara et al., 2022).

Ensuring sustainability

Two factors contributed to sustainability. First, the government introduced legislation to underpin the programme. A law guaranteeing free maternal and newborn health services in public health facilities, and a law legalising the provision of abortion care in specified circumstances which has increased the proportion of abortions carried out in health facilities from 27 per cent in 2008 to 53 per cent in 2014. Second, the management and financing of the Health Extension Programme, such as salaries for health extension workers and rehabilitation of health posts was decentralised to the regional and districts (woreda) levels, which created local owenership (Assefa et al., 2017; Akwara et al., 2022).

What were the results?

Monitoring of the programme's impact has shown a number of improvements. The maternal mortality rate in women of reproductive age has declined although data disaggregated by age are not available (Assefa et al., 2017). There has also been an increase in the levels of safe abortion and a decline in unsafe abortion and its consequences (Moore et al., 2008).There has been a substantial decline in the national levels of child marriage (based on reports by young women aged 20–24 years) with a 9 per cent reduction between 2000 and 2016. Modern contraceptive use among 15–19-year-old women has increased by 34 per cent between 2000 and 2019 with a 38 per cent increase in post-partum contraception between 2000 and 2016 which has reduced rapid repeat pregnancies and the associated health risks. There has been a small 3 per cent decrease in births to adolescents aged 15–19 between 2000 and 2019, but a large decline in childbearing in the early adolescent years, reducing the associated poor maternal and child outcomes (Akwara et al., 2022).

***Argentina*[3]**

How teenage pregnancy was put on the national agenda

Since the 1990s Argentina has recognised adolescents as autonomous drivers of their sexual and reproductive health and wellbeing, in line with the Convention on the Rights of the Child (Ref). One expression of this is that the country started providing adolescents with access to contraception, albeit in limited jurisdictions (Hospital General de Agudos Dr. Cosme Argerich. Ciudad de Buenos Aires, Argentina, 2009).

However, high rates of adolescent pregnancy – particularly high levels of unplanned pregnancy persisted with an estimated seven out of ten pregnancies to under-20s unplanned. To tackle this obvious lack of autonomy in reproductive health decision-making, over the past 15 years the government has planned and executed a set of nationwide measures (Ministry of Health, 2019).

Planning scale-up

To equip adolescents with the knowledge and skills to look after their reproductive and sexual health and to provide easy access to services, the government put in place the following four measures. Some were adolescent specific; others covered the population as a whole but made a specific reference to adolescents.

In 2003 a National Programme of Sexual and Reproductive Health was established under Law 25.673, which laid the groundwork for national policies aimed at promoting sexual and reproductive health. Adolescents were included as a group to be addressed (Argentina, Law 25673).

In 2006 the country passed the Comprehensive Sex Education Law (CSEL), this legislation introduced mandatory sex education in all educational institutions and educational levels across the country. Implementation of the legislation has built adolescent understanding and fostered their demand for sexual and reproductive health services (Argentina. Law 26150).

In 2014 there was an Amendment to the Civil and Commercial Code (2014) to include adolescents. This legally permitted individuals over 13 years old to access medical care without parental consent in matters related to their sexual and reproductive health, including contraceptive methods, legal interruption of pregnancy and mental health services (Rofman et al., 2022).

In 2017 a National Plan for the Reduction of Unintended Pregnancy in Adolescence (the ENIA Plan) was published. This multisectoral strategic plan set clear objectives, listed a plan of work and allocated funds. The plan marked a huge departure from the past and drew on the learning from the England strategy. Central to it was guaranteed freedom of choice, three complementary services – the provision of long-acting contraceptives, access to Voluntary Interruption of Pregnancy (VIP) – and strengthened sexual health counselling in secondary schools. To address inequalities, implementation focused on areas with higher rates of adolescent pregnancy (Ministry of Health, 2019).

How scale-up was managed

Beginning in areas of high rates, implementation was rolled out nationwide in a phased manner. After 20 years of implementation, both sexuality education and sexual and reproductive health services have become widely available. However, being a federal nation these laws and policies – especially the sensitive ones such as the CSEL – were applied to varying degrees in different jurisdictions.

The ENIA Plan led to stepped up efforts to reach adolescents by integrating existing and innovative tools. But, while it contributed to a nationwide decrease in adolescent fertility, its focus was limited to certain areas of the country. The need remains for the ENIA tools to be available to adolescents across the entire country.

To complement the public health approach, efforts to empower adolescents were driven by the country's strong feminist movement. Further ongoing communication campaigns like #PUEDODECIDIR (puedodecidir.org) – 'You can decide' played a key role in helping young people take charge of their lives and reach out and demand for services and support.

Finally, a combination of public health, legal and social welfare approaches were used to reduce pregnancies in younger adolescents under 15.

Building support and addressing resistance

Support was provided by a political establishment which created an enabling environment for sexual and reproductive health across the life course with supportive laws and policies; funding, to translate them into action; social acceptance of adolescent sexuality; and a strong feminist movement. The political and social commitment to addressing inequity, and a functional health, education and social welfare system – despite the long-running financial crisis, were crucial to focusing on girls 'left behind', including those who were very young.

Ensuring sustainability.

Three key issues will impact the sustainability of Argentina's progress. First, whether the laws and policies described above continue to influence governmental decision making. Second, whether there are adequate funds to continue the work being done and to expand to areas of the country not fully covered. Third, whether adolescent demand that has been generated and the community support that has been built, will press for continued action and investment. Given the enormous political changes that have occurred, there are questions both in financial terms, for example funds for the acquisition of contraceptives, and in wider support for programmes aimed to build gender equality and address inequity. The role of progressive province governments and the UN agencies is key to maintaining the agenda through political changes.

What were the results?

The under-20 adolescent fertility rate in Argentina has decreased from 33.7/1,000 in 2013 to 13.7/1,000 in 2021, a reduction of 59 per cent (Ministry of Health, 2023b). Within this substantial reduction in the adolescent fertility rate, a significant decrease was achieved in pregnancies in young people under 15.

Further, the country has reduced mortality and morbidity resulting from abortion. In 2021 the country recorded zero adolescent deaths from unsafe abortions, reflecting the result of an effective comprehensive approach (Ministry of Health, 2023b). In parallel to reductions in births to adolescent mothers, maternal mortality has also reduced (Ministry of Health, 2023b)

***England*[4]**

How teenage pregnancy was put on the national agenda

In the late 1990s England had a high rate of teenage pregnancy which had shown no sustained downward trend and was out of line with similar Western European countries. The incoming government positioned teenage pregnancy as a cause and consequence of inter-generational inequalities which required collective multi-agency action. Previous governments' efforts had relied on the health sector, with little result. Strong advocacy from NGOs and medical organisations kept lack of progress high on the political agenda. A new Social Exclusion Unit was commissioned to identify the reasons behind the high rates and develop a comprehensive strategy, consulting with young people, NGOs and professional organisations. The ten-year goal of halving the under-18 pregnancy rate, commitment to sustained resources, and launch by the Prime Minister secured the strategy as a national priority (Social Exclusion Unit, 1999).

Planning scale-up

Scale-up was integral from the start, with the ten-year strategy framed around four themes: joined up action; improved relationships and sex education in school and easy access to free youth friendly contraceptive services; a communications campaign to reach young people and parents; and co-ordinated support for young parents. The programme was delivered by multiple agencies working together in all 150 local government areas, to reach an agreed local target. Fundamental to the scale-up effort was the establishment of a structure which consisted of a national unit, nine regional teenage pregnancy co-ordinators and 150 local co-ordinators, and multi-agency partnership boards. A local implementation grant contributed to partnership building and joint implementation.

How scale-up was managed

Resourcing and maintaining the national, regional and local structures throughout the ten-year programme enabled both the monitoring and support of effective implementation. Regular network meetings were held to maintain momentum and morale, identify and address problems and share effective practice Accurate and up-to-date national and local conception data provided a regular review of progress. A mid-strategy review comparing areas with similar demographics, but contrasting progress found that those that were applying all the recommended actions had demonstrated reduced rates. This validated the strategy's multi-component approach and confirmed that England's high rates were not inevitable if the right actions were taken. More prescriptive guidance was issued together with a self-assessment tool for local areas to review their actions. Direct engagement of government ministers and senior leaders in poor-performing areas, combined with tailored support, helped to accelerate progress.

Building support and addressing resistance

The evidence-based strategy was strongly endorsed by NGOs and professional organisations with some specific guidance co-badged with medical and nursing institutions. Trust was enhanced by the appointment of experts to an Independent Advisory Group, charged with holding the government to account with an annual report to Parliament of the Strategy's progress. Its expertise was influential with local senior leaders and helped the government respond to negative media reporting by a small but vocal minority on the 'dangers' of sexuality education and providing confidential contraception to under-16s. The national unit convened forums for NGO and inter-faith organisations to bring stakeholders together to explain and provide updates on the Strategy and discuss any concerns.

Ensuring sustainability

Visible national and local political leadership was provided through the ten years with the strategy goal maintained as a national priority. To help integrate the strategy into mainstream services, the actions and goals of were embedded in wider government programmes aimed at improving health, education and economic outcomes. Sustaining progress beyond the end of the strategy and through a change of government and dismantling of the structures posed challenges. However, the strategy had established awareness that adolescent pregnancy needed to be addressed and that the right actions had impact. Ministers called for further progress. Local leaders called for continued support and updated national guidance was published. The adolescent pregnancy rate indicator was included in the public health dataset for monitoring national and local progress. Legislation for compulsory relationships, sex and health education in all schools (ages 5–16), recommended by the Independent Advisory Group from the start of the Strategy was passed in 2017 and implemented in 2020. The challenges of maintaining progress within a government policy of austerity and widening inequalities are described in Chapter 5.

What were the results?

Between 1998, the Strategy baseline and 2021, England's under-18 conception rate has fallen by 72 per cent from 46/1,000 15–17-year-olds to 13/1,000, a fall in numbers from 46,000 to 12,400 (Office for National Statistics, 2023). However, despite the significant progress inequalities persist, requiring further concerted action. England's teenage birth rate remains higher than comparable Western countries; teenagers are at highest risk of unplanned pregnancy, with 52 per cent of under-18 conceptions ending in abortion; despite reductions in all local areas there is a seven-fold difference in rates; and outcomes for young parents and their children remain disproportionately poor.

***Thailand*[5]**

Thailand, like many other countries, has a decreasing overall birth rate, but the rate among 10- to 19-year-olds increased substantially during the 2000s; rates reached their peaks at 53.4 per 1,000 women aged 15 to 19 and 1.8 per 1,000 women aged ten to 14 in 2012 (Bureau of Reproductive Health, Department of Health, Thailand, online). Within less than a decade, however, these rates have reduced by more than half to 21.0 and 0.8 respectively in 2022 (Thailand Public Health Statistics, 2021).

Central to the progress made in the substantial reduction in adolescent births is that recognition of the *rights* of young people was enshrined in the ground-breaking adolescent pregnancy law. It is the acceptance of this fundamental entitlement that made the Thai approach to the issue of adolescent pregnancy so enlightened (Act for Prevention and Solution of the Adolescent Pregnancy Problem, Thailand, 2016).

Led by the Department of Health, Ministry of Public Health, with support from various organisations – such as Thai Health Promotion Foundation (ThaiHealth), non-health Ministries, UN agencies, the media and the private sector – several initiatives were taken between 2012 and 2015. In 2012, a multi-sector delegation from Thailand made a study visit to England and the Netherlands. Among the key findings from the study visit was the importance of a whole system approach to tackling teenage pregnancy in England during its ten-year strategy implementation.

In 2013, ThaiHealth supported provincial authorities to implement pilot projects – informed by England's ten key factors – in 20 provinces; and lessons learned from the evaluations enabled replication in other provinces. The *Young Love* campaign was launched involving roadshows to schools to talk about safe sex and teenage pregnancy and to distribute condoms to young people, alongside a television broadcast to raise public awareness. National standards for Youth-Friendly Health Services were developed for health care workers (Department of Health, Thailand, UNICEF, UNFPA, WHO, undated).

In 2014 a programme of free long-acting reversible contraception to young people to prevent repeat pregnancy was introduced (Inthavong, S., Pantasri, T., Morakote, et al., 2022). and the first National Conference on *Healthy Sexuality: Adolescent Pregnancy* was held (Thai Health Promotion Foundation (a), 2013). Over 2000 participants took part and national and international experts were engaged. The event created high awareness about the issue of teenage pregnancy among various stakeholders and was followed by a further high-profile national event in 2017 (Thai Health Promotion Foundation (b), 2017).

During 2015, with the leadership of parliamentarians and the Department of Health, the teenage pregnancy bills were introduced using rights-based and multi-sectoral approaches. The *Act for Prevention and Solution of the Adolescent Pregnancy Problem, B.E. 2559 (2016)* was approved in the Parliament followed by enactment in 2016. A national committee was established – chaired by the Prime Minister – along with sub-committees dealing with the five identified strategic themes of the national strategy: school-based education, involving families and communities, improving health services, developing support and welfare for pregnant young women, and improving data collection and knowledge management.

What characterises the Thai approach are: (1) the clear recognition of rights and entitlements, and their specific mention right at the centre of the Adolescent Pregnancy Act itself and the inclusion of young people in the national committee, (2) the multi-sectoral approach to the problem with clear roles of duty bearers mandated in the law, (3) the empowerment of local authorities to lead the local implementation, (4) the development of a national strategy setting a goal to halve adolescent birth rates within ten years (Bureau of Reproductive Health, Department of Health, Thailand, undated), and (5) the establishment of an Independent Advisory Group (based on the England model), comprising a diverse group of experts and young people themselves to help guide the implementation of the national strategy (Department of Health, Thailand, undated). Further background information is provided in a collection of 'Success Stories' from the WHO's South East Asia Regional Office (WHO Regional Office for South East Asia, 2021).

Among other challenges faced are the need to scale up comprehensive sexuality education and youth-friendly health services to achieve national coverage, and empowering those involved to build public support and resist the negative opposition that inevitably accompanies progress in the area of adolescent sexual and reproductive health. Close working with key media outlets is also very important.

8.6 Countries, communities and families are being left behind

Despite these excellent nationally led examples, and even though there has been progress globally, it has been slow and uneven, with many countries, communities and families being left behind. To meet the Sustainable Development Goals' call of leaving no one behind, there is a pressing need to understand and address this inequity. A recently published UNFPA report titled "Childhood in motherhood" reiterates that, while progress has occurred in reducing adolescent pregnancy and childbearing, the pace has been slow. It notes that the global decline translates to about three percentage points per decade for the past six decades (UNFPA, 2022b).

An intersecting web of factors at the micro, meso and macro levels contributes to this (28). Studies in SSA, LAC and South-East Asia point to adolescent first births being more common among the poorest and rural residents with births among the youngest age group (< 16 years) concentrated among these populations (Chandra-Mouli et al., 2021; Neal et al., 2016; Neal et al., 2018; Neal et al., 2019). Progress in reducing adolescent first births has been particularly poor among these vulnerable groups, leading to increasing inequity. For instance, in LAC, there has been little progress in reducing adolescent first births over the past few decades in Haiti (modest decline), Bolivia and the Dominican Republic (plateau in the decline), and Colombia and Peru (increase) (Neal et al., 2018).

There is a pressing need for initiatives that seek to understand who is being left behind, and work with them to identify why this is happening, and what can be done with them to address the situation. The work of the Women's Centre of Jamaica (WCoJ) over four decades illustrates this well. The WCoJ responded to the lack of opportunities for pregnant adolescents to continue their education if they became pregnant, the limited to no re-entry opportunities for adolescent mothers, and the high rates of second births. The organisation piloted the provision of a package of actions to pregnant and parenting adolescents, their male partners and their families: continued education, counselling, school placement support, child-care and parenting skills building, and family planning counselling and service provision, in a safe environment. With support from the Government of Jamaica and partners both within and outside the country, the initiative moved steadily from a pilot to a nationally scaled up programme that has been sustained for 40 years and replicated in other Caribbean countries. It has also contributed to shaping national policies and procedures on school retention and re-entry for pregnant and parenting adolescents. Finally, a body of studies has demonstrated the effectiveness of the initiative in maintaining low levels of rapid repeat pregnancies and assuring school completion and continued education (Amo-Adjei et al., 2022).

Notes

1 With thanks to Galina Lesco for contributing this case study.
2 With thanks to Lemessa Oljira for contributing this case study.
3 With thanks to Fernando Zingman for contributing this case study.
4 The detail of the England strategy and its implementation is described in the first edition of *Teenage Pregnancy and Young Parenthood: Effective Policy and Practice*. Routledge, 2018.
5 With thanks to Dr Bunyarit Sukrat, Dr Wiwat Rojanapithayakorn and Rattanaporn Ingham for contributing this case study.

References

Amo-Adjei, J., Caffe, S., Simpson, Z., Harris, M. et al. (2022). "Second Chances" for Adolescent Mothers: Four Decades of Insights and Lessons on Effectiveness and Scale-up of Jamaica's Programme for Adolescent Mothers. *American Journal of Sexuality Education*, 1–34.

Bivol, S., Thompson, R. and Pejic, D. (2013). *Youth friendly health services in Republic of Moldova*, in *Youth-friendly health policies and services in the European Region*, Baltag, V. and Matheison, A. (Eds). Copenhagen: WHO Regional Office for Europe, pp. 95–114.

Bose, K., Martin, K., Walsh, K. et al. (2021). Scaling Access to Contraception for Youth in Urban Slums: The Challenge Initiative's Systems-Based Multi-Pronged Strategy for Youth-Friendly Cities. *Frontiers Global Women's Health*, 1(2), 673168.

Chandra-Mouli, V. and Akwara, E. (2020). Improving access to and use of contraception by adolescents: what progress has been made, what lessons have been learnt, and what are the implications for action? *Best Pract Res Clin Obstet Gynaecol*, 66, 107–118.

Chandra-Mouli, V., Akwara, E., Engel, D. et al. (2020). Progress in adolescent sexual and reproductive health and rights globally between 1990 and 2016: what progress has been made, what contributed to this, and what are the implications for the future? *Sexual and Reproductive Health Matters*, 28(1), 1–11.

Chandra-Mouli, V., Ferguson, J., Plesons, M. et al. (2019). The Political, Research, Programmatic, and Social Responses to Adolescent Sexual and Reproductive Health and Rights in the 25 Years Since the International Conference on Population and Development. *Journal of Adolescent Health*, 65, S16–S40.

Chandra-Mouli, V., Neal, S. and Moller, A. (2021). Adolescent sexual and reproductive health for all in sub-Saharan Africa: a spotlight on inequalities, *Reproductive Health*, 18(Suppl 1), 1–18.

Chandra-Mouli, V., Parameshwar, P., Parry, M. et al. (2017). A never-before opportunity to strengthen investment and action on adolescent contraception, and what we must do to make full use of it. *BMC Reproductive Health,* 14, 85.

Chung, W.H, Kim, M.E. and Lee, J. (2018). Comprehensive understanding of risk and protective factors related to adolescent pregnancy in low- and middle-income countries: A systematic review. *Journal of Adolescence*, 69, 180–188.

Family Planning 2030. (2021). *Commitment resource kit: Developing bold and transformative commitments for adolescents and youth.* FP2030, Washington, DC.

Global Financing Facility (2022). *Financing for results to improve ASRH and wellbeing: Entry points for Action.* International bank for reconstruction and development/Global Financing Facility, Washington, DC. www.globalfinancingfacility.org/sites/gff_new/files/GFF-Financing-results-improve-ASRHR_0.pdf.

Global Sustainable Development Goals Indicator Platform (2024). https://unstats.un.org/sdgs/dataportal.

Herat, J., Plesons, M., Castle, C. et al. (2018). The revised international technical guidance on sexuality education – a powerful tool at an important crossroads for sexuality education. *BMC Reproductive Health,* 15(1), 185.

Liang, M., Simelane, S., Fortuny Fillo, G. et al. (2019). The state of adolescent sexual and reproductive health. *Journal of Adolescent health,* 65, S3–S15.

Neal, S., Channon, A., Chandra-Mouli, V., Madise, N. (2020). Trends in adolescent first births in sub-Saharan Africa: a tale of increasing inequity? *International Journal for Equity in Health,* 19(151).

Neal, S., Ruktanonchai, C., Chandra-Mouli, V. *et al.* (2016). Mapping adolescent first births within three east African countries using data from Demographic and Health Surveys: exploring geospatial methods to inform policy. *BMC Reproductive Health*, 13(98).

Neal, S., Harvey, C., Chandra-Mouli V. et al. (2018). Trends in adolescent first births in five countries in Latin America and the Caribbean: disaggregated data from demographic and health surveys. *BMC Reproductive Health*, 15(1), 146.

Neal, S., Ruktanonchai, C., Chandra-Mouli, V. et al. (2019).Using geospatial modelling to estimate the prevalence of adolescent first births in Nepal. *BMJ Global Health,* 4(suppl 5), e000763.

Petroni, S., Steinhaus, M., Stevanovic Fenn, N. et al. (2017). New Findings on Child marriage in sub-Saharan Africa. *Annals of Global Health*, 83(5–6). doi:10.1016/j.aogh.2017.09.001.

Philippine Statistics Authority and ICF. (2018). *Philippines National Demographic and Health Survey 2017.* Quezon City, Philippines, and Rockville, MD,: PSA and CF.

Southern African Development Community (2024). *The Sexual and Reproductive Health and Rights score card for the Southern African Development Community.* www.sadc.int/pages/sexual-reproductive-health-and-rights-scorecard.

Sully, E.A., Biddlecom, A., Darroch, J. et al. (2020). *Adding It Up: Investing in Sexual and Reproductive Health 2019.* New York: Guttmacher Institute.

The Global Fund (2022). *HIV information note. Allocation Period: 2023–25.* The Global Fund, Geneva.

United Nations Children's Fund. (2020). *Action to end child sexual abuse and exploitation.* New York: UNICEF.

United Nations Children's Fund. (2021). *Towards Ending Child Marriage: Global trends and profiles of progress.* New York: UNICEF.

United Nations Department of Economic and Social Affairs (2024a). *Births by five-year age group of mother, region, subregion and country, annually for 1950–2100 (thousands).* UNDESA. Online edition [cited 3 January 2024] https://population.un.org/wpp/Download/Standard/Fertility.

United Nations Department of Economic and Social Affairs (2024b). *World Population Prospects, 2022 Revision: Age-specific fertility rates by region, subregion and country, 1950–2100 (births per 1,000 women) Estimates.* UNDESA. Online edition [cited 3 January 2024] https://population.un.org/wpp/Download/Standard/Fertility.

United Nations Population Fund (2022a). Motherhood in childhood: the untold story. New York: UNFPA.

United Nations Population Fund (2022b). *Not on pause: Responding to the Sexual and Reproductive Health Needs of Adolescents during the COVID-19 crisis.* New York: UNFPA.

WHO (1993). *The health of young people: A challenge and a promise.* Geneva: WHO.

WHO. (2011). *WHO Guidelines on preventing early pregnancy and poor reproductive outcomes in adolescents in developing countries.* Geneva: WHO.

WHO. (2020). *Global status report on preventing violence against children.* Geneva: WHO.

Yakubu, I. and Salisu, J.W. (2018). Determinants of adolescent pregnancy in sub- Saharan Africa: a systematic review. *BMC Reproductive Health*, 15(15).

Zambia Statistics Agency, Ministry of Health, Zambia and ICF. (2018). *Zambia Demographic and Health Survey 2018.* Lusaka, Zambia, and Rockville, MD: Zambia Statistics Agency and Ministry of Health, Zambia.

Case study references

Act for Prevention and Solution of the Adolescent Pregnancy Problem (2016). Thailand, B.E.2559.

Akwara, E., Worknesh, K., Oljiira, L. et al. (2022). Adolescent Sexual and Reproductive Health and Rights in Ethiopia: Reviewing progress over the last 20 years and looking ahead to the next 10 years. *BMC Reproductive Health*, 19, 123.

Argentina (2002). *Ley 25673 Programa Nacional de Salud Sexual y Procreación Responsable [National Law 25673 National Program of Sexual Health and Responsible Procreation]. (2002).* Retrieved 24 February 2024.

Argentina (2006). *Ley 26150 National Comprehensive Sexual Education Program [Internet].* 2006 (retrieved February 2024).

Assefa, Y., Damme, W.V., Williams, O.D. et al. (2017). Successes and challenges of the millennium development goals in Ethiopia: lessons for the sustainable development goals. *BMJ Global Health*, 2, e000318.

Assefa, A., Degnet, A. and Andinet, D.W. (2009). Impact evaluation of the Ethiopian Health Services Extension Programme, *Journal of Development Effectiveness*, 1(4), 430–449.

Bivol, S., Thompson, R. and Pejic, D. (2009). *Youth friendly health services in Republic of Moldova*, in *Youth-friendly health policies and services in the European Region*, Baltag, V. and Matheison. A. (Eds). Copenhagen: WHO Regional Office for Europe, pp. 95–114.

Bureau of Reproductive Health, Department of Health, Thailand. https://rhdata.anamai.moph.go.th/index.php/adolescentadd/adolescentadd_1; https://rhdata.anamai.moph.go.th/index.php/adolescentadd/adolescentadd_2.

Chandra-Mouli, V., Baltag, V. and Ogbaselassie, L. (2013). Strategies to sustain and scale up youth friendly health services in the Republic of Moldova. *BMC Public Health*, 13, 284.

Carai, S., Bivol, S., Chandra-Mouli, V. (2021). Assessing youth-friendly-health-services and supporting planning in the Republic of Moldova. *BMC Reproductive Health*, 12(1), 98.

Department of Health, Thailand, UNICEF, UNFPA and WHO (n.d.) *Policy brief – Improving youth friendly health services in Thailand*. UNICEF. Improving Youth-Friendly Services (YFHS) in Thailand.pdf (unicef.org).

Hospital General de Agudos Dr. Cosme Argerich. Ciudad de Buenos Aires, Argentina (2009). *Adolescencia Un Servicio Amigable para la Atención Integral de la Salud*.

Inthavong, S., Pantasri, T., Morakote, N., Muangmool, T., Piyamongkol, W., Pongsatha, S. and Chaovisitseree, S. (2022). Change of contraceptive preference after the free-LARC program for Thai teenagers. *BMC Women's Health, 22*(1), 1–7.

Lesco, G., Squires, F., Babii, V. et al. (2019). The feasibility and acceptability of collaborative learning in improving health worker performance on adolescent health: findings from implementation research in Moldova. *BMC Health Serv Res*19, 339.

Ministry of Health (2019). *National Strategic Plan Argentina Health 2019–2023*. www.argentina.gob.ar/sites/default/files/documento_oficial_plan_2019.pdf.

Ministry of Health (2023a). *Informe de Monitoreo ENIA Anual 2022*: Informe trimestral de Monitoreo enero-marzo 2021; salud.gob.ar.

Ministry of Health (2023b). *Selected Health Indicators for the 10–19-year-old population in Argentina – Year 2021* (Bulletin Number 169). Secretariat of Access to Health, Sub-Secretariat of Medicines and Strategic Information, National Directorate of Epidemiology and Strategic Information, Directorate of Health Statistics and information.

Moore, A.M., Gebrehiwot, Y., Fetter, T. et al. (2016). The Estimated Incidence of Induced Abortion in Ethiopia, 2014: Changes in the Provision of Services Since 2008. *International Perspectives on Sexual and Reproductive Health*, 42, 3, 111–20.

Office for National Statistics (2023). Conception statistics, England and Wales, 2021. London: ONS.

Republic of Moldova (2022). *National Bureau of Statistics of the Republic of Moldova*. https://statistica.gov.md/en; www.statistica.md/pageview.php?l=en&idc=407.

Rofman, R., della Paolera, C., Camisassa, J. et al. (2022). *Odisea demográfica. Tendencias demográficas en Argentina: insumos claves para el diseño del bienestar social*. Buenos Aires: CIPPEC, UNICEF and UNFPA. www.unicef.org/argentina/documents/odisea-demografica-tendencias-demograficas-en-argentina-insumos-claves.

Social Exclusion Unit (1999). Teenage Pregnancy. London: SEU, Cmnd 4342.

Thai Health Promotion Foundation (a) (2013). www.thaihealth.or.th/?p=222232 (in Thai)

Thai Health Promotion Foundation (b) (2017). www.thaihealth.or.th/?p=240608 (in Thai)

Thailand Public Health Statistics (2021). https://spd.moph.go.th/wp-content/uploads/2022/11/Hstatistic64.pdf.

United Nations Children's Fund (2018). *Ending Child Marriage: A profile of progress in Ethiopia*, UNICEF, New York. https://data.unicef.org/resources/child-marriage-in-ethiopia.

WHO Regional Office for South East Asia (2021). *Success Stories in Reproductive, Maternal, Newborn, Child and Adolescent Health from WHO South-East Asia Region*. SEARO, New Delhi, chapter 4.

Epilogue

It has been a real privilege to talk to so many people to research and write this second edition. Three themes have stood out.

First, the huge impact of the work on young people themselves. The strategy was always about making a difference to young people's lives. Equipping them with the knowledge, skills and confidence to make safe, consensual, well-informed choices about relationships, sex, pregnancy and sexual health, and for young parents to be able to fulfil their ambitions without stigma or judgement. The impact of the work that has continued in the wake of the strategy is no different, with each case study described in the book contributing to young people's confidence, wellbeing and sense of agency, as illustrated by these short quotes. A young woman seeking to prevent pregnancy by accessing a pharmacy condom scheme, and a young mother and father accessing support from a local Voluntary and Community Sector (VCS) service.

> *"They (the pharmacists) were excellent. They were so accommodating, and I felt my needs were validated. They were constantly smiling and gave me all the information I needed to know".*
>
> *"In my experience, WILD has helped me change for the better and supported me through difficult life events. I don't normally put my trust in professionals/workers, but I have with WILD and I'm so glad I did".*
>
> *"There's a lot of the stuff centred on like, the mother, so it was one of the people that was supporting my girlfriend with the pregnancy. . . . she mentioned that there was a local charity. I just had to message them on Facebook and stuff and get into it, and it was really good. I learned baby first aid with them. It was really good".*

Second, the continuing tireless efforts of individuals in local areas, and the invaluable contribution of the VCS and political and organisation collaborations. Interviewing commissioners and practitioners in local areas and collating the many case studies has been inspirational. There have undoubtedly been major challenges, but I was reminded again of the dogged determination of those involved in teenage pregnancy work to get things right for young people. Remarkable too has been the huge and invaluable contributions from national voluntary sector organisations, notably the Sex Education Forum, Brook, and the Association for Young People's Health, the cross-party political alliance of the All-Party Parliamentary Group on Sexual and Reproductive Health, and the organisational collaborations of the English HIV and Sexual Health Commissioners and the Advisory Group on Contraception. They have all played a critical advocacy role in maintaining a focus and holding government to account.

Third, I am struck by the stark need for further national action. Progress cannot and should not hinge on local champions or VCS organisations and professional collaborations. Leadership and investment are needed from national government to re-state the priority and embed the principles of the strategy into universal provision, enabling local areas to use their resources to focus on targeted support and early help for those most in need.

An immediate priority is ensuring effective implementation of relationships and sex education (RSE); only then will young people reap the benefits of statutory status. This will require investment in trained confident teachers and involvement of young people to ensure RSE meets their needs in an increasingly complex world. But it also requires government to speak out about the health and safeguarding benefits of RSE – the reason for the overwhelming parliamentary majority for statutory status. Politicisation of RSE has consequences, serving only to rob children and young people of the knowledge and skills they need to take care of themselves.

Essential too is national investment to ensure that all services, including sexual and reproductive health and support services for young parents, are young people friendly, with well trained staff. This would create a 'no wrong door' approach, widening access to trustworthy and non-judgemental advice and reducing the need for dedicated young people's services. The revised *You're Welcome* criteria are much needed, but universal implementation of the criteria is at risk without sufficient funding for local areas to review their services, address gaps, and invest in staff training.

Securing high-quality RSE in all schools and youth friendly services in all communities will embed primary prevention for the current and future cohorts of young people and sustain progress in the long term. But equally pressing is the need to halt and reverse the upward trends in the wider determinants for early pregnancy and poor outcomes for young parents and their children. All have been impacted by austerity and further exacerbated by the COVID-19 pandemic. Long term investment is essential to prevent widening inequalities, but urgent action is needed now to reach out and support teenagers who have not returned to school after the pandemic, and the growing number of 15–16-year-olds taken into local authority care. Failure to act now risks leaving a cohort of young people at high risk for early pregnancy and, if they become young parents, poorer outcomes for them and their children. Deep concern about the impact of growing inequalities on the wider aspects of children and young people's physical and mental health, education, and economic security has been widely voiced by medical organisations (Academy of Medical Royal Colleges 2023) and the Voluntary and Community sector (Joseph Rowntree Foundation, 2023). The Conservative Government's decision to fund only 11 per cent of the recommended budget needed to support an education covid recovery plan drew particularly strong criticism (*Times Education Supplement*, 2024).

Much of the focus for urgent action is rightly on investment in early years – from pre-conception through pregnancy and into the first five years of childhood – a critical period that lays the foundation for mental and physical health and wellbeing for later life. But equally important is a focus and investment in young people to support them in their journey into adulthood, with a holistic approach to policies affecting all aspects of their lives. This was the policy landscape set by the Labour Government between 1997 and 2010, in which the teenage pregnancy strategy led the way in effective joint working – with agencies such as Connexions, drug and alcohol services, youth offending teams and the healthy schools and extended schools programmes, all benefitting from the synergy with the others.

The rewards from investing in an integrated youth policy, and the consequences of not doing so, are set out in a fascinating review: *Trends in Adolescent Disadvantage. Policy and Outcomes for Young people under Labour, the Coalition, and the Conservatives, 1997–2019* (London School of Economics, 2023). The review demonstrates the clear link between investment and improved outcomes, and charts the reversal of progress once funding was cut and the scaffolding of services to reach and support all young people was dismantled. It is clear that the local areas who have contributed to this edition are trying their best to sustain partnership working, but join-up, leadership and investment at national level are essential. The task for the new Labour Government is to develop a new coordinated youth strategy, with a laser focus on reducing inequalities – drawing on the learning from the past, harnessing the knowledge and passion of local areas and the Voluntary and Community Sector organisations sector and involving young people to ensure the strategy is fit for the 21st century. National investment in RSE and young people friendly sexual health services together with a well-resourced youth strategy will provide the secure policy context for the next chapter of the teenage pregnancy strategy and prevent the legacy of a brilliant programme of work from unravelling.

References

Academy of Medical Royal Colleges (2023). Securing our healthy future. Prevention is better than cure.

Joseph Rowntree Foundation (2023). Destitution in the UK 2023.

Times Educational Supplement (2024). Feature. Sir Kevan Collins: "We did nothing. We gave up, it was pathetic."

Index

Abortion, abortion as proportion of conceptions 8, 10, 13, 17, 24, 69; improving access to 50, 56, 94; abortion support for pregnant teenagers case studies Walsall, 120, 121, Bristol, 150; abortion (international case studies) Moldova 199, 200; Ethiopia, 201, 202; Argentina, 204
Accelerated Action for the Health of Adolescents (AA-HA!) xii
accountability, see senior leadership, self-assessment
adolescence, x, 45, 98, 195, 203
adverse childhood experience, association with teenage conceptions, 16, 82, 153, 164, 165. *See* also care experienced children and young people.
antenatal care, protective benefits of, 19, 20, 156, involvement of fathers, 165
Argentina 5, 193, 197, 198, 202–204 (case study). *See* also, international
Aspinall, P.J. 17
austerity, fiscal choice, impact of 1, 2, 3, 81, 103, 104, 108, 110, 111, 112, 152, 179, 206, 213. *See* also funding and poverty.

Barking and Dagenham, *see* local implementation case studies, 132–133, 147–148
Barnsley, *see* local implementation case studies 119–123
Berrington, A.M. 15, 16, 18–20
Bozon, M. 13
breastfeeding, rates of, 154; impact of support programmes, 157, 160, challenging barriers to sustained (case study) 161
Bristol, *see* local implementation case studies, 150–151
Brook. Conundrum study 30, 147; service access guidance (s), 49, 70; digital services 95–97, digital communications, 146, 147; Confidentiality and safeguarding: Sexual Behaviours Traffic Light Tool, Spotting the Signs, informing young people, 134–136; case studies, South Tees, 136, 137; Dudley, 138; Camden & Islington, 140; Salford, 142

Camden and Islington, *see* local implementation case study, 140–141
care experienced children and young people, association with teenage conceptions, 45, 64, 82, 99; targeted prevention for 51, 60, 100; support for care experienced young parents, 185–186 (case study); *see* also local implementation, 145–146 (case study)
Cheshire and Merseyside, *see* local implementation case study, 122–123
Childcare funding (Care to Learn), *see* Young Parents.
Catholic schools, 51. *See* also faith schools
children: impact of early conceptions on 19–20; outcomes for 153–156
Clarke, Kerry 77
Clayton, C, 188. (notes)
Colleges, guidance for on-site sexual health services, 67, 70; *see* also, relationships and sex education, and local implementation, case studies.
Colquhoun, Anne 51, 54
communications, strategy media campaigns, for young people, 52–53,

65–66, 71–72; for parents, 53, 66, 71–72; communications guide for local areas, 66; *see* also local implementation, case studies.
comprehensive sexuality education, x, xi, 25, 197, 199, 207. *See* also relationships and sex education.
condoms, campaigns 52, 65, 71; improving access to, guidance, 70, 142, 147–148, 173. Condoms (international case studies) Moldova, 199, Thailand, 206. *See* also local implementation, case studies, and contraception
confidentiality, young people's concerns, 45, 49; measures to address concerns, 49, 50, 133–136; See also Brook confidentiality and safeguarding.
Connexions service. *See* youth services
contraception: impact of, 13, 24, 30; variations in levels of use 12–13; strategy focus on, 46, 49–51, 68–69; media campaign to promote, 52–53; media campaign to normalise discussion of, 71–72; implementing youth-friendly services, guidance on 49, 56, 57, 74, 98, 213; in education and non-health settings, 50, 67, 76; digital services, 95–97. *See* also Teenage Pregnancy Strategy, access to contraception, developments 2018–2023, and local implementation, case studies.
cost of living crisis, impact of, 2, 99, 104, 108, 110, 155, 179, 182, 187. *See* also austerity and poverty
Covid-19 pandemic, impact of, xi, xii, 82, 84, 85, 88, 92, 93, 97, 99, 100, 104, 105, 108, 110, 111, 153, 155, 166, 179, 187, 213, 214
Croydon, *see* local implementation case studies, 137–138, 141–142

Darroch, J.E. 9, 13
data, use in monitoring progress: local monitoring dataset, 72; use in targeted prevention: 64–65; managing scale-up, 205. See also, local implementation case studies, 123–126
Department for Children, Schools and Families, 50, 67, 72, 73
Department for Education, 73, 74, 85, 87, 91, 100, 129, 145, 168, 169, 170
Department of Health and Social Care, 84, 85, 86, 92, 95, 100, 107, 114, 145, 187
depression, *see* mental health
Diamond, L. 14
disadvantage, *see* poverty
domestic abuse, young parents experience of, 155, 156, 159, 160
Dudley, *see* local implementation case study, 138–139

economic wellbeing, *see* poverty
education: attainment as risk factor for early pregnancy, 15, 45, 65, 153; support for young parents 165–169; Case studies, 167–169; *see also* relationships and sex education
Elander, J. 14
emotional health *see* mental health
England *see* Teenage Pregnancy Strategy (TPS) for England and international.
Ermisch, J. 16
Essex, *see* local implementation case study, 131–132
Ethiopia, 193, 197, 198, 200–202 (case study). *See* also, international.
Ethnicity, 15, 17, 49, 53, 65, 124, 134; RSE in diverse communities (case study), 129–130
Extended Schools Programme, guidance for on-site sexual health services, 50, 66, 67, 214

faith schools, relationships and sex education. *see* Teenage Pregnancy Strategy, developments in relationships and sex education (2018–2023) and local implementation case study 86–87
Family Planning Association (VSO) 51, 56
Family Nurse Partnership, 122, 150, 159, 160–165, 170, 178
fathers *see* young fathers
foster carers, developing skills and confidence in RSE, case studies: 144–145, 145–146
funding, strategy local implementation grant 47, 56, 67, 76, 205; funding cuts, impact of, 81, 92, 93, 94, 95, 99, 105, 119, 152, 214; *see* also, childcare funding.

General practice 49, 53, 95, 100; case studies involving general practice: 133–134, 142–143
Germany 13

Government: Conservative, 38, 44, 214; Coalition, 38, 73, 81, 103, 152, 214; Labour, 38, 43, 44, 47, 73, 86, 214
Grimsby Dads Collective (case study), see also Young Dads Collective 180–181

Hamlyn, C. 48
Hashem, F. 17
Hawkes, D. 16, 19, 21
Holder, Rhiannon 52
Housing for young parents, *see* Young Parents.
Hughes, B. (Baroness Hughes of Stretford) 63, 68

Iceland 9
inequalities 9, 10, 43, 74, 82, 84, 86, 153, 155, 186, 203, 204, 206, 213, 214; widening of, 2, 100, 101, 108, 111, 114, 182, 187
Ingham, R. 13, 14, 32, 37
Integrated Care Systems, Integrated Care Boards, *see* joint working and local implementation, case studies.
International Conference on Population and Development x, xii, 195, 196. *See* also, international
international, trends and context of adolescent childbearing 193–195; global response to 195–196; national responses to, 197–207; lessons from effective programmes, Ethiopia, Argentina, England, Thailand 197–198; continuing inequalities, 207–208
Islington, *see* local implementation case studies 143–144

Japan 9
joint working, principle of strategy 45, 47; collaborative partnerships 53–55; integration with government programmes, 55–56, 72, 78; developments since 2010: 84–86, 104, 107, 111. *See* also local implementation case studies and senior leadership.

Kiernan, K. 15
Kirby, D. 26
Kontula, O. 13

Ladlow, L. 188. (notes)
Lambeth, *see* Well Centre
leadership *see* senior leadership
Lees, J. 70
Lindberg, L. 29, 30, 31
local implementation: ten key factors for effective local strategies, 61, 62, 63; case studies illustrating: senior leadership & accountability, 119–123; strong use of data and local intelligence, 123–125; improving relationships and sex education in schools and colleges, 126–131; youth friendly contraception and sexual health services, 131–134; advice and contraception in non-clinical and youth settings, 136–138; targeted prevention for young people at risk, 139–141; workforce training on relationships and sexual health for non-health practitioners, 141–143; supporting parents and foster carers with relationships and sex education, 143–146; good communication to deliver information and service publicity, 146–148; options support for pregnant teenagers, referral for abortion or antenatal care, post-pregnancy contraception, 149–150. Teenage Pregnancy Prevention Framework and self-assessment tool 75, 84, 106, 110
Local Government Association 75, 84, 95, 102, 106, 119, 152, 178, 182, 187
Looked after children (see care experienced children and young people)
low/middle income countries x, 24, 193

Macdonald, A. 69
Maddow-Zimet, I. 29
Martinez, Anna 56
maternity services, *see* young parents.
media, role of 79, 84, 91; social media, role and influence of: 32, 108, 109, 122, 129, 136, 137, 143, 147, 148, 198. *See* also, media
mental health, affecting young parents 11, 19, 20, 153, 154, 155, 156, 175, 182, 198. Case studies addressing young parents mental health: 164, 167, 181, 183, 184, 185, 186
Moldova 193, 197, 198–200 (case study). *See* also international
Morinis, J. 20, 154
mothers *see* young mothers

National Healthy Schools Programme (NHSP) 49, 55, 73, 66, 67, 72, 75, 108, 214. *See* also local implementation case studies 125, 126, 127
Neale, B. 188 (notes)
Netherlands 9, 13, 14, 24, 32, 33, 162, 206
Nichols J. 5, 75, 101
non-governmental organisations (NGOs) see also Voluntary and Community Sector Organisations (VSO)
Northern Ireland 21 (Notes)
Nottingham *see* local implementation case study, 129–130
Nottinghamshire *see* childcare funding case study

outreach programmes, guidance on, 70, 93, 95, 96, 98; see also, targeted prevention.

parenthood *see* young parents
Parentline Plus helpline role in campaign 53, 65, 71
parents: role of 28, 32, 33; media campaign to reach, 53, 65–66, 71; support for communication with children, 100; *see also* local implementation case studies 143–144, and Teenage Pregnancy Strategy, developments in relationships and sex education (2018–2023).
partnerships *see* joint working
Pevalin, D.J. 16
Pharmacies 50, 71, *see* also local implementation case studies 132–133, 147–148. *See* also condoms
poverty, impact on teenage conceptions, 14, 45, 74, 98–99, 108, 112, 153, 175, 187; impact on young parents and their children, 154, 155; disadvantage of pre-existing, 153, 155, 161, 179, 188; digital poverty, 109, 111, 174. *See* also austerity and cost of living
practitioners (non-health), importance of engagement with, 51, 53, 61, 64, 67, 105; essential role of trusted advisers 158; communication with partner agencies (case study) 109; effective communication with 148–149 (case study); see also workforce training
primary care *see* general practice and pharmacies
public health, x, 1, 3, 37, 38, 56, 63, 75, 81, 84, 85, 93, 97, 103, 104. *See* also local implementation, case studies
Public Health England i, 75, 84, 85, 92, 94, 97, 102, 115 (notes), 119, 145, 148, 154, 178, 182, 187

Quail, K. 55

Rademakers, J. 32
relationships and sex education, RSE (school based), evidence for 25–30, 37; abstinence-only, abstinence-plus, 25, 26, 29, 30, 31; strategy focus on, 45, 48, 50; statutory status 69–70, 86, 87; developments in RSE 2018–2023, 87–92; *see* also local implementation case studies
reproductive health, 92, 93, 94, 106, 107, 202, Reproductive Health Programme, 85 *See* also Women's Health Strategy
Richmond, *see* local implementation case studies, 125–126, 127–128, 144–145

safeguarding, protective benefits of RSE, 27, 91; safeguarding needs of young parents and their children, 156, 160, 164, 172, 176, 178, 183, 184, 185, See also Brook confidentiality and safeguarding.
Salford, *see* local implementation case studies, 142–143
Santelli, J. i, 26, 30, 31, 70
Schalet, A. 33
schools *see* relationships and sex education, National Healthy Schools Programme, Extended Schools Programme; contraception; local implementation, case studies
Scotland 14, 21 (notes), 27, 35, 36, 151 (notes), 154
second and subsequent pregnancy, support with post-pregnancy contraception, *see* local implementation case studies 149–150
self-assessment of local programmes, 61, 66, 68, 72, 75, 106, 110, 114, 205
senior leadership (local), importance of 60, 61, 72, 75, 78, 94, 107, 111; direct ministerial contact with, 63;

see also local implementation case studies: 119–123
sex and relationships education (SRE) *see* relationships and sex education.
Sex Education Forum 26, 27, 48, 50, 56, 69, 70, 76, 86–91, 106, 125, 129, 130, 144, 175, 213, 130 (case study), 144, 145–146 (case study) 175, 213
sexual abuse, 89, 107, young parents experience of, 155, 195
sexual activity, variations in levels of 12, 13, 28, 29, 30, 31
sexual competence, 17, 32–34
sexual exploitation, 105, 156; case studies, 127, 128, 136, 144–145, 150, 156. See also Brook, Spotting the Signs.
sexual harassment (in schools), 88, 89, 90, 91; *see* also local implementation, case studies
sexual health services: *see* contraception, local implementation, case studies
sexual information, other sources of 31–32
Singh, A. xii
Singh, S. 13
Smith, D.M. 14
Smith, T. 14
Social Exclusion Unit 38, 44, 48, 152, 204
South Korea 9
South Tees, *see* local implementation case studies, 122–124, 136–137
special educational needs and disability, supporting RSE for young people with (case study) 130–131
Speakeasy programme 66; *See* also parents
Sure Start Plus programme 156–159; see also young parents, effective support for
Surrey *see* local implementation case study, 126–127
Sustainable Development Goals xii, 92, 196, 207. *See* also, international
Sweden 9, 13, 33, 179
Switzerland 9

targeted prevention for young people at risk 11, 34, 37, 46, 53, 64, 95, 104, 109, 124. *See also* local implementation case studies, 136–141
Tarrant, A. 188. (notes)
Teasdale, G. 55, 73
Teather, S. 74
teenage birth rates, international variations in 13, 14, 24, 43. *See* also teenage conceptions
teenage conceptions, definition of term 7–8; research challenges 11–12, international variations 13–14, regional variations 14–15, individual characteristics 15–17; degrees of intentionality 17–18; impact of 18–21
teenage conception rate reduction, evidence for 24–34, 37–38; intervention rationale 10, 34–37
Teenage Pregnancy Prevention Framework, *see* Teenage Pregnancy Strategy and local implementation.
Teenage Pregnancy Strategy (TPS) for England: rationale for, and development 42–46; first phase of implementation (1999–2005) 46–56; second phase of implementation (2005–2010) 46–73; mid-course review, 59–60; keeping the focus beyond the end of the strategy (2010) 73–78; what happened next at national level (2018–2023): data, 81–83; government policy 83–86; relationships and sex education, 86–92; contraception access, 92–97; youth policy, 97–101; what happened next at local level 2010–2018: 101–104, 2018–2023, 104–110, summary of key issues (2010–2023) 111, 113; recommendations for further action, 114–115; applying the learning internationally, 197–198, 204–206 (case study). *See* also, local implementation, ten key factors for effective local strategies, case studies.
Teenage Pregnancy Strategy, support for young parents 46; *see* young parents.
Teenage Pregnancy Coordinators, role of: 47, 48, 49, 56, 61; co-ordinator role post 2010: 75, 81, 102
Teenage Pregnancy Independent Advisory Group (TPIAG) role of 47, 51, 74, 86, 112, 205
Teenage Pregnancy National Support Team (TPNST), role of 63, 68, 75
Teenage Pregnancy Unit, role of, 47–48, 102; Teenage Pregnancy Unit post 2010: 75

Thailand 193, 197, 198, 206–207 (case study). *See* also, international.
Thomas, R. 51
TPS *see* Teenage Pregnancy Strategy (TPS) for England
training *see* workforce training
Trivedi, D. 26

United Nations 91, 92, Rights of the Child (UNCRC), 155, 200
United Nations Children's Fund (UNICEF), 9, 13, 24, 26, 37, 196
United Nations Educational, Scientific and Cultural Organisation (UNESCO), xi, xii, 26, 29, 89, 91
United Nations Population Fund (UNFPA) x, xi, xii, 10, 29, 196, 207
United States of America (USA), teenage conception rates reduction, 30–31
Unity Schools Trust, *see* local implementation case study, 128–129

van Zessen, G. 14, 32

Wales, 21 (notes) 35, 36, 99, 147, 151 (notes)
Walsall, *see* local implementation case studies 119–121, 149–150
Wandsworth, *see* local implementation case studies, 125–126, 127–128, 144–145
Wellings, K.G. 17, 25, 33, 38, 76, 82, 91, 152, 30, 33
Well Centre *see* local implementation case study, 133–134
Whiteley, C. 68
whole system approach, importance of, 3, 4, 37, 61, 62, 84, 85, 101, 107, 114, 119, 127, 135, 206. *See* also, joint working
WILD Young Parents 155, 156. *See* also Young Parents case study 184–185
Women's Health Strategy, 85, 93, 94, 95, 107
workforce training 51, 77, 104, 105, *see* local implementation case studies 141–143
Working with Men, 50
World Health Organisation (WHO) x, xi, xii, 5, 56, 98

Young Dads Collective (YDC) 179–180
young fathers: impact of early conceptions on, 19; experience and needs of, 174–176; services response to, 176–178; co-creation of support pathways for, 179–180; dedicated support for, 164–165, 180–181 (case studies); experience of employment post pandemic, 181–182
young mothers: impact of early conceptions on, 11, 18; outcomes and influencing factors 153–156; sustaining breastfeeding, 161 (case study)
young parents: Framework for supporting teenage mothers and young fathers, 75, 182, 187; effective support for 157–164 (*see* also Family Nurse Partnership); support into education and training, 165–171, 167–169 (case studies); Childcare funding for (Care to Learn) 152, 169–171, 170–171 (case study); housing for: impact of poor housing on outcomes 19, 155, 157; supported housing pilot evaluation, 171; experiences and support needs of young parents study, 172; supported housing provision (case study), 173; NHS specialist maternity team for, 183–184 (case study); VCS sector support for, 184–185 (case study); local authority service support for, 185 (case study); support for care experienced young parents, 185–186 (case study). Recommendations for further action: 186–188
youth services and youth workers, importance of, 47, 51, 60, 99, 101, 214; decline of, 99, 103, 104; Connexions Service, 51, 60; loss of, 103, 104, 169; *see* also Teenage Pregnancy Strategy, youth policy developments 2018–2023, and local implementation, case studies
You're Welcome, *see* contraception, youth friendly services guidance; Teenage Pregnancy Strategy, youth policy developments 2018–2023.